# Finance for Purchasing Managers

# Finance for Purchasing Managers

## Understanding the Financial Impact of Buying Decisions

RICHARD FRANCE

Routledge
Taylor & Francis Group

LONDON AND NEW YORK

First published in paperback 2024

First published 2013 by Gower Publishing

Published 2016 by Routledge
4 Park Square, Milton Park, Abingdon, Oxon OX14 4RN

and by Routledge
605 Third Avenue, New York, NY 10158

*Routledge is an imprint of the Taylor & Francis Group, an informa business*

**British Library Cataloguing in Publication Data**
A catalogue record for this book is available from the British Library.

**The Library of Congress has cataloged the printed edition as follows:**
France, Richard (Accountant)
    Finance for purchasing managers : understanding the financial impact of buying decisions
/ by Richard France.
        pages cm
    Includes bibliographical references and index.
    ISBN 978-0-566-09171-1 (hardback) – ISBN 978-1-4094-6419-8 (ebook) – ISBN 978-1-4094-6420-4 (epub)  1.  Industrial procurement--Management.  2.  Purchasing--Management.  3. Finance.  I. Title.

    HD39.5.F73 2013
    658.15 – dc23

                                                                                    2013003125

ISBN: 978-0-566-09171-1 (hbk)
ISBN: 978-1-03-283832-8 (pbk)
ISBN: 978-1-315-58239-9 (ebk)

DOI: 10.4324/9781315582399

# Contents

# List of Figures

# About the Author

Richard France is a Chartered Accountant (FCA) and has an MBA from Henley Business School. Having qualified, he became Finance Director of a 300-employee manufacturing business followed by a 20-year period combining lecturing at University with financial consultancy and training work in his own company. Prior to his current full-time role lecturing in Finance and Accounting at Manchester Metropolitan University, he spent several years working for PMMS Consulting Group, which is an International niche consultancy company specialising in Purchasing Training and Consultancy. His role was to develop the key financial skills required of buyers in both the public and private sectors. He has worked with many well-known public companies in retail, services and manufacturing, from where much of his source material has come.

# Preface

This book has been written with both the student and the practising purchasing professional in mind. It has been written so that the reader at whatever level can pick out their required sections.

For instance, the first-time student can read through the relevant sections and ignore some of the Advanced Issues. Similarly, the practitioner can go straight to the Advanced Issues without necessarily having to wade through the basics. However, it is common for many practitioners to need to quickly brush up on the basics first, before moving on to the more Advanced Issues. When reading the Advanced Issues, it is assumed that the previous level has been read and understood, and therefore this level builds on the prior knowledge and adds more practical aspects.

This book is, first and foremost, a finance book aimed at the non-financial manager or aspiring manager, but it is written from the perspective of a purchasing manager. Therefore, frequent references are made to the purchasing role, as well as to purchasing models such as supply positioning.

Richard France

# PART I
# *Financial Analysis of Suppliers*

# 1

# The Role of Finance from a Purchasing Perspective

The role of purchasing has changed significantly over the last 30 years, particularly in the UK. There are various reasons for this, but primarily it is because the country has moved from being fundamentally a strong manufacturing economy to being significantly more service orientated. Due to the increasingly high costs of labour, many large multinational manufacturing organisations have reduced their manufacturing in the UK and made direct investments in countries where the labour costs are significantly cheaper. Clearly, the industries to be hit by this strategy are those where a significant element of the costs arise from direct labour and where a company may buy items in for perhaps one quarter to a half of the costs of manufacturing those items itself. As a low labour cost country gets near to the capacity of its useable labour, there will be significant inflation that will then push up the manufacturing costs, as has happened in South Korea. Manufacturers will then move to the next country where there is still a significant amount of under-utilised labour that will operate for a low cost. Outsourcing in this way may have significant corporate social responsibility (CSR) issues if using under-age labour or working excessive hours. This places further responsibility on the buyer to ensure their company is not damaged by negative publicity associated with poor CSR practice. This is, of course, in addition to any moral or ethical views the buyer or the buyer's company may have in this regard.

Many industries in the United Kingdom have virtually ceased to exist where they have been traditionally large employers of low-skilled labour. For instance, the clothing and pottery industries both employ a small fraction of the numbers they used to employ 30 years ago.

What do these changes mean for the buyer?

Fundamentally, buyers are purchasing supplies that are significantly further along in the value chain. For instance, in the engineering sector 30 years ago, a buyer might have purchased raw steel in large quantities in sheet or rod form, and then the company would add value to the raw material to turn it into a complete engineered part. This is still the case when purchasing for an overseas manufacturer, but often the buyer seeks to purchase either the completed part itself or a significant element of that completed part (perhaps 20, 30 or 40% of its final value). This means that the buyer needs a higher level of expertise in the product make-up and specifications, as well as being responsible for a higher value of external spend. In other words, the buyer's role has become more vital to the success of an organisation, which gives greater credibility and responsibility to the role of the buyer. Essentially, organisations have sought, due to the volatility of demand, to turn the fixed costs of manufacturing into the variable costs of buying in.

Good sources of supply, therefore, have become a principal resource of the company, and the buyer and these sources need protection. As part of this process, the buyer needs a higher level of awareness of the financial stability of the sources of supply, as well as a sound financial understanding of what make up the supplier's cost structures. A close liaison is therefore needed between the buyer and the accountant in an organisation, both to inform and to learn from each other in order that both may improve in the quality of their respective decision-making processes.

The broad role of finance is to plan and control the finance in a company by ensuring the company is able to fund the shorter-term working capital – this is the timing difference between converting inventory into Accounts Receivable and then into cash received, but aided by credit from suppliers (explained later in more detail) – and fund longer-term purchases of Non-current Assets to ensure the capacity to meet demand. Additionally, the control of costings and pricing is critical to ensure that the organisation is able to make ongoing profits to aid in its development. There is a critical difference in the public sector, in that there is a fixed, limited amount that can be spent, and the organisation is tasked with ensuring that the public obtain best value from the money spent. Essentially, this means break-even budgeting rather than profit maximization.

Historically, in many organisations, the purchasing function was subsumed under the finance function, but this has changed in the last 20 to 30 years so that there is a separate purchasing function often commanding a board appointment in organisations that have heavy buying-in costs. There should still, however, be a close relationship between the two, as overall control of costs falls into the remit of the finance function, and bought-in costs fall under the remit of the purchasing function. Each should support the other with their respective skills.

In a large organisation, there are traditionally two key accounting roles. The first is that of the financial accountant, usually at director level. The financial accountant will be responsible for the more strategic aspects of an organisation's finances. This will include:

- reporting to shareholders;

- raising finance through a share issue or from a bank;

- producing year end accounts;

- liaising with the auditors;

- optimising taxation strategy;

- filing of significant company documents;

- ensuring the soundness of all financial systems;

- overall financially controlling the organisation;

- managing the treasury function; and

- ensuring adherence to accounting standards and (where appropriate) stock exchange requirements.

The second role is that of the management accountant. This role will be responsible for the supply of management information, such as:

- the production of monthly management accounts;

- the production and control of budgets;

- short-term cash budgeting;

- the allocation of costs across departments in the organisation;

- the management and control of costs within an organisation;

- the production of costing information for both products and departments; and

- cost/benefit analysis and Capital Investment Appraisals, although the calculations could be undertaken or supervised by the financial accountant (for example, valuing companies for the purpose of purchase or sale).

These lists are by no means exhaustive, and the tasks contained in the roles frequently overlap. In a small company, all of the tasks are undertaken by one accountant. In a larger company, there may also be a separate company secretary, whose responsibility is predominantly administrative and procedural with regard to filing documents, shareholder recording, formal meeting arrangements and recording. (However, the formal position of a company secretary still exists in all companies and, in small companies, it is often another duty taken by a director.) In very large companies, there will be many accountants in each area of operation, so that a Finance Director would oversee the work of both finance and management accountants.

The financial accountant's role traditionally would be more likely to turn into a board appointment simply by the more strategic nature of the role. However, with the closer alignment and merging of the disciplines, the management accountant's role may well be strategic in some organisations (for instance, when involved in a Business Process Re-engineering project or in a Benchmarking exercise).

## Types of Accounting Qualification

There are various types of accountancy qualification that reflect the roles undertaken. The financial accounting role is traditionally taken by a Chartered Accountant (ACA) or, in the USA, a Certified Public Accountant (CPA). Trained primarily in the profession by undertaking both accounting, audit and taxation work, this qualification is generally regarded (at the risk of offending holders of other accounting qualifications) as the 'leading' qualification due to its higher entry requirements, level of failure in examinations, and acknowledged more strategic content of the training (for instance, the high company law content). Approximately 85% of FTSE 100 boards have at least one ACA qualified member. A minority of students now train in 'approved' industrial organisations rather than in a professional practice.

The management accounting role is traditionally taken by a Chartered Cost and Management Accountant (CIMA). This qualification has developed over the years and has caught up significantly in stature with the Chartered Accountancy qualification and there have been possibilities of a merger with the Chartered body. The training is in the workplace with an organisation, rather than in a professional office, and so there tends to be limited exposure to different types of organisation compared to that of a Chartered Accountant, although more in depth at the place of work. It is a highly regarded qualification, and the best for a management accountant.

A further qualification, namely Chartered Certified Accountant (ACCA), is a hybrid of the two, and a person can train through an auditing company or in industry. It is a highly rated qualification and is a fast growing global organisation.

Additionally, in the public sector the most sought-after and highly rated qualification is with the Chartered Institute of Public Finance and Accountancy (CIPFA), and there was also consideration of this institute merging with the Chartered Accountants.

The main qualification for a company secretary is a 'Chartered Secretary', obtained through the Institute of Chartered Secretaries and Administrators (ICSA), and this is very much a finance role specialising in corporate governance.

All of the Institutes are 'Chartered', causing some confusion, but the term 'Chartered Accountant' traditionally refers to the Institute of Chartered Accountants where one qualifies as an Associate (ACA) or Fellow (FCA).

## Accounting Standards

Accounting standards are set by the national standard setters of the relevant countries. They may or may not subscribe to the International Accounting Standards Board (IASB) recommendations. It is the intention of the IASB to create a single group of globally enforceable standards to which all national bodies subscribe. In the UK, the standards used were called the Statements of Standard Accounting Practice (SSAP – first published in 1971), which have been replaced by Financial Reporting Standards (FRS). Publicly quoted companies normally subscribe to producing accounts using International Accounting Standards (IAS), and each new standard is given a number, such as IAS 1 (which is about how financial statements are presented). The number of these is 41, although some have been removed. Any newly created standards are now called International Financial Reporting Standards (IFRS), of which there are 13 currently in existence; so there are both IASs and IFRSs with which to comply. There are also Generally Accepted Accounting Principles (GAAP), which are whole bodies of accounting methods in use in particular countries and cover much wider areas than IFRSs. For instance, the UK GAAP encompasses the UK Companies Act 2006. There are also Statements of Recommended Practice (SORP) which supplement accounting standards in particular industries.

Currently, all public companies are required to publish accounts using IFRS regulations; for years commencing after 1 January 2015, all accounts in the UK will be published under IFRS regulations, and so all the accounts and accounting terms used in this book will reflect this, although reference is made to the terms currently in use.

The implications of this 'red tape' are that, hopefully, it makes accounting statements more accurate, more dependable and easier to compare, nationally and internationally. There is a cost of compliance and in financial accounting to ensure compliance, with implications for financial reporting, directors' responsibilities, risk management and control processes.

# 2

# Types of Organisation, the Main Accounting Statements and their Primary Use

## Types of Organisation

There are various types of organisation, and some may have differing treatment of aspects of their accounts. The following is a brief description of the main types.

### SOLE TRADER

A person who trades in their own name and is personally liable for all the business debts incurred. The profits are taxable at personal tax rates as if all of the profits have been taken as income, irrespective of the drawings. It is the cheapest and simplest form of trading structure to set up.

### PARTNERSHIP

This occurs where two or more persons work together in a situation as above. Partners are 'jointly and severally' liable for the partnership debts; in other words, if one partner is unable to pay their share, the others are liable. There should always be a written partnership agreement to support the capital introduced, share of profits and division of work although frequently this is not the case.

### LIMITED COMPANY (LIMITED BY SHARES OR GUARANTEE)

This body is a separate legal entity from either the owners (shareholders) or managers (directors). The directors' salaries are treated like that of any other employee for tax purposes and pay 'Schedule E' tax. These salaries are therefore tax deductible (unlike the drawings of a sole trader).

It is governed by the Companies Acts (updated 2006) and must register all shareholders, directors, debentures and yearly accounts.

A 'private' limited company (suffix, 'Ltd') has at least one shareholder and must have at least one director. Until April 2008 it also had to have a secretary. The company's articles of association may require more than one director in any event. Its shares may not be traded on a stock market.

A 'public' limited company (suffix, 'PLC') has a company secretary, at least two directors (one may be the secretary) and two shareholders, and needs a minimum of £50,000 issued share capital of which 25% must be paid up. It is not the same as a 'quoted' company, which means quoted on a recognised stock market. The 'Limited' term means the shareholders have limited liability, in the sense that they can lose no more than the shares that they own, up to the indebtedness of the company. A company may be limited by guarantee, meaning that, rather than receiving shares, members may 'guarantee' either a limited or unlimited amount.

## PUBLIC SECTOR ORGANISATION

This is the section of the economy that handles the supply of goods and services on behalf of the government at national, regional or local level. Whilst public sector accounting as such is not discussed in this book, the assumption is that the buyer for public sector services will be dealing, to a great extent, with private sector organisations.

## ASSOCIATED/SUBSIDIARY COMPANY

A company is a subsidiary of another if more than 50% of its voting shares are owned by the 'holding' company. Between 20% and 50% ownership, the company is known as 'associated' if there is also a 'significant' degree of influence by the holding company over its financial and operational policies (for example, a board member).

## CHARITABLE COMPANY

This body is governed by the Charity Commission and must be a non-profit-making organisation, meaning any surpluses remain for the benefit of the organisation. It must have a charitable purpose and be a 'voluntary' organisation. It can be unincorporated, incorporated or a trust. If incorporated, it is also governed by the Companies Acts.

## CO-OPERATIVES

In the UK there is no legal definition for a co-operative, but a key organisational difference is that it is run for the benefit of members not investors. Membership changes over time, and current members manage the business on trust for future members. Each member exercises one vote. Membership cannot be restricted artificially. Increasingly, co-operatives are set up as companies limited by guarantee or by shares. Co-operatives are set up to give the members either greater combined power in the market or greater purchasing power. Co-operatives account for over 20% of agricultural production in the UK (compared to 50% in France).

The emphasis of this book is on private and public limited company finance issues, and focuses on the buyer from these bodies or from a public sector organisation that deals with these bodies.

## Principal Accounting Statements

There are three principal accounting statements that are published as part of a company's financial reporting:

- income statement (formerly profit and loss account);

- balance sheet (or statement of financial position); and

- cash flow statement.

Comparisons are usually provided with the previous year figures (USA – two previous years). Other statements are contained in the internal budgets of an organisation, which are principally projections of profitability, capital spend and cash.

## INCOME STATEMENT

The income statement shows how the company has traded over the past period. It may be drawn up over any length of time but monthly, quarterly or annually are the most common, although published accounts are annual, except in exceptional cases.

It summarises the *trading* transactions of the company under the two main headings of 'income' and 'expenditure'. If the income is greater than the expenditure, the company is said to have made a profit. A loss is incurred where the expenditure is greater than the income.

A simple income statement would look as follows:

| | |
|---|---|
| Sales | 100,000 |
| *Less* Costs | 90,000 |
| = Profit | 10,000 |

This can be related to one's personal circumstances where the sales could be regarded as one's net income. The costs could be all of one's personal expenses during the year such as food, clothing, electricity, motor expenses etc. The balance at the year end is hopefully a surplus! This is then either invested as savings, invested in one's house, or spent on a holiday! With a business, it is either invested in the business, put into savings or other businesses, or given out to shareholders as a 'dividend'.

## BALANCE SHEET

The balance sheet (or statement of financial position (SOFP)) is drawn up at the end of an income statement accounting period and is a statement of what is owned by the company on that date and also what is owed by the company. These are known as assets and liabilities.

A simple balance sheet would look as follows:

| | | | |
|---|---|---|---|
| Assets | 25,000 | Liabilities | 20,000 |
| | | Capital | 5,000 |
| | | | 25,000 |

This shows that this company owns £5,000 more than it owes and the 'capital' figure is therefore the net value or 'net worth' of the company. As the company makes a profit, so the value of the assets rises and so does the capital or net worth of the business.

In a personal situation, one could relate the balance sheet to the following:

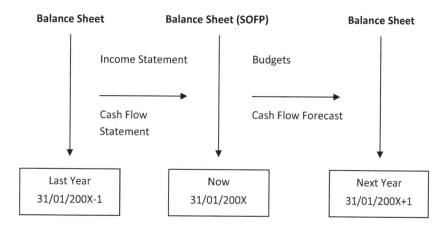

**Figure 2.1**   **Diagram of Statements for a Company with a 31 January Year End**

- you *own* a house, car, furniture, clothing, food, lawnmower, cash in the bank etc; and

- you *owe* a loan on the house, money to the bank (overdraft), credit card debts, bills for services such as electricity and oil etc.

Hopefully, you own more than you owe, and this balancing figure is known as your capital or 'net worth'.

## CASH FLOW STATEMENT

The cash flow statement is a summary of the past year's transactions, written in a form which links the profit earned to the movement in cash between year ends. It is like a summary of the history of the cash book, but in a somewhat complex manner, and it is mainly read by financial analysts and other accounting trained professionals. However, it is part of the published accounts and, as such, can show very useful information that would not be immediately obvious from the income statements and balance sheets.

A cash flow forecast, not part of the published financial statements, is part of the budgetary control process and is covered later in some detail. It is a means of estimating the cash requirements of the business in the short and medium term.

## Who is Interested in Accounting Statements?

There are many parties interested in accounting statements. These are known as 'stakeholders' in the business. In addition to the directors, there are the shareholders, bank, employees, customers, suppliers, tax authorities, environmental groups etc.

Each stakeholder will have a different reason for looking at the accounts, although all will usually wish to see that the company is making a profit and is solvent.

Some of the stakeholders and their requirements could be summarised as follows:

| For Whom | Requirements |
|---|---|
| Government/ HMRC | To pay Corporation Tax |
| Shareholders/Sponsors | Capital growth & Dividend |
| Directors/Managers | To be able to manage the organisation |
| Bank | Security of the assets /Ability to repay loan from profit |
| Employees | The primary need for Job Security |
| Customers | They will normally seek continued supply ability |
| Suppliers | They will seek payment and then further orders |
| Pressure Groups | To Apply Pressure |

To apply pressureThe pressure groups would encompass equal opportunities groups, environmental groups, local and national authorities. The result is that there is great difficulty in satisfying all of these parties in one set of statements. For instance, the bank is only interested in the value of the assets if the company is forced to cease trading, whereas the directors would be more likely to value the assets at their current replacement value. So which value should be used?

These stakeholders need to be satisfied and 'managed' and they all have differing requirements. The bank requires repayment of its loans, the shareholders require a dividend, the directors need information with which to manage the company, environmental groups need to be satisfied that the organisation is not upsetting the local ecology etc. They are sometimes split into primary and secondary stakeholders. Primary stakeholders are those with a direct relationship with the organisation (often contractual) such as employees or suppliers, whereas secondary stakeholders might be a local environmental group. Secondary stakeholders are, however, not necessarily less important.

One way of categorising these stakeholders is by relating their power or influence to their interest in the organisation.

For instance, consider a football club. Most clubs are heavily in debt to the bank which has a high indirect interest in the success of the club. They must be involved as key players. The police who ensure safety at matches have high influence and power to close a match down, but they actually have little direct interest in the club. It would be important that they are kept here, as undoubtedly their interest would increase if the ground violence became worse. The individual football supporters have high interest but low influence. Again they should be managed in order to stay in this quadrant by keeping them informed. If they are not kept informed, they might get together or utilise the press and suddenly become high power as well as high interest. The press again would be a key player, although having no contractual relationship with the club. The players would have high interest but generally low power (other than the occasional superstar). The local residents would have low power but high interest, so again they need to be kept happy so that they do not seek to group into a power base and so influence the club in a direction it does not wish to go. The low interest, low power group might be such as residents who live on the other side of the town. Provided they are not inconvenienced in any way, they would need little by way of communication other than traffic information on match days. Managing a club to satisfy these stakeholders (both current and future) would give greater longevity to a club. For instance, consider the ways in which Manchester United are developing their fan base in the Far East. (See further Question 1 in the Appendix.)

## Books of Account

Companies are controlled by recording their transactions in a set of books. There are four main books of account, of which the first three are referred to as books of 'prime' entry, as the detail of transactions are entered in these:

- cash book;

- sales ledger;

- purchase ledger; and

- nominal or general ledger.

## CASH BOOK

The cash book records all receipts and payments into a business in much the same way that an individual would record their own bank movements on the copies of their cheque stubs and paying-in books. It will therefore maintain a running balance of cash position at the bank. This book is a 'mirror' of the statements received from the bank and is, of course, not usually a book but maintained on a computer. It is, however, the same principle as a book, in that it uses 'debits' and 'credits'. A debit is the left-side entry (which represents something coming into the account) and a credit is a right-side entry (which represents something going out of the account). If there is more on the left than on the right (that is, a net debit balance), there is money in the bank, which is said to be 'in credit'. If in reverse, the bank is overdrawn. The reason that the bank is 'in credit' when we have money 'in the bank' is that the bank will owe us and therefore, in the bank's books, they will show a credit balance, whereas in our books it will be a debit balance! There will, however, always be differences between the cash book and the bank because of the timing differences of cheques being paid into and out of the bank. The process of agreeing the cash book to the bank statement is known as a 'bank reconciliation'. This is an essential process for proving accuracy and also recording items such as bank charges and interest that are only obtained from the bank statement.

If a company fails to control its cash properly, it is seriously jeopardising its long-term survival, and keeping this book correctly is fundamental to this process. It is the centre of the company's accounting system.

Another related book is used called the petty cash book, and this summarises the incidental items that are paid for by physical cash rather than by cheque. This will cover such items as sundry office expenses and travel payments for employees. It is managed like the cash book except, as it uses cash, it cannot be physically overdrawn (that is, negative cash). There has been many a fraud perpetrated through this book, as removing cash is often difficult to prove unless the culprit is actually seen doing it. It is therefore desirable to keep all the transactions through petty cash to a minimum.

## SALES LEDGER

A ledger is simply a book of account or a record. The sales ledger is a record of all the invoices sent to your customers (debits – on the left) and with the corresponding payments received from the customers (credits – on the right). Customers normally trade on credit (if the supplying organisation is not retailing) and so will constantly be in a position of owing for supplies received, and there will therefore be a debit (left-hand side) balance on this ledger representing the invoices which the customers have yet to pay. This balance is termed as 'accounts receivable' (or 'receivables'). The action of controlling this ledger by controlling the 'credit' allowed to customers is known as 'credit control', and is vital to the continued survival of the company. The money received from customers is the primary revenue and therefore the life-blood of the organisation.

## PURCHASE LEDGER

The purchase ledger works on the same principle as the sales ledger, except in reverse. It uses purchase invoices (on the credit side) rather than sales invoices, and it uses cheques paid to the suppliers (debit side) instead of cheques received from customers. Similarly to the sales ledger, there is usually a balance of bills outstanding that have yet to be paid. These are termed 'accounts payable'. Most cost items have an invoice and would be recorded in the purchase ledger, so a full analysis of all purchases can be obtained through this ledger. Wages, for instance, would not have an invoice and therefore only show in the cash book.

## NOMINAL LEDGER

This book summarises the financial affairs of the organisation. The information contained in the analysis of the previous three books of prime entry are summarised and recorded in the nominal ledger. From this is produced a 'trial balance' (a summary of all the 'debits' and 'credits' – explained later), and from that is produced an income statement and a balance sheet. It would contain details of all expense accounts, income accounts, assets, liabilities and capital sources.

There are, of course, many other records kept, such as inventory records, fixed asset records, payroll details and VAT records, but a business with several million pounds sterling turnover can function reasonably adequately with just the above main books of account.

## DOUBLE ENTRY BOOK-KEEPING

These books interlink by the 'double entry' book-keeping system (oldest surviving publication by an Italian monk and mathematician named Luca Pacioli in 1494). Money received from customers increases the bank balance and decreases the sales ledger (accounts receivable).

Money paid to suppliers decreases the bank and also the purchase ledger (accounts payable). Money drawn from the bank for the petty cash tin reduces the bank and increases petty cash.

At the end of a period, all the transactions and balances are summarised in a trial balance, where the left-hand side balances ('debits') should always equal the right-hand side balances ('credits'). Adjustments are then made (such as depreciation and closing inventory valuation) and, from this adjusted trial balance, an income statement and balance sheet are drawn up.

# 3

# Income Statements

## Broad Introduction

As previously stated, the income statement is a summary of the income and expenditure for a given period. It summarises the trading between two balance sheet dates and therefore is not a statement 'as at' a particular date but a statement 'for a period to' a particular date.

The first figure on an income statement is the 'sales' (or 'turnover' as it is sometimes called). For accounting purposes, a sale is normally executed when your company has supplied its part of the contract, whether goods or services. This means that an invoice can be sent to the customer, and this invoice becomes the 'sale' in the accounting system. It should be noted that a sale is not made either when goods are ordered or when goods are paid for. It is only when invoiced. It is a similar situation for all costs in an income statement, in that a cost is not necessarily a cost for a period if it is paid for in that period. It is a cost if the cost was 'incurred' during that period. This is known as the 'accruals' concept, in that all costs build up or 'accrue' during an accounting period, even if paid for outside that period. These costs are 'matched' to the income-producing period.

There is a basic rule for income statements in that they are nothing to do with the timing of cash being received or paid. It is a statement summarising what has been 'incurred' or what cash would be received or paid if no credit was given or taken. It is about invoices. Invoices sent out to customers are sales, whether or not paid for in that period. Invoices received from suppliers are costs, whether or not paid for in that period, although they need to be consumed in that period. Wages, of course, would not have associated invoices.

The resulting profit generated is therefore not a real or physical item like cash. It is a 'notional' item representing an improvement in the overall net assets and so purely an accounting concept. It is an increase in value of the business.

## Income Statement Sections

There are three main sections to an income statement:

- **Trading Account** – This is the buy and sell part of the statement, shown as the sales less the cost of sales, giving the gross profit. This term is now fading, due to the use of IFRS terminology, but does serve to describe well this section.

- **Overheads** – The running costs of the business are deducted from the gross profit to arrive at the operating profit.

- **Other Costs and Income** – Other costs (and non-operating income) such as financing costs are deducted, along with taxation, to arrive at the profit after tax.

### Example 1    Simple Example of an Income Statement

| | | |
|---|---|---|
| Sales | 3,000 | |
| *Less* Cost of Sales | 2,000 | |
| Gross Profit | 1,000 | Trading account ends here |
| *Less* Overheads | 300 | |
| Pre-Tax Profit | 700 | |
| Taxation | 200 | |
| After Tax Profit | 500 | |
| Dividend | 200 | These figures are strictly a part of |
| Retained Profit | 300 | the balance sheet |

## TRADING ACCOUNT

The cost of sales consists of the purchases used by adjusting the purchases of a product or service by movements in opening and closing inventory (that is, Opening inventory + purchases – Closing inventory). Other items may go into cost of sales, such as direct wages for a manufacturing company, but manufacturing companies' accounts are more complicated as they have differing stages of inventory – raw materials, work-in-progress and finished inventory. The gross profit percentage (GP/Sales × 100) is mainly influenced by changes in buying and selling prices rather than volume of trade. The absolute level of gross profit is affected by volume. Not all companies have a trading account, as they may have no direct cost of sales (such as a small consultancy company).

## OVERHEADS

Overheads are costs such as heat, light, power, administrative salaries, motor expenses etc and are largely unaffected by small alterations in turnover levels. All items that are purchased are deducted from sales to arrive at the profit; the question is how and at what stage is it deducted? If it is all used up during the year, such as telephone calls, it is all deducted. If an insurance bill relates in part to the following year, only that part which relates to the year in question is deducted, the balance being carried forward. For instance, a motor vehicle is deducted in stages over its useful life, which is known as 'depreciation'.

The overheads are deducted from the gross profit to arrive at the operating profit or profit (earnings) before interest and tax, known as PBIT (EBIT). Interest is then deducted (or added if received) to arrive at pre-tax profit.

## OTHER COSTS

Interest on loans (if there are any) and taxation are then deducted, which will leave the 'earnings' or after tax profit, which can be divided between dividends and retained profits. The dividend is then deducted to arrive at the retained profit, but these two figures are shown here just to show the link with the balance sheet, which is where they would be shown.

**Example 2**

Take a look at the following list of figures of Argonaut Ltd and arrange them into an income statement:

| | |
|---|---|
| Sales | 25,000 |
| Motor Expenses | 2,000 |
| Salaries | 4,500 |
| Depreciation | 1,400 |
| Loan Interest Paid | 800 |
| Taxation | 700 |
| Dividend Declared | 550 |
| Sundry Overheads | 2,500 |
| Interest Received | 4,000 |
| Cost of Sales | 16,000 |

**Answer**

| | | |
|---|---:|---:|
| Sales | | 25,000 |
| *Less* Cost of Sales | | 16,000 |
| Gross Profit | | 9,000 |
| *Less* Overheads | | |
| Motor Expenses | 2,000 | |
| Salaries | 3,900 | |
| Depreciation | 2,000 | |
| Sundry Overheads | 2,500 | |
| | | 10,400 |
| PBIT | | −1,400 |
| Interest Received | | 4,000 |
| | | 2,600 |
| Loan Interest Paid | | 800 |
| | | 1,800 |
| Taxation | | 700 |
| | | 1,100 |
| Dividend Declared | | 550 |
| Retained Profit for Year | | 550 |

Note how the interest received would distort the underlying profitability of the company if it was added to sales as income and therefore adjusted before the profit before interest and tax (PBIT).

Some key issues to be addressed are:

- What was the level of sales last year?

- Has the gross profit improved?

- Have the overall overheads stayed level?

- Is the PBIT higher than last year? (Currently a loss!)

- What is the likely projected sales and gross profit?

- The company is making a profit solely due to interest received, and the dividend is paid out of that. It is, in simple terms, not worth trading like this on an ongoing basis. The shareholders would make more just by earning out of the interest.

## Depreciation

Depreciation has been introduced in this example above and is frequently a source of confusion. The problem with depreciation is that it is not actually paid to anybody. It is a notional cost, by which is meant that no cash changes hands. Depreciation is that portion of value of a fixed asset, such as a motor car or machine, that has been 'consumed' during the time period. A non-current or fixed asset is one that remains in the company after the year end (that is, it is not completely used up), and is explained more fully in Chapter 4.

### DEPRECIATION METHODS – STRAIGHT LINE

Depreciation can well be described as a means of spreading the cost of an asset over its useful life. For instance, if you buy a machine costing £100,000 and expect it to last five years, the depreciation could be calculated as being one-fifth of the cost each year (or £20,000). This method is known as the 'straight line' method and creates an even spread of depreciation over the life of the asset. The assumption in this case is that the asset is worthless after five years. However, this may not necessarily be the case, and it may be that you expect the machine to be worth £20,000 in five years' time. In this case, the overall depreciation for five years would be £80,000 and this figure should be spread evenly over the five years (that is, the yearly depreciation would be £80,000 divided by five – £16,000).

The transactions for five-year straight line would look as follows:

| Year No | Value (Opening) | Depreciation | NBV (Net Book Value) |
|---------|-----------------|--------------|----------------------|
| Year 1 | £100,000 | £16,000 | £84,000 |
| Year 2 | £84,000 | £16,000 | £68,000 |
| Year 3 | £68,000 | £16,000 | £52,000 |
| Year 4 | £52,000 | £16,000 | £36,000 |
| Year 5 | £36,000 | £16,000 | £20,000 |

The assumption is that the asset could be sold for £20,000 after Year 5, which would be the value in the company balance sheet (examined in Chapter 4) after five years. This is, of course, an estimate and, in all likelihood, it would not be sold for exactly that figure. This does not matter, as the final bookkeeping would take account of this by showing a profit or loss on sale. For instance, if the machine was sold after five years for £16,000, the income statement would show a loss on sale of assets of £4,000 pounds. If it was sold for £23,000, the income statement would show a profit on sale of assets of £3,000. Therefore, a profit or loss on sale of an asset is effectively an adjustment to the depreciation, which has either been over- or under-charged. However, the cautious assumption for depreciation when using the straight line method is to assume that the asset becomes valueless at the end of the depreciated period, unless the asset is expected to be sold with some life left in it. For instance, a contract might be for three years, after which a machine being used in that contract would be sold as having no further use in the company and would have significant life and value remaining.

Organisations are required to decide upon various accounting policies, and the method of depreciation is one of those policies. With the straight line method, the time period is agreed between the finance director and the external auditors on the basis of assessing the fairest estimate of the life of the asset. If a long time period is used, the yearly depreciation will be less, therefore showing a higher profit in the accounts and also a higher asset value, which shows the relative importance of a realistic estimate.

## DEPRECIATION METHODS – REDUCING BALANCE

A second, much-used method is the 'reducing balance' technique, which is best described by looking at the figures for purchasing a £100,000 machine, as before. Effectively, the depreciation percentage is decided upon (in this case, 20%), and this is then applied each year to the 'reduced balance value'.

The transactions for 20% reducing balance would look as follows:

| Year No | Value (Opening) | Depreciation | NBV (Net Book Value) |
|---------|-----------------|--------------|----------------------|
| Year 1  | £100,000        | £20,000      | £80,000              |
| Year 2  | £80,000         | £16,000      | £64,000              |
| Year 3  | £64,000         | £12,800      | £51,200              |
| Year 4  | £51,200         | £10,240      | £40,960              |
| Year 5  | £40,960         | £8,192       | £32,768              |

This method clearly shows higher depreciation in the earlier years, which is closer to the real valuation in many instances, such as with motor cars where a 25% rate is commonly used. With this method, the asset never reaches zero value, although in practice it may be 'written off' after so many years as it may have been scrapped.

If a smaller percentage is used, the yearly depreciation will be less, therefore showing a higher profit in the accounts and also a higher asset value. Once again, a realistic rate is necessary to avoid distortion of the profits.

Accounting policies such as depreciation methods should be stated in the published accounts, and therefore any change to accounting policies should be viewed with considerable caution as these methods should be applied consistently year to year. An organisation may use several methods for depreciation but should *consistently* apply the same method to the same block of assets. For instance, cars might be at 25% reducing balance, plant and machinery on ten-year straight line, and IT equipment on 50% reducing balance.

Depreciation can often be a source of excess profit concealment in a supplier's quotation by being included more than once, and this is discussed in the next chapter.

## Advanced Issues

In reality, the income statement can become a little more complex, particularly in the trading account, where we might be looking at management accounts. For instance, the cost of sales may be broken down as in the following accounts extracts:

**Example 3    Income Statement (trading a/c section)**

| | | |
|---|---:|---:|
| Sales | | 300,000 |
| *Less* Cost of Sales | | |
| Opening Inventory | 28,000 | |
| Materials Purchased | 100,000 | |
| Total | 128,000 | |
| *Less* Closing Inventory | 32,000 | |
| Materials Used | 96,000 | |
| Direct Wages | 43,000 | |
| Cost of Sales | | 139,000 |
| Gross Profit | | 161,000 |

Here, the cost of sales is broken down into a split between materials (used) and direct wages. The direct wages relate to those who provide the service or make the product. For instance, in a manufacturing company they would be the wages of those on the 'shop floor', such as machine operators. They add value to the materials bought in. You will notice the 'materials used' figure is added to the 'direct wages' and not the 'materials purchased'. Otherwise, if we wished to simply reduce the profit (to pay less tax, for instance), we could purchase extra materials just before the year end to eliminate some of the margin. Instead, we take the materials purchased and adjust it for inventory movements, by adding the opening inventory and deducting the closing inventory, to arrive at the materials that we have actually consumed or 'used'.

The closing inventory figure is one of the most commonly abused figures in accounts, and manipulation of this comes under the heading of 'creative accounting'. For instance, if we wished to show a gross profit of £20,000 more, we simply need to over-value (falsely) the closing inventory figure by £20,000. The closing inventory becomes £52,000 and, because this is deducted, the materials used figure falls to £76,000 and the cost of sales falls to £119,000, making the gross profit £181,000. This is a misrepresentation of the figures, and the auditors should spot this and prevent its occurrence. However, it is worth being aware of, as some companies do try to manipulate figures to show what they would like to show rather than the facts. (Enron and WorldCom are recent well-known examples of accounting misrepresentation.)

Another figure that is sometimes extracted in certain industries is earnings before interest, tax, depreciation and amortisation (EBITDA). Amortisation is the name given to depreciation on intangible assets such as goodwill, which is discussed later. The reason this is used is that it can sometimes be a better comparator in industries where there is very heavy capital expenditure, such as 'telecoms', and the differing depreciation policies adopted by companies could have a distorting effect. It also gives a loose approximation to the cash generative ability of the company to repay loans, as depreciation is not a cost that affects the cash flow of an organisation.

The figures for Argonaut Ltd (in Example 2 above) would look as follows:

**Example 4**

**Income statement**

| | | |
|---|---|---|
| Sales | | 25,000 |
| *Less* Cost of Sales | | (16,000) |
| Gross Profit | | 9,000 |
| *Less* Overheads: | | |
| Motor Expenses | 2,000 | |
| Salaries | 3,900 | |
| Sundry Overheads | 2,500 | |
| | | (8,400) |
| EBITDA | | 600 |
| Depreciation (and Amortisation) | | (2,000) |
| PBIT | | (1,400) |
| Interest Received | | 4,000 |
| | | 2,600 |
| Loan Interest Paid | | (800) |
| | | 1,800 |

| | |
|---|---|
| Taxation | (700) |
| | 1,100 |
| Dividend Declared | (550) |
| Retained Profit for Year | 550 |

This shows a positive EBITDA figure and, as this figure is sometimes used as a simplistic view of cash generation, it is therefore better than the negative PBIT figure shown after depreciation. The reason is that depreciation is a cost that is not actually paid out and so does not affect cash generation. (See further Question 2 in the Appendix.)

# 4

# Balance Sheet – Statement of Financial Position

## Introduction

As already briefly explained, a balance sheet is a statement of what you own and what you owe. In business language, this is a statement of assets and liabilities at one point in time.

If we were to list all our assets in one column and all our liabilities in another column, with the net difference added to the smaller column, not surprisingly the two columns would balance. Hence, the term 'balance sheet' is created, although this 'difference' figure is not simply plugged in to make it balance:

|        | Assets | Liabilities |                              |
|--------|--------|-------------|------------------------------|
|        | X      | X           |                              |
|        | X      | X           |                              |
|        | X      | X           |                              |
|        | X      | X           |                              |
|        | X      | X           | Difference between two columns |
| Totals | XX     | XX          |                              |

This form of statement would be easy to understand but it would not convey enough information to the readers of the statement, particularly investors, accountants and business managers.

It is therefore drawn up in what is known as a vertical format under five major headings. These headings are known as follows:

- non-current assets (fixed assets)

- current assets

- members' equity

- non-current liabilities (creditors due > 12 months)

- current liabilities (creditors due < 12 months)

The net worth (or members' equity) is the sum of the shareholders' investment and the profits made to date. This is the balance sheet value of the company, and should not be confused with the market value, which is what a buyer of an organisation would be prepared to pay for it; and the balance sheet value would only be a part of that, as the value would also be influenced by reputation, market share, brand identity etc.

An example is as follows, and it is recommended that you keep referring to this example as you read this part:

## Example

| 1. Non-current Assets | Cost | Depn | NBV |
|---|---|---|---|
| | 1,200 | 200 | 1,000 |
| 2. Current Assets | | | 400 |
| Total Assets | | | 1,400 |
| 3. Members' Equity | | | |
| Share Capital | 300 | | |
| Reserves | 200 | | |
| Shareholders' Funds | | | 500 |
| 4. Non-current Liabilities | | | |
| Creditors Due > 12 months (eg Loans) | | | 600 |
| 5. Current Liabilities | | | 300 |
| Members' Equity and Liabilities | | | 1,400 |

The difference between the assets and liabilities is the members' equity. This could be regarded as liabilities, because they are effectively owed to the shareholders, although there is no liability to repay them unless the company is liquidated.

It is perhaps a good time to introduce the concept of 'companies' and their 'shareholders'.

## Companies and Shareholders

A company is regarded as a separate legal entity from either those who manage it or those who own it. The owners are known as 'shareholders' who delegate the management of their company to managers known as directors. The directors are just like any other employee except with more onerous responsibilities. The owners or shareholders become shareholders by investing money in the company in return for a 'share' of that company that will be in proportion to the amount of money invested. It is like dividing a cake. For example, Michael, Bruce and Jimmy set up a company and Michael invests £1,500, Bruce invests £800, Jimmy invests £600.

The company would look as follows:

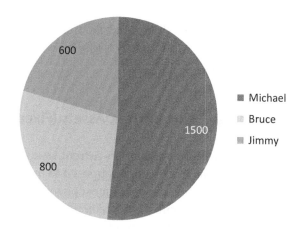

**Figure 4.1     The Relative Share Proportions of the Company**

A company is regarded as a separate legal entity.

The total value of that company is £1,500 + £800 + £600 = £2,900.

Michael would own over half of the company and therefore effectively have control of the company. He would own 1,500 £1 shares, Bruce would own 800 £1 shares, and Jimmy would own 600 £1 shares. Suppose the company made a profit of £1,450 after tax and 'retained' that profit (that is, it did not distribute it as dividend); in that case, the company would be bigger at the end of the year by that profit of £1,450. However, there would be just the same number of shares distributed between Michael, Bruce and Jimmy. The company would now be worth £2,900 starting capital plus £1,450 profit retained = £4,350.

Each share was originally purchased for £1 (called the 'face', the 'par' or the 'nominal' value). What do you think each share is now worth?

The calculation is straightforward:

Value of company ÷ No of shares

= 4,350 ÷ 2,900

= £1.50 per share.

This therefore gives an indication in part of why share prices fluctuate on the stock market.

There can be different types of shares, but the normal share in the UK is called an 'ordinary' share (USA – Common Stock). These usually carry voting rights equivalent to the number of shares held.

## Balance Sheet Headings – Non-current Assets (Fixed Assets)

The first heading on a balance sheet is the non-current assets. These are often referred to as assets that you mean to keep, as opposed to those that you mean to sell. Of course, you will probably dispose of most of your non-current assets over time, but they are purchased with a view to increasing the capacity of the company and with a longer-term view in mind.

Ownership of land and buildings is generally considered good on a balance sheet because its value is usually rising rather than depreciating, and it is considered very good security (USA – collateral) for a bank or lending institution. (Although the recent mortgage crisis caused by the global banking sector's lack of adherence to its own basic code has caused property values to fall.)

Non-current assets are listed in order of the most 'fixed' first. By fixed, it does not mean physically fixed, but it does mean fixed in the balance sheet, in the short term at least.

Examples are as follows:

*Tangible*:

- land and buildings

- plant and machinery

- fixtures and fittings

- office equipment

- motor vehicles

- investments

*Intangible*:

- goodwill, patents, brands

Investments are shares in or loans to other companies. Intangible (untouchable) assets have been the subject of much accounting discussion in the UK, as some other countries will not include intangibles such as brands on the balance sheet due to the difficulty in valuing them and the distorting effect on the overall balance sheet.

Goodwill arises upon the take-over of a company when more is paid for that company than the value of the assets.

Question: Why pay more for a company than the value of the assets?

Answer: Because, when you buy a company, you buy the future earning ability of that company (that is, customers, orders, contacts, products, technology etc).

Patents are a legal right to protect a product which then cannot be copied by another company. Product distribution rights, trademarks and copyright may also fall into this category.

Brands are separately registered brands belonging to a company which may be capable of being sold separately, such as Perrier or McDonalds. The higher the brand value placed on the balance sheet, the higher the apparent net worth of that company. (Brands are independently valued by specialists, such as the top management consultancies or Interbrand – a global branding consultancy company – although brands are usually only shown on a balance sheet if they have been purchased.)

These intangibles are depreciated like tangible non-current assets, but the term used is 'amortisation'.

A fixed asset is not a fixed asset because it fits into one of the above categories. The main factor in its categorisation is how it is used. For instance, a motor dealership would not have all their cars on a balance sheet as non-current assets. They are clearly goods for resale and therefore inventory. This would be the same for a property developer with a bank of land.

## Balance Sheet Headings – Current Assets

These are short-term assets or 'transient' assets, in that they are always changing due to their composition. For example, the bank account in a company is changing in balance every day due to transactions. By short term is meant within 12 months.

This is the second heading, and they are listed in order of reverse liquidity, which means that the furthest away from cash is placed first.

The main items are:

- inventory

- short-term investments

- accounts receivable (and prepayments)

- bank

- petty cash

### INVENTORIES

Inventories are at three stages in the process: raw materials, work-in-progress, and finished goods. Additional inventories can be consumables, such as stationery. Inventories should be valued at the lower of cost and net realisable value. By this is meant that, if an item of inventory purchased for £20 can be sold for £25, it should be valued at £20. However, if it will cost £7 to make it saleable, the net realisable value would be £25 – £7 = £18 and this should be the new inventory value.

## SHORT-TERM INVESTMENTS

These are shares in or loans to other companies that are intended to be liquidated within a year of the balance sheet date.

## ACCOUNTS RECEIVABLE AND PREPAYMENTS

Prepayments (that is, bills paid in advance) are added onto accounts receivable (money owed to the company as a result of sales made for which no money has yet been received). Bad debts (money not expected to be paid for goods) are deducted from accounts receivable. Accounts receivable were formerly referred to as debtors.

## BANK

The bank figure is what the company's own cash book states is in the bank (that is, it is reconciled for unpresented cheques). This means that allowance is made for cheques paid into or out of the bank that have not yet shown through the bank statements. If the bank is overdrawn (in other words, the company owes the bank), it is not shown here under current assets as a negative, but it is shown under current liabilities.

## PETTY CASH

This is the balance of money left on the company's premises.

## Balance Sheet Headings – Members' Equity

The total of this block is the net difference between the assets and liabilities.

The capital is the 'share capital', and this is the 'issued' share capital as opposed to the 'authorised' share capital. The difference is that, as part of a company's rules and regulations, it will have a maximum number of shares that it may issue without needing a change in its regulations, which can be onerous. This maximum is known as the 'authorised' share capital. The issued share capital is the number and amount in value of shares actually issued in return for money or commitment to pay. (They can also be issued in return for other shares in a takeover situation.) Added to this may be a share premium account (USA – Capital surplus), which is a surplus arising from issuing shares above their 'face' (par) value. Clearly a share which has a face value of £1 and was originally issued ten years ago would normally be worth considerably more today (because the company has grown through retained profits). So, a further issue of shares would be at the same 'face' value but the investor would pay a higher price. In other words, one might pay £3.50 per share and receive a £1 share. The £2.50 excess paid would represent the growth in share value since the original share issue.

The reserves are a general term for all undistributed profits and they may be split into different reserve funds which are essentially the same total fund. The main two differences in reserves are revenue reserves and capital reserves.

Revenue reserves are the accumulated profits of a company which may be distributed to shareholders by way of dividend. They may also be referred to as retained profits, earnings to date or accumulated funds.

Capital reserves arise when, for instance, the non-current assets are re-valued upwards and this effectively increases the net asset value of the company. It must therefore have the effect of increasing the overall capital value, and this increase is called a capital or 'revaluation' reserve. This reserve cannot be distributed by way of a dividend to shareholders.

The total of the share capital and reserves is known as equity value or members' equity.

## Balance Sheet Headings – Non-current Liabilities

These are often referred to as 'creditors due over 12 months' and are principally long-term loans, either from a bank or a finance company.

They are often secured on the assets of a company and are the last deduction in arriving at the 'total net assets' of a company or its 'total net worth'.

Accounts are drawn up with the underlying objective in the UK that they show a 'true and fair view', and this phrase overrides even accounting standards when compliance with them would not provide the required true and fair view.

In showing a true and fair view, four key accounting concepts are assumed.

First, it assumes (for instance) that the assets have been depreciated at a rate that shows a fair write down of the asset based on a fair estimate of its life. Once a depreciation method has been agreed, it should be applied 'consistently'. This is true of all accounting policies and is known as the 'consistency' concept. Once a policy is agreed between the directors and the auditors, it should (normally) be maintained and applies similarly to all other policies.

Secondly, it assumes all valuations will be based on what is known as the 'going concern' concept. This concept in accounting assumes values in a balance sheet as if the business were continuing. This is not the same as the resale value of the assets on liquidation.

Thirdly, it assumes that the 'accruals' concept is used (mentioned earlier). That is that costs 'accrue' during a period and, irrespective of when they are paid, it is the cost that the company has 'incurred' in doing its business during the accounting period.

A fourth and final fundamental accounting concept is the 'prudence' concept. This assumes that, in making valuations, a cautious or prudent approach is taken. For instance, inventory is valued at the lower of cost and net realisable value. A company should not take a profit until it crystallises (that is, the item is actually sold).

## Balance Sheet Headings – Current Liabilities

These are 'creditors due within 12 months'. The elements are as follows:

- accounts payable and accruals

- short-term loans

- bank overdraft

*Accounts payable and accruals* – these may be trade (suppliers), expenses (such as electricity, telephone) or government (taxation). Accruals are bills not yet received for expenses incurred prior to the balance sheet date.

*Short-term loans* – these are that part of any loan repayable within 12 months. So, whilst they may be loans taken out for repayment in the short term, such as a loan to cover a short-term inventory purchase, they are more commonly that portion of any long-term loan that has to be repaid within 12 months of the balance sheet date.

*Bank overdraft* – the bank figure is what the company's own cash book states is owed to the bank (if it is an overdraft); that is, it is reconciled for unpresented cheques. In published accounts, there is one heading for short-term bank loans and overdrafts.

If the current liabilities are subtracted from the current assets, this net figure is referred to as 'net current assets' and should always be positive in the very least in order to ensure that there are adequate assets for paying short-term bills (in other words, the current assets are greater than the current liabilities).

This figure is the *working capital* of the company, and it is extremely important that the elements of this are managed correctly as if, for instance, too much money is invested in inventory, the company may find it cannot afford to pay its other day-to-day bills. Similarly, if too much money is owed to the company and not paid on time, paying a creditor's bills will be difficult.

The total assets always equals shareholders' equity total plus the total of the long- and short-term liabilities.

## Question

Convert into a balance sheet and assess the liquidity:

| | |
|---|---|
| Petty Cash | 1,000 |
| Shares | 70,000 |
| Land and Buildings | 150,000 |
| Bank Overdraft | 40,000 |
| Motor Vehicles | 20,000 |
| Reserves | 90,000 |
| Inventory | 70,000 |
| Accounts Receivable | 49,000 |
| Accounts Payable | 60,000 |
| Plant and Machinery | 30,000 |
| Loans (Long-term) | 60,000 |

## Answer

**Assets**
Non-current Assets (Fixed)

| | | |
|---|---|---|
| Land and Buildings | 150,000 | |
| Plant and Machinery | 30,000 | |
| Motor Vehicles | 20,000 | |
| | | 200,000 |

**Current Assets**

| | | |
|---|---|---|
| Inventory | 70,000 | |
| Accounts Receivable | 49,000 | |
| Petty Cash | 1,000 | |
| | | 120,000 |

**Total Assets**  | 320,000 |

Equity and Liabilities
Shares and Reserves

| | | |
|---|---|---|
| Shares | 70,000 | |
| Reserves | 90,000 | |
| | | 160,000 |

**Non-current Liabilities – Loans**    60,000

Current Liabilities

| | | |
|---|---|---|
| Accounts Payable | 60,000 | |
| | | 100,000 |

Total Liabilities and Shareholders' Equity   | 320,000 |

It should be noted that the layout is not always shown this way, and published accounts tend to show the figures in one vertical line as this facilitates comparison with the previous year. This balance sheet is shown using the International Accounting Standards, and the current UK GAAP presentation (for non-quoted companies) for the next two years until change would be as follows:

### Example      UK GAAP Presentation

| **Fixed Assets** | | |
|---|---|---|
| Land and Buildings | | 150,000 |
| Plant and Machinery | | 30,000 |
| Motor Vehicles | | 20,000 |
| | | 200,000 |
| **Current Assets** | | |
| Stocks and WIP | 70,000 | |
| Debtors | 49,000 | |
| Petty Cash | 1,000 | |
| | 120,000 | |
| **Current Liabilities** | | |
| Bank Overdraft | 40,000 | |
| Creditors | 60,000 | |
| | 100,000 | |
| **Net Current Assets** | | 20,000 |
| Total Assets less Current Liabilities | | 220,000 |
| Loans | | 60,000 |
| Total Net Assets | | 160,000 |
| Shares and Reserves | | |
| Shares | | 70,000 |
| Reserves | | 90,000 |
| | | 160,000 |

Note the following name differences between UK GAAP and International Accounting Standards:

| **UK GAAP** | **IAS** |
|---|---|
| Profit & Loss A/c | Income Statement |
| Balance Sheet | Balance Sheet or SOFP |
| Fixed Assets | Non-Current Assets |
| Capital & Reserves | Members Equity |
| Stock | Inventory |
| Debtors | Accounts Receivable |
| Creditors | Accounts Payable |

The indenting of current assets and liabilities is purely to separate them out from the other main figures and does complicate the view (although it shows the short-term working capital), but the five headings are still in essence the same.

When assessing the liquidity, the question is how easily the company can pay its short-term bills. This lies in its working capital, or its current assets and current liabilities. Using ratio analysis, we can look at the ratio of current assets to current liabilities (ratios are covered in Chapter 6), but in simple terms we can just examine the actual figures that make up the working capital (net current assets). The inventory is clearly a proportionally high figure. The accounts receivable are lower than the accounts payable and there is a significant overdraft. Therefore the money receivable in the short term does not cover what is needed to pay the short-term bills, and this company is therefore under the control of the bank because of the overdraft. It must reduce its inventory, get its money in quickly and pay it out slowly. It may need to raise further long-term finance if these working capital actions are not enough, so it will then look to its non-current assets for security for further borrowing. It is currently borrowing £100,000 (loans and overdraft), and the land and buildings are valued at £150,000, so it would appear that further funds could be available on security, provided the company was profitable enough to repay the extra interest and loans. Otherwise, further private share capital would need to be raised from investors. (See further Question 3 in the Appendix.)

## Advanced Issues

There are a few extra refinements with which a practitioner ought to be familiar.

The non-current assets would be placed in order of the most fixed, or longest life, first (that is, land and buildings). Current assets are placed in order of reverse liquidity. This means the furthest away in life cycle from cash is placed first (inventory?), followed by accounts receivable and then money in the bank. The current liabilities would be placed normally with the loans and overdrafts first, followed by all other accounts payable.

The basic balance sheet would be quite simple for published accounts, with the complications being in the notes. It is often said that 'the devil is in the detail', and the notes are where one finds statements about bank facilities, loan repayment dates, contingent liabilities (such as a possible law suit cost contingent on losing the case) and underfunding of pension funds, for instance. The following is an imaginary extract of Premslack plc for the six months to September 2011 (with IAS alterations).

### Example

| Balance sheet summary | £million |
|---|---|
| Tangible Non-current Assets | 250 |
| Intangible Non-current Assets | 50 |
| Other Non-current Assets | 34 |
| | 334 |

Current Assets

| Total Inventory | 59 |
|---|---|

|  | Accounts Receivable and Prepaid | 130 |
|  | Intra Group Accounts Receivable | 58 |
|  | Other Current Assets | 20 |
|  | Cash and Equivalents | 27 |
|  |  | 294 |
| TOTAL ASSETS |  | 628 |

EQUITY AND TOTAL LIABILITIES
MEMBERS' EQUITY

|  | Ordinary Share Capital | 121 |
|  | Retained Profits | 20 |
|  | Capital Reserves | 24 |
|  | Preference Shares | 10 |
|  |  | 175 |
|  | Less Minority Interests | 28 |
|  |  | 147 |

Long-term Liabilities

|  | Long-term Debt | 206 |
|  | Other | 19 |
|  | Provisions | 13 |
|  |  | 238 |

Current Liabilities

|  | Trade Creditors | 187 |
|  | Loans and Overdrafts | 9 |
|  | Due within Group | 17 |
|  | Other Creditors | 30 |
| Total |  | 243 |

| Total Equity and Liabilities |  | 628 |

Some of these headings need explanation.

In the current assets and liabilities there are 'Intra Group Accounts Receivable' and 'Due within Group'. As these are group accounts, they are at zero because they cancel out within the group but, if these were not 'group' accounts, they could show figures that might imply the holding company was 'milking' the subsidiary by not repaying the loans (in other words, the money was due back to the subsidiary but never being paid and on permanent loan).

In current liabilities, there are short-term loans. This might imply the company has taken out short-term loans, but more likely is that this is the element of a long-term loan that is repayable within 12 months. For instance, if a £50,000 loan was taken out over five years, this would show as £10,000 as a short-term loan and £40,000 as a long-term loan.

In the Capital and Reserves is a **Share Premium** account. This occurs when new shares are issued at above their par value which is normal as a share which has a par value of 20p might be worth several pounds. So a new shareholder would pay the market price of, say, £1.30. The excess above the 20p (£1.10) would be classified as share premium. For all intents and purposes the Share Premium account can be treated just as share capital and so not normally repayable.

**Capital Reserves** are 'Revaluation' reserves and occur normally when properties are re-valued.

**Minority Interests**. These occur where there are group accounts. Group accounts are produced where there is more than one company in the 'Group'. Put simply, all the figures of each company are added together but with intra group transactions eliminated. The group accounts therefore show the effects of the total trading of the group with the outside environment. Minority Interests are those shares that are owned by investors outside the group. For instance, if a company was taken over and 20% of the shares stay with the current owner, these would rank as minority interests and would be deducted from the capital value of the group to show the true ownership value of the group to the group investors.

# 5

# Cash Flow Statements

## Cash Flow Statements (or Statements of Cash Flow)

The cash flow statement is probably the most confusing of the three statements and it is best described as a highlighting mechanism for movements in the items that affect the bank balance. What the statement does is to show how a given level of operating profit (or loss) converts itself into a movement in the bank balance. One might reasonably expect, without prior knowledge, that, if a company made a profit of £345,000, the cash position would improve by £345,000. To put it another way, it answers the question that a client once put to me as follows: 'You told me I made £37,000 profit last year, how come my bank balance has got worse by £17,000?' The sort of thing that causes this difference is capital expenditure, which uses cash but does not show in the computation of profit. Also, it depends when customers pay their bills, as profit is taken at the point of invoice (and not when paid); if the accounts receivable increase, that will make the cash position worse.

The cash flow statement is designed to show:

- relationship between profit and cash movement during the period;

- sources of cash for the period;

- how the cash has been used; and

- material movements in assets and liabilities.

It is produced by:

- adjusting the profit for non-cash items; and

- calculating the movements of assets and liabilities between balance sheets.

The sources and uses of the funds are as follows:

| Source of Funds | Use of Funds |
|---|---|
| Profit (adjusted) | Loss |
| Sale of assets | Purchase of assets |
| Reduced inventory and accounts receivable | Increased inventory and accounts receivable |
| Increased accounts payable | Decreased accounts payable |
| Share issue | Share buy-back |
| Increased loans | Decreased loans |

The easiest way to demonstrate a cash flow statement is to work through a simple example of two years' balance sheets:

### Example

| | Year 1 | Year 2 |
|---|---|---|
| ASSETS | | |
| Non-current Assets | 500 | 700 |
| Inventory | 100 | 130 |
| Accounts Receivable | 300 | 250 |
| Bank | 300 | (100) |
| Total Assets | 1200 | 980 |
| LIABILITIES | | |
| Accounts Payable | 200 | 300 |
| Loans | 650 | 230 |
| Shares | 100 | 150 |
| Reserves | 250 | 300 |
| Total Capital and Liabilities | 1200 | 980 |

For the sake of simplicity, we shall assume that the increase in reserves represents the profit for the year. We start with this figure at the top of the statement and adjust it for what creates, and what uses, cash; and the resulting balance at the end should equal the movement in the bank. If the movements in each item are recorded on a statement on the basis of whether they improve cash (source) or use cash (use), we end up with a statement as follows:

| Sources: | |
|---|---|
| Profit | 50 |
| Reduction in Accounts Receivable | 50 |
| Increase in Accounts Payable | 100 |
| Share Issue | 50 |
| Total Sources (A) | 250 |
| Uses: | |
| Purchase of Non-current Assets | 200 |
| Increase in Inventory | 30 |

| | |
|---|---|
| Loan repayments | 420 |
| Total Uses (B) | 650 |
| Movement in Bank (A – B) | (£400) |

This shows that, although there was a profit of £50, the major items are an improvement in cash from holding back on payment of bills (accounts payable) but there has been a purchase of fixed assets of £200 and loans of £420 have been repaid. In other words, the statement 'highlights' the major movements in funds. (Also shown is the finance raised from a share issue of £50 and a reduction in accounts receivable which would imply the bank would be worse off by £50 if the accounts receivable stayed at the same level of £300.) (See further Question 4 in the Appendix.)

## Advanced Issues

The reality is that the cash flow statement evolved from what was previously called a 'sources and application of funds statement' and is a more complicated version, as various sections are netted off against each other. Rather than the sources and uses of funds being listed in total, they are listed under specific headings created by their differing cash flow management requirements, as follows:

- CASH FLOWS FROM OPERATING ACTIVITIES
  - Operating profit, depreciation, working capital movement
    - Interest Paid
    - Tax Paid

- CASH FLOWS FROM INVESTING ACTIVITIES
  - Non-current Asset Movements
  - Interest and Dividends Received

- CASH FLOWS FROM FINANCING ACTIVITIES
  - Share and loan movements and dividends paid

- NET MOVEMENT IN CASH

- CASH AT BEGINNING

- CASH AT THE END

There are essentially three main headings which net down to the movement in cash.

The first heading is the 'Cash Flows from Operating Activities', where we take the operating profit and the depreciation is then added to it to create the 'adjusted' profit. This is because the depreciation does not affect the cash position and is purely a 'notional' cost. Then the working capital movement excluding bank (inventory, accounts receivable, accounts payable) is added and interest paid and tax are deducted. It is desirable that this net figure is positive, as this is the underlying cash generation figure for the company.

The second heading is the 'Cash Flows from Investing Activities', which basically shows the effects on cash flow of buying or selling non-current assets. This would include the purchase and sale of whole companies as well. Interest and dividends from investments would also be shown here.

The third heading is the 'Cash Flows from Financing Activities', which shows the effects of loans received or paid off, share issues and dividends paid.

These three headings added together would account for the 'Overall Movement in Cash' which, when added to the opening bank balance, would reconcile with the closing bank balance.

**Example**

A detailed example of two years' balance sheets and the cash flow statement for Rumper Ltd might look as follows:

**Balance Sheet as at 30 June (£million)**

|  | 2012 | 2011 |
|---|---|---|
| Non-current Assets |  |  |
| Cost | 119 | 85 |
| Depreciation | (37) | (26) |
|  | 82 | 59 |
| Current Assets |  |  |
| Inventories | 40 | 34 |
| Accounts Receivable | 24 | 26 |
| Bank | 13 | 10 |
|  | 77 | 70 |
| TOTAL ASSETS | **159** | **129** |
| Members Equity |  |  |
| Ordinary Shares of £1 Each | 29 | 26 |
| Retained Profit | 65 | 43 |
|  | **94** | **69** |
| Long-term Loans (10%) | **10** | **20** |

| Current Liabilities | | |
|---|---|---|
| Trade Accounts Payable | | |
| Taxation | 15 | 12 |
| Dividend | 17 | 13 |
| | 55 | 40 |
| Total Equity and Liabilities | **159** | **129** |

- no non-current assets were sold or re-valued during year;

- of the loans, £10 million were paid off at the end of 2008;

- operating profit is £55 million; and

- note that the tax and dividends in the cash flow statement should be those actually paid during the year.

A cash flow statement for the year to 30 June 2009 would appear as follows:

| | | |
|---|---|---|
| **Operating Profit** | | |
| (Movement in Profits plus Tax+divi+Interest) | | |
| (65–43+17+15+2) | | 55 |
| Add depreciation | | 11 |
| Adjusted profit | | 66 |
| Add Working Capital Movement | | |
| (– Inventory Inc + Decrease in Accounts Receivable + Increase in Accounts Payable) | | 4 |
| | | |
| **Cash Flow from Operating Activities – Inflow** | | 70 |
| Less Taxation | -12 | |
| Less Interest Paid (£10m @ 10%) | -1 | -13 |
| **Net Cash Flow from Operating Activities – Inflow** | | 57 |
| | | |
| *Investing Activities* | | |
| Purchase of Non-current Assets | | -34 |
| | | |
| **Net Cash Inflow before Financing** | | 23 |
| | | |
| *Financing* | | |
| Issue of Shares | 3 | |
| Loan redemption | -10 | |
| Dividends Paid (during year) | -13 | -20 |
| | | |
| **Increase in Cash & Cash Equivalents** | | 3 |

This reconciles to the movement in all the bank accounts.

The interpretation of this would be as follows:

- The company made an operating profit of £55 million but the cash only improved overall by £3 million.

- The net cash flow from operating activities should be compared with last year and also it should be positive. In this case, it is + £57 million. This means the company is generating cash from its day-to-day activities. Ideally, the movement in the bank (cash and cash equivalents) would also be positive. However, it is often the case that this is negative in any given year when heavy investments are made, but one would expect in the longer term that these would be paid for out of operating cash flow plus the finance raised from the financing activities.

- One would then examine all the more significant figures to establish the 'primary' reasons for the change in the bank situation. In this case, the primary reason for the cash not being higher is the large purchase of non-current assets and the amount of the loan that has been repaid, as well as the dividend to shareholders.

# 6

# Interpretation of Accounts

## Introduction

This chapter covers the means of assessing a company's 'financial' performance, based on a detailed study of the previous statements described. It may refer to a company's own figures where a buyer may be assessing their own company against a budget for instance, or more commonly where assessing a supplier's accounts. This is done by looking at the absolute figures, trends, calculating and assessing ratios and the limitations of ratios.

The first stage of interpretation of accounts should be to examine the absolute figures over a period of ideally three years or more. This will give us an idea of trends without needing any detailed calculations of figures. Remember that, in order to calculate a trend, you need three years of accounts to give you two years of movement. If this movement is in the same direction, we have the beginning of a trend. The problem with comparing only two years of accounts is that there will always be some movement from one year to the next, and so to interpret this as a trend could be completely erroneous. Having said that, for the purposes of the following exercises, only two years' accounts will be used to limit the information on the page, and movements will be interpreted as a trend (purely for reason of simplicity).

## Where to Start?

It is always best to start with sales, as this will determine many of the cost changes as well as changes in some of the balance sheet items – particularly the working capital. Let us assume sales have increased by 10%.

Then we should run down the income statement, noting down any major changes over the periods. It may be that, if sales have increased 10% and the materials have increased 20%, there is immediately apparent a problem with the materials costs irrespective of any ratios. There might be a similar issue with the direct wages and other costs. The overheads would not be expected to rise as much as 10%, as these are predominantly 'fixed' costs (covered in detail in Part II) and so should rise little, if at all. We should then follow on with the balance sheet, noting down any large movements. If inventory, for instance, has grown 15%, we would assume that there is a loss of control of inventory (unless we had reason to believe that the company had made a deliberate policy to hold more inventory, for instance through a comment in the published accounts). Similarly for accounts receivable, if they had risen 25% (with sales only rising 10%) they are having problems getting their money in. We track the other movements of assets and liabilities. If a cash flow statement has been produced, this will highlight all these movements on the balance sheet and so short circuit a little of our analysis. We can establish what has used cash and what has created it. This overview approach is essential, as it gives a 'gut' feel about the company which often tells us 80% of the situation without needing ratios.

For instance, it tells us:

- What the level of the sales are and what the growth is.

- Whether the company is profitable.

- Whether the company has money in the bank.

- Whether the company has long-term debt.

- Whether the company is buying or selling its non-current assets.

- Whether the company is stockpiling or having problems with its accounts receivable or accounts payable.

It must be stressed that this provides a very useful overview which can be refined by the use of ratio analysis.

## What are Financial Ratios?

Financial ratios are ratios that are used to assess a company's performance over a period of time.

If one was given a ratio on a company and asked what it meant, it would be very hard to give a sensible explanation without first knowing a little more about the company and the context within which the ratios were produced.

It is therefore important to decide why the ratios are being produced and how they will be interpreted before they are produced. All ratios are 'relative' in their interpretation, and we must therefore pick sensible bases against which to interpret the ratios so produced. We therefore compare the ratios produced with these bases or comparators.

There are three basic comparators used.

1.  **Compared to Budgets** – Here the ratios are compared with what the company thought it ought to have done. This would only be available for internal comparison. This comparison could only be used on internal accounts due to the access to information.

2.  **Compared to History** – Here the ratios are compared with what the company achieved in the last year.

3.  **Compared to the Competition** – Here the ratios are compared either with the industry average or key competitors.

## Limitations to Financial Ratios

When interpreting financial ratios of external companies, in addition to interpreting them with regard to industry norms, history etc, it is also necessary to take a view on other aspects of potential significance which may have an effect on the interpretation. For instance:

- **Accounting policies** – Two companies may depreciate assets at different rates, causing a distortion in the profits.

- **Type of trade** – There is little use in comparing the ratios of an engineering company with those of a restaurant, although return on capital can be universally applied.

- **Year end date** – Two companies may have different financial year ends and, as the balance sheet is drawn up on one particular date at the year end, any ratios utilizing balance sheet figures may be open to wide interpretation due to seasonality or effects of a major event.

- **Size of company and stage of growth** – Again, a large multinational will have very different ratios from a small sub-contract engineering company.

These limitations do not mean that comparisons are not worthwhile but they do mean that caution should be applied to the interpretations. For instance, when assessing internal figures, care must be taken when comparing to internal budgets drawn up under different market conditions.

We shall now examine the detail of the ratios most commonly used and then look at applying them to an example.

## Ratio Groups

Ratios may be grouped together in blocks to give a better feel for the interpretation. The basic areas under which ratios may be grouped are as follows:

- **Profitability** – How profitable is a company? Indicators include ROCE, ROS, GP%, materials, labour, overheads/sales.

- **Financial Status (Liquidity and Gearing)** – How stable is the company? Indicators include current, acid test, gearing, interest cover.

- **Activity** – How efficient is the company? Indicators include inventory, accounts receivable, accounts payable, AUR, fixed asset turnover.

- **Other Useful Ratios** – Indicators include sales and profit per employee.

These headings will become clear as they are explained. They seek to summarise the ratios by asking the questions: How profitable is a company? How stable is a company? How efficient is a company? Are there any other useful ratios?

## Profitability Ratios

### RETURN ON CAPITAL EMPLOYED (ROCE)

This ratio is probably the single most important ratio. It is known as the 'primary' ratio and is arrived at by expressing the operating profit as a percentage of the total long-term capital employed in the company. Although the capital employed is taken from the balance sheet and should therefore (like any other balance sheet item) be 'averaged' (by adding the previous year and dividing by two), it is common practice to take the year end figure.

RATIO: $\dfrac{\text{Profit before interest and tax}}{\text{Capital employed}} \times 100$

The profit is taken before interest and tax, due to the distorting effect of these two items which are little to do with the basic trading of the company. The capital employed is made up of three items – the share capital, the reserves and the long-term loans from the bank (if they exist).

The significance of this ratio is that it measures the 'overall efficiency' of the business and is one of the few ratios which can be used across any type of business, as it measures the return the company is producing compared to the capital put in. Clearly, a company which is high risk needs to be showing a high rate of return to attract investors or banks; and similarly a safe, stable company does not need to show such a high return. The ROCE is not an indicator of risk, but it should reflect the level of risk in the longer term.

A critical factor is what investors may get 'risk free' if their money is invested in, say, government stocks or a bank – although banks have been shown recently not to be without significant risk. If that is 5%, any company should be showing a return in excess of that as compensation for the risk. A basic measure of risk is the volatility of the profits and, for public companies, the volatility of share price is used. A target ROCE of 20% is often used, although this is highly dependent upon the industry sector; and, when assessing key suppliers, a ratio significantly above this may imply that the supplier is charging excessively for its services. '10 to 12% ROCE target needed to be competitive in the capital markets' (PricewaterhouseCoopers). The engineering group Siemens adopted a ROCE target for 2009 of 14–16%, and BMW adopted a target of 26% by 2012.

## RETURN ON SALES (ROS)

This ratio measures what percentage of sales are turned into profit. It is desirable to have as high a percentage as possible and, in some ways, this ratio measures the degree of competition in an industry.

RATIO:       $\dfrac{\text{Profit before interest and tax}}{\text{Sales}} \times 100$

Where there is high competition, the tendency is for this ratio to be small (1–3%). It does not necessarily mean that there is a low return on capital. A company could have a low ROS, have high volumes but need little capital investment and so create a high ROCE.

A target of 10% is often used but, in reality, it is because it is a nice round number! Some companies may have > 20% ROS and it is likely that they will have limited competition, but they will probably also have high ROCE simply because their profit percentage is very high. The buyer should beware of the supplier wanting a price hike when he says 'we are not making any money as we are only making 2% on sales'. They may be making 30% on their capital!

## GROSS PROFIT RATIO

This ratio measures any movements in the gross margin percentage or the buy and sell part of the business as shown in the trading account. In a buyer's own company, this is the section where they can directly influence the net profit by buying better; the gross profit increases with a resulting net profit rise.

RATIO:       $\dfrac{\text{Gross profit}}{\text{Sales}} \times 100$

Note that gross margin and gross profit mean essentially the same. ('Margin' is actually the term for the percentage, and 'profit' the term for the absolute.) It is computed the same as return on sales, except the gross profit is used rather than the operating profit. It tends to measure the effects of changes in either material buying prices, selling prices or production efficiency. It may also indicate a change in the product mix. For example, if the sales are the same each year but selling less of the high-margin products, the gross profit percentage will fall. Year on year, it should be the aim of a company to keep this ratio the same or to increase it. Where this ratio begins to fall, alarm bells should ring and the following two ratios should be examined to give better interpretation.

(These ratios are not available for published accounts, as the breakdown of the cost of sales is not available.)

## MATERIALS TO SALES RATIO

This ratio measures changes in materials to sales; so, where the gross profit has fallen, this ratio might show in part why.

RATIO:        $\dfrac{\text{Materials}}{\text{Sales}} \times 100$

It is clearly desirable for this to be as low as possible.

## DIRECT LABOUR TO SALES RATIO

Like the above ratio, it measures changes to direct labour costs or usage to sales, and may explain a movement in the gross profit ratio.

RATIO:        $\dfrac{\text{Labour}}{\text{Sales}} \times 100$

This is not the total labour used but the direct labour used on the factory if the company is in manufacturing or the wages of those 'at the coal face'. For instance, a consultancy company's direct wages would be that of the consultants operating on the clients work and not those of the administrators or head office directors.

## OVERHEADS TO SALES RATIO

This ratio may be applied to any overhead in the income statement where a comparison may prove useful. This is particularly true of variable and semi-variable costs that may change in proportion to changes in sales such as selling costs, transport costs etc.

RATIO:        $\dfrac{\text{Overhead}}{\text{Sales}} \times 100$

As sales rise, costs such as salaries and telephone should fall as a percentage of sales. A constant monitoring of all overheads as a percentage of sales is useful, to give warnings of any costs that are out of control. When suppliers expand, this is often an area that causes worry, as their overheads can grow at an alarming rate if uncontrolled (for example, directors awarding themselves large bonuses).

## Financial Status Ratios

These ratios are mainly taken from the balance sheet and express the short- and long-term solvency or liquidity of the company.

### CURRENT RATIO

This ratio is a measure of the adequacy of the working capital in a company and is expressed not as a percentage but as a true ratio expressed 'to one', such as 2:1 or 3.5:1. It is calculated by relating the current assets to the current liabilities as follows:

RATIO:     $\dfrac{\text{Current Assets}}{\text{Current Liabilities}}:1$

The current assets should always be greater than the current liabilities as an absolute minimum, but really we are looking for a ratio of 1.6:1 to 2:1 as a guide. If the ratio is significantly less, the company may have trouble paying its bills. If it is significantly more, perhaps the management of the working capital is inefficient, and better use could be made of the inventory or money in the bank. This ratio should always be interpreted alongside the following 'acid test' ratio, as different industries also have different ratio norms. What is important is the trend in this ratio as, if it is going down, it could be a sign that the company is losing money.

### ACID TEST RATIO

Also called the liquid or quick ratio, this ratio is similar to the current ratio, except that the liquid assets are used instead of the current assets. It is really looking at the 'very short-term' liquidity in the company.

RATIO:     $\dfrac{\text{Liquid Assets}}{\text{Current Liabilities}}:1$

(The liquid assets are usually taken as the current assets less the inventory, as the inventory (in all its forms) can often take many months to turn back into cash.)

An ideal ratio is 1:1, which would mean that the short-term money coming into the company (accounts receivable and bank deposits) would cover the short-term money which could go out (accounts payable and bank overdraft). In other words, it is a state of cash equilibrium. A company might exist on a lesser ratio, so a guide might be 0.6:1 to 1:1. Once again, the trend in this ratio is all important and also whether the company is retailing or manufacturing. For instance, a supermarket may exist comfortably on a ratio of 0.4:1 because it has very high inventory turnover (covered below) and comparatively few accounts receivable, as its customers pay immediately (or paid within a week by a credit card company).

It should be noted that, if, for instance, all the figures double, these ratios would remain unchanged and would not necessarily highlight underlying problems with the working capital. A necessary refinement or explanation of these ratios would be found in the activity ratios described later.

These two ratios together are what would be used when examining a company's 'liquidity'. By liquidity we mean a company's ability to turn current assets into cash quickly and pay its bills.

## GEARING RATIO

This ratio (USA – 'leverage') is an expression of the longer-term solvency of the company and it relates the amount of long-term borrowed capital in a company to the amount of capital contributed by the shareholders. Unfortunately, there are several expressions for this ratio and so each needs to be interpreted differently. The two most common are:

RATIO 1:     $\dfrac{\text{Loan Capital}}{\text{Capital (Shares + Reserves + Loans)}} \times 100$

This expression is referred to as 'accountants gearing' and shows what percentage of the total capital is borrowed.

So a company with £50,000 in loans and £100,000 in shares and £100,000 in reserves would have gearing of:

$$\frac{50{,}000}{(100{,}000 + 100{,}000 + 50{,}000)} \times 100$$

$$= 20\%$$

By this expression, a company cannot be over 100% geared (unless wildly insolvent – that is, its reserves are a greater minus figure than its shares are positive).

RATIO 2: $\dfrac{\text{Loan Capital}}{\text{Shares + Reserves}} \times 100$

This expression is referred to as the 'Debt:Equity Ratio' and shows the relative debt to owners' funds. It exaggerates the level of debt as a percentage, so that a company with 50% gearing with Ratio 1 would have 100% gearing with Ratio 2. In fact, these would be the cut-off percentages for defining a high geared company. High geared means high borrowing, and most 'blue chip' companies would ensure their gearing was less than 100% (or 50% for Ratio 1) to show a lower risk of failure.

The calculation of the example above would be as follows:

$$\frac{50{,}000}{(100{,}000 + 100{,}000)} \times 100$$

$$= 25\%$$

This is a moderately 'low geared' company, in that its gearing (borrowing) is low. A 50% to 100% geared company would be medium geared, and over 100% is a high gearing and therefore is inherently a risky company. A 100% geared company effectively means that half its total capital is borrowed.

It is therefore very important to know which ratio is being used, as there are also other formulae used for a gearing measure.

## INTEREST COVER

This ratio shows the ability of a company to cover its interest payments to the bank and will give an indication of its borrowing power.

It is calculated from the income statement (profit and loss account) as the profit before interest divided by the interest and expressed as 'number of times'.

RATIO:     Profit before interest ÷ Interest

The more times the interest is covered by the profit, the safer the company is. Prior to the recent banking crisis, anything less than twice (or three times) covered would be viewed as high risk. Now the cover often needs to be a minimum of six times!

If a company has high gearing, it is in a higher risk position, but this risk would be mitigated by having a high interest cover of greater than, say, ten times. In other words, it is making a high level of profit (or interest rates are very low). If a company has high interest cover, it also implies that it is better able to pay back its loans as well as their interest, but the loan repayment periods would need to be addressed to better assess this aspect.

These four ratios therefore give a 'snapshot' view of the company's ability to meet its short- and longer-term obligations.

## Activity Ratios

There are five major activity ratios, which are called 'activity' because they refer to a company's activity in a certain area (that is, the speed at which they turn things over). They are calculated by relating a balance sheet figure to an income statement figure.

The first three measure aspects of the working capital.

### INVENTORY TURNOVER

This ratio expresses the speed with which inventory is turned over or utilised. Again, there are several expressions which are used, depending upon whether you are assessing internal trends or comparing with an external company. The problem with comparing with external companies is that you rarely have the information needed to make a direct comparison with your own company.

The correct ratio is as follows:

RATIO: $\dfrac{\text{Cost of Sales}}{\text{Average inventory}}$

Text books will often show average inventory as being the (opening + closing inventory)/2 but, in reality, the closing inventory is the one usually used in ratio analysis, as taking the average of opening and closing inventory only gives the average of the year-end inventory, rather than the monthly or weekly which would be the point in order to eliminate seasonal fluctuations.

Sales may be used instead of 'cost of sales', as the cost of sales figure is often inconsistent with its contents in external accounts, due to certain figures being included in cost of sales in some companies' accounts and not in others. It will, of course, give a very different figure, but the trend or comparison is what is important rather than the figure itself. As high an inventory turnover as possible should be sought, which will require carrying minimal inventory. However, if too little inventory is carried, customers will not be properly serviced. The ratio can be broken down using raw materials, work-in-progress and finished inventory. It can also be expressed as days in inventory by dividing into 365. So, four times per year turnover would equate to carrying 91 days inventory.

## ACCOUNTS RECEIVABLE RATIO

This ratio expresses the amount of time it takes to collect one's debts and, once again, caution should be used, as a true average accounts receivable figure is rarely available, and so seasonal trends can have a very distorting effect on the accounts receivable figure.

RATIO:     $\dfrac{\text{Trade Accounts Receivable}}{\text{Credit Sales}} \times 365$

Trade accounts receivable are the accounts receivable from normal trading and, clearly, cash sales should where possible be eliminated from the sales figure. When the result is multiplied by 365, this gives an average payment time expressed in days. This needs to be as low as possible for cash flow reasons. An increasing trend of debtor days can indicate any of the following:

- poor quality goods (delivery, manufacturing or service problem);

- a poor credit control (management problem); or

- selling to companies who cannot pay on time (a marketing problem).

It can be distorted by the treatment of bad debts. One to two months should be a guide, so over three months must be a concern. This ratio is distorted by the VAT element in the accounts receivable. It is useful to compare this ratio with the buyer's own company payment terms for obvious negotiation levers.

It is critical in that it indicates the speed with which the primary source of revenue is turned into cash.

## ACCOUNTS PAYABLE RATIO

This ratio expresses the amount of time it takes to pay one's debts and, once again, caution should be used, as a true average accounts payable figure is rarely available, and so seasonal trends can have a highly distorting effect. Additionally, it is often impossible to determine which purchases are on credit, so it is common to relate the accounts payable to the sales simply to obtain a trend although, even then, there may be differences due to the mix of cash and credit purchases.

RATIO:     $\dfrac{\text{Trade Accounts Payable}}{\text{Credit Purchases}} \times 365$

This needs to be as long as possible for cash flow reasons, but that is not usually the best policy. If accounts receivable are collected quickly, accounts payable can be paid quickly and discounts gained. If this ratio is too long – three months or more – it could well imply second-tier supplier problems and may indicate to a buyer a potential delivery risk.

Ideally, the debtor days and creditor days are roughly the same, showing that the money comes in at the same time as it goes out.

## ASSET UTILISATION RATIO (AUR)

This ratio (also called 'capital turnover') relates the capital to the sales, and it is as follows:

RATIO:     $\dfrac{\text{Sales}}{\text{Capital}}$

It is such an all-encompassing ratio that it has limited use, but it does give an indication of how the capital employed in a company has been used to generate sales and therefore can be a warning sign if it starts to fall. It can also be used to indicate the degree of extra finance required to fund an expansion in that, if the sales/capital is, say, 3.5, and the company wishes to increase its sales by £17.5 million, it will require approximately 17.5 ÷ 3.5 = £5 million in extra finance from the bank or shareholders.

It is also, along with return on sales, known as a secondary ratio. If return on sales is multiplied by this ratio, the result will be the return on capital employed:

ROCE = ROS × Sales/Capital (AUR)

For example, where profit = 20,000, sales = 100,000 and Capital = 50,000:

20 ÷ 50 = (20 ÷ 100) × (100 ÷ 50)

40% = 20% × 2

It therefore follows that, in order to improve ROCE, a company needs to maximise its profit on sales and minimize its capital requirement to generate sales.

## FIXED ASSET TURNOVER

This ratio is similar to the AUR except that, rather than using the total capital employed, it uses only the non-current assets:

RATIO: $$\frac{\text{Sales}}{\text{Non-current Assets (Tangible)}}$$

The relevance of this ratio is that, when a company expands its tangible non-current assets, it is usually done in order to expand its sales. Therefore, an increase in non-current assets one year should be met with a proportional increase in sales. There is usually a lag in time after spending on non-current assets before it shows in a sales increase, so several years' figures should be used to establish a useful trend. This ratio should be as high as possible, but the depreciation and asset replacement policies can considerably cloud the interpretation.

However, if this figure is too high it might indicate a lack of replacement of non-current assets and, to a buyer looking at a supplier's accounts, this could imply future capacity or quality problems.

## Other Useful Ratios

There are many ratios which may also be usefully used, and each industry will have its own key ratios. However, employee ratios are often used, such as:

RATIO: $$\frac{\text{Sales}}{\text{Number of employees}}$$

or

RATIO: $$\frac{\text{Profit}}{\text{Number of employees}}$$

These are additional barometers in determining a company's success and are often used by direct sales companies. The profit per number of employees may be an indicator of overstaffing if it starts to fall.

Retailers will use sales per square foot, and supermarkets use inventory turnover and margin per area of shelf or floor space.

Additionally, investment ratios are of great importance such as earnings (profit) per share, dividend cover and yield, price/earnings ratio. These are covered in Part IV.

## Example

The following example of Superstick Glue Ltd shows an income statement and balance sheet that need analysis. There were five employees:

| Income Statement | | Balance Sheet | |
|---|---|---|---|
| | | Non-current Assets | 200,000 |
| Sales | 250,000 | | |
| Materials | (135,000) | Current Assets | |
| Direct Wages | (10,000) | Inventory & WIP | 70,000 |
| Gross Profit | 105,000 | Accounts Receivable & Prepaid | 49,000 |
| Overheads | | Petty Cash | 1,000 |
| Sundry Overheads | (25,000) | Total Current Assets | 120,000 |
| Motor | (7,000) | Total Assets | 320,000 |
| Depreciation | (12,000) | Equity | |
| Salaries | (45,000) | Ordinary Share Capital | 70,000 |
| Total Overheads | (89,000) | Revenue Reserves | 90,000 |
| Operating Profit | 16,000 | Shareholders' Funds | 160,000 |
| Loan Interest | (4,000) | | |
| Net Profit (Pre-tax) | 12,000 | Loans | 60,000 |
| Corporation Tax | (4,000) | Current Liabilities | |
| Net Profit after Tax | 8,000 | Trade Accounts Payable | 60,000 |
| Ordinary Dividend | (3,500) | Other Accounts Payable | |
| Retained Profit for year | 4,500 | Bank Overdraft | 40,000 |
| | | Total Current Liabilities | 100,000 |
| | | Equity & Liabilities | 320,000 |

## Answer

| | Current Year | Previous Year |
|---|---|---|
| PROFITABILITY | | |
| ROCE | 7.27% | 8.40% |
| ROS | 6.40% | 5.00% |
| Gross Profit | 42.00% | 44.00% |
| Mats/Sales | 54.00% | 51.00% |
| Wages/Sales | 4.00% | 5.00% |
| Sundry Overheads | 10.00% | |
| Motor | 2.80 | |
| Deprec | 4.80% | |
| Salaries | | |
| Total Overheads | 35.60% | 39.00% |
| FINANCIAL STATUS | | |
| Current | | |
| Acid Test | 0.50 | 0.60 |
| Gearing 1 | 27.27% | 20.00% |
| Gearing 2 | 37.50% | |
| Interest Cover | 4× | 6× |
| ACTIVITY | | |
| Sales/Inventory | 3.57× | 5× |
| Inventory T/o (Times) | 2.07× | 3.80× |
| Accounts Receivable T/O (Days) | 71.54 | 65 |
| Accounts Payable T/O (Days) | 156.43 | 120 |
| Fixed Asset T/O | 1.25 | |
| EMPLOYEE RATIOS | | |
| Sales/Employee | 50,000.00 | 52,000.00 |
| Profit/Employee | 3,200.00 | 3,400.00 |

These ratios have been calculated exactly as per the previously outlined methods. The interpretation would be as follows.

In terms of absolute figures (this would normally be done over two years or more):

- The company is profitable and paying a dividend.

- There are substantial non-current assets.

- The working capital (net current assets) appears inadequate although it is positive – there is too much inventory, the accounts receivable are less than the accounts payable, and there is a bank overdraft.

- There are loans but well below the value of the property.

- There is significant net worth.

In summary, the working capital is underfunded but there is adequate security to cover further loans, as the non-current assets are worth £200,000 (assuming some is property or other good security) and the loans and overdraft combined are £100,000.

In terms of ratios (these can be compared with the previous year's ratios):

- *Profitability*
  - ROCE is poor and falling.
  - The ROS has improved slightly due to a cut in overheads.
  - The gross profit percentage has fallen primarily due to increased material costs.

- *Financial Status*
  - The current and acid test are worryingly low and falling.
  - The gearing has increased, whilst the interest cover is falling, which again spells problems if this trend is not arrested.

- *Activity*
  - This is the real problem area.
  - The inventory turnover has fallen significantly, which means either they cannot sell the inventory or they are becoming very inefficient.
  - The debtor collection time has slipped from 65 to 71 days and is edging towards the dangerous.
  - The creditor payment time has moved from 120 to 156 days, which is likely to mean they are on stop with some suppliers.

- *Employee Ratios*
  - Both sales and profit per employee have fallen significantly (note there were five employees).

The net result of this analysis is that the working capital is in a poor state and needs rectifying by better working capital management, and it is likely also that additional finance is needed. If this was a supplier, the buyer would be ill-advised to proceed until certain that the issues had been addressed. The management accounts since the balance sheet date would need examination, or some form of performance guarantee or performance bond should be demanded. (See further Question 5 in the Appendix.)

## Advanced Issues – Published Accounts and Availability of Information

The general principle with ratios is that they are just another tool for interpretation of a company's trading ability and should not be used as a sole means in making a judgment of their ability to supply your needs satisfactorily. When making any judgment about a company, no single ratio tells the full story, and ratios should be linked together for interpretation purposes. For instance, in the example at Question 5 in the Appendix, there is a huge inventory increase causing the inventory turn to fall, and this can be linked with the increase in warehousing and distribution.

Ratios support other things that are known about a supplier's company, such as the absolute balance sheet and income statement information, quality aspects, cost, delivery, ease of doing business, length of relationship etc.

There are two major questions that need to be answered when interpreting a supplier's accounts. First, is the company stable and is it feasible to do business with them? Secondly, if there is a choice of suppliers, which is the most appropriate from a financial viewpoint?

## Relevance of Supply Positioning

It is appropriate to bring in a well-known model from supply chain theory which is called the 'supply positioning' model. This model below was developed by P.T. Steele and T.I. Elliott-Shircore of PMMS Consulting Group Limited, first published in Purchasing and Supply Management in 1985. This 2 × 2 matrix is used for supply positioning to categorize supplies by mapping their business risk against the value of business as in Figure 6.1.

Where the supplies fit will depend on how we, as buyers, interpret and use the figures in the accounts.

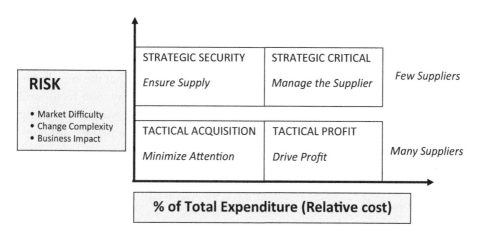

Figure 6.1    The Supply Positioning Model

## STRATEGIC SECURITY

In this quadrant, this might be an occasional purchase but an extremely high risk one, such as a small important part in an aeroplane engine. Price is not a key factor here and ensuring that the supply is available is critical. There tend to be few suppliers in this quadrant, so we are not concerned if the supplier is making huge profits as it represents a small spend to us and the important aspect is that the supplier is going to stay in business. If the finances are good or stable, there is no problem; but, if the supplier looks to be going out of business, this increases the risk to us of an already risky part supply. It may be that we choose to help the supplier in some up-front financial way, such as up-front payment or tooling purchase on their behalf, or even investment in the supplier depending on the level of risk. We are ideally looking for a profitable company with a strong balance sheet in this quadrant with good liquidity and low gearing.

## STRATEGIC CRITICAL

In this quadrant, we have a very high spend with long-term contracts and have limited choices of where else to procure our supplies. It is essential that the supplier is stable (strong balance sheet) as well as making a good level of profit in order to re-invest. It should have a solid ROCE (say, >20%) and steady gross margin. There should be good liquidity and gearing should ideally be less than 40% (allowing another 10% for expansion loans) and all other ratios stable.

## TACTICAL ACQUISITION

In this quadrant, we have low spend and low risk so, as buyers, we need to spend time up-front to arrange a medium-term contract so that the supply can then require minimum attention. Price is not key but aggravation factor and buyer time can be high if this is not managed well. We do not wish to be dealing with a supplier in this quadrant who is likely to go out of business as, although it is not a big spend, it could cost a disproportionate amount of time to re-source the supplies. A stable supplier in this area is required (sound balance sheet with good inventory turnover) although a very low level of profitability is acceptable.

## TACTICAL PROFIT

In this quadrant (sometimes called the 'leverage' quadrant), there is a high percentage spend but there are many alternative suppliers, so theoretically it would not be a major issue if the supplier became insolvent. However, given the choice, we would all prefer to avoid the issues around undependable supplies and therefore it would be better to have a supplier in this quadrant who is going to be around for a while. Contracts will be short term in order to play the market, and buyers will be using a hard negotiation approach and generally not being concerned if the supplier's profit is minimal, as there are always other suppliers. We therefore would wish to see good liquidity and very modest profits for our suppliers in this area and, if we have a major part of their business and they are making a ROCE above 20%, we are not negotiating hard enough.

The above, of course, are generalized comments and there are always situations that will not fit into set analytical tools, but they should at least help to temper the way in which we interpret a supplier's financial statements.

# 7

# Sources of Information Used in Costing and Negotiation

## General

There is a significant lack of up-to-date financial information in some areas and most notably in small companies. The first problem is that, if a company is not quoted on a stock market, its figures may be neither adequate nor available in certain cases. A publicly quoted company will not only be governed by company law but also by stock exchange rules and therefore there are additional publishing requirements. For instance, interim accounts of a quoted company are published. The normal latest publication date of accounts for a public company is seven months from the end of the company's financial year end, and for a private company the maximum is ten months. This means that the information could be significantly out of date. Also note that a public company is not necessarily 'quoted' on a stock market, so would not be subject to the additional stock exchange rules.

The second problem is to do with size, in that there is only a limited amount of information needed to be published for smaller companies. For instance, a small company would only need to publish a balance sheet but not an income statement or cash flow statement. The income statement would need to be produced for Her Majesty's Revenue and Customs (HMRC) but not published.

To be a 'small' company, at least two of the following conditions must be met (2009):

- annual turnover must be £5.6 million or less;

- the balance sheet total must be £2.8 million or less;

- the average number of employees must be 50 or fewer.

For a medium company, no cash flow statement would need to be published.

To be a 'medium-sized' company, at least two of the following conditions must be met (2009):

- annual turnover must be £22.8 million or less;

- the balance sheet total must be £11.4 or less;

- the average number of employees must be 250 or fewer.

*(Source:* www.companieshouse.gov.uk)

The third problem is that the company might be a part of a group, in which case there are complex rules about publication of accounts for a group structure. Generally speaking, a group (where there is more than one company and one is a subsidiary of the other) will publish accounts for both the group (known as 'consolidated accounts') and also the biggest single trading company. Consolidated accounts are created by adding all the group's accounts figures together and deducting any inter-company transactions. They are best described as the summary of the group's trading with the outside world. The figures will show side by side as 'group' and 'company'. This presents a problem if you are trading with a company in the group that is not the main trading company and is registered outside the UK, as the accounts will be prepared but will not be in the public domain.

## Dealing with a Lack of Information

### SMALL COMPANIES

The lack of a cash flow statement is not so significant, as an estimated one can be produced by examination of the two previous years' balance sheets; but the lack of an income statement is significant, as having neither a sales nor a profit figure makes the financial assessment of a supplier very thin. One can try to make assumptions about these two aspects. For instance, if the accounts receivable are £240,000 and the normal payment time in the trade is two months, one might deduce that the turnover was approximately $240,000 / 2 \times 12 = £1,440,000$. Also, one can examine the growth in net assets and make the assumption that this is all retained profit (a share issue would also cause a growth in net assets, but this would be apparent on the balance sheet).

This figure would be after dividend and tax, and so one could at least assume some level of profit but no more.

The main analysis would therefore need to rest with the balance sheet. This would involve the following:

- An assessment of year-on-year trends in the main figures.

- Are they investing in non-current assets?

- Has the retained profit increased year on year?

- What are the changes in accounts receivable compared to the changes in accounts payable?

- What has happened to the inventory value?

- Assessing the balance sheet ratios of gearing, current and acid test.

- Are they cash rich or heavily indebted?

- Are there any changes in accounting policies?

Other key aspects would need to be considered for action. For instance, if they are a potential new supplier, they are likely to be helpful in providing information, and there is no reason why they could not provide either an income statement or up-to-date management accounts since the last accounting reference date. This would be a similar situation with information about a group subsidiary. A client of mine once had this problem, and their supplier was not prepared to release the accounts of the subsidiary. It was solved by my client's finance director visiting the supplier and viewing the subsidiary accounts at the supplier's premises. This is a common situation within the USA, where private company accounts are not filed at all in a public depository. If a supplier is unwilling to allow any viewing of their accounting information, one can only assume the worst, or at least treat it as another risk factor.

Small companies (as defined above) do not need to produce 'audited' accounts, where the figures are subject to much greater depth of checking, and less reliance is put on covering statements from directors. This is a further risk, and a small company may by choice have their accounts audited (at a significantly greater cost) in order to give a greater degree of comfort to those with contractual dealings with them. Additionally, accounts signed by the directors carry more weight than unsigned 'draft' accounts, which should be treated with a high degree of caution.

A final important aspect is whether there is any 'auditor's qualification' in their audit report. This means that the auditor has a fundamental disagreement with the board of directors over a significant item or items in the accounts and therefore feels it necessary to make an 'excluding' statement. Companies would seek to avoid a qualification at all costs, as this might affect the HMRC's acceptance of the accounts for tax purposes and also affect their relationship with their bank. Examples of these issues might be the method of valuation of inventory or when 'revenue' is recognized as having been earned (that is, in which year?).

## Information to be Used in Purchasing and Negotiation

The type of purchasing information that we are looking to create might include the following (which is not an exhaustive list):

- How old are the accounts, and when are the new accounts due to be published?

- Do the accounts and ratios shows a stable situation?

- Do the accounts and ratios show an excessive profit situation or an excessive loss situation?

- Do the accounts contain any auditor's qualification?

- Has either the managing director or financial director resigned from the company?

- Are there potential second-tier supplier problems?

- Is the company in the hands of its lenders?

- Are there any dependency issues with the supplier, and what are the sizes of any further orders and any contracts that might cease with the supplier?

- Where would we position the supplier in the supplier positioning matrix, and how does this affect our judgement of the supplier's financial capability?

- Has the supplier the capacity to deal with the required orders?

The negotiation information that we might hope to create could look as follows:

## NEGOTIATION STRENGTHS

- Are we in a position to demand assurances of the supplier or cross-guarantees within the supplier's group?

- Do we have negotiating leverage due to our proportion of the supplier's business?

- Has the supplier lost business to other customers?

- Is the supplier's cash flow tight and therefore could we gain significant price benefit by having an early settlement agreement with the supplier?

- Have divisions within the supplier's group lost business and have others gained? Can we use this movement to our benefit?

- Have there been significant changes in the supplier's gross margin and could this be due to pricing issues with customers? Again, can we use this for our benefit?

## NEGOTIATION WEAKNESSES

- We are very dependent on the supplier to the extent that, if we tried to cut price, would this prejudice the supplier's finances so significantly that it might create financial problems for them?

- If we seek alternative suppliers, might the supplier be forced into liquidation, causing many lost jobs resulting in significant bad publicity on our business planning ability?

- Do we have adequate leverage on the supplier's volumes to negotiate price effectively?

## Corporate Social Responsibility (CSR) Issues

'Corporate Social Responsibility is the continuing commitment by business to behave ethically and contribute to economic development while improving the quality of life of the workforce and their families as well as of the local community and society at large' (The World Business Council for Sustainable Development in its publication 'Making Good Business Sense' by Lord Holme and Richard Watts).

- Does our proportion of the supplier's business have a significant effect on employment in the supplier's geographic place of business?

- Have the supplier's gross margins increased significantly? Could this imply quality issues that might be experienced by our customers further down the line? Could this also imply outsourcing to low labour cost countries? What might be implications of poor CSR policies at these outsourced companies?

- Does our supplier have robust CSR policies and are these followed through when they outsource their supplies?

- What is their average pay per employee and has this decreased?

# PART II

# Costing, Pricing and Cost Modelling

# 8

# Introduction to Costing

Cost accountancy is concerned with the analysis of income and expenditure, and many such costs are not immediately identifiable with a particular division, department or product. To not include these costs would understate the real cost of the product and by properly measuring and allocating costs, the following benefits arise:

- The process of analysing costs can considerably affect the attitude of the staff involved. If something is seen to be measured, those responsible for it will be careful with the expenditure.

- 'Make or buy' decisions are easier. By that we mean that we can make a decision on whether it is better to buy a product or service in or to make it ourselves. Information is made available on which comparison with outside tenders is made easier.

- Sources of waste are revealed. We can measure against what we think it should cost and show up overspend or wastage.

- The problems of losing contracts unwittingly through overpricing or accepting jobs at a loss are reduced because of a clear understanding of the costs incurred in providing a product or service.

Having established the benefits of costing, it is necessary to classify the costs into their various categories. Costs can be classified into two main headings when assessing cost behaviour. A 'fixed cost' remains unchanged within given output parameters. A 'variable cost' varies with changes in the level of activity. It can vary proportionately to sales or production. This concept is explored fully in Chapter 11.

Within these two classifications of fixed and variable costs are the various elements of costs, namely:

- materials (direct and indirect);

- labour (direct and indirect); and

- expense (direct and indirect).

The sum of the three elements of cost is the total cost of a product or service.

The sum of the indirect costs is often described as overheads.

A direct cost is a cost which is traceable directly to the product, and whilst in theory all costs can be traced to a product, in practice the cost has to be of such significance that it is worth tracing to a given product. There is always a financial cost in controlling a cost, and the cost of that control must be more than offset by the benefits attained in controlling that cost.

An example of a company which manufactures wooden tables is as follows:

- *Direct material* – wood, metal, varnish, packaging.

- *Direct labour* – wages to wood turner, varnisher etc.

- *Direct expense* – royalty to designer.

- *Indirect material (variable)* – glue, nails, cotton waste, machine lubricant.

- *Indirect labour (variable)* – work checkers, toolsetters.

- *Indirect expenses (variable)* – electricity, water, gas (power only).

- *Indirect material (fixed)* – stationery.

- *Indirect labour (fixed)* – salaries, wages of personnel or accounts office.

- *Indirect expense (fixed)* – rent/rates.

The fixed overheads are the sum of the fixed indirect material, labour and expenses. These costs in total may constitute a large sum that is spread across the whole company and, for ease of control, they are usually departmentalised, and cost centres are set up and managed along the lines of executive responsibility. Divisions might be under the headings of production, personnel, sales, distribution, research and development etc. Some of these costs shown as indirect (such as gas) in another company may be separately measured and classified as direct, due to the significance of the cost (such as the heating costs of a kiln in pottery manufacture).

## Product Costing

Products are costed by their three constituent elements of materials, labour and overheads. Materials and labour are easily measured for a given product or service, but the allocation of overheads is where the difficulty lies.

### MATERIALS

Materials are easily measured in units such as length, weight, area, flow speed, volume displacement etc, and these units are then multiplied by the purchase price per unit to give the cost of material. It should be the actual material *consumed* in making a product and not the material *in* the product which is the basis for the costing (in other words, waste is costed for). The effects of how inventory is accounted for will affect the costing and, in inflationary times, the inventory cost per unit will rise. Materials may be costed as weighted average, last in first out (LIFO), first in first out (FIFO) or standard cost. (Note: LIFO is specifically disallowed in IAS 2.) Weighted average is a means of averaging the cost of an item in a market with price fluctuation.

For example, if 40 items are bought at £1 each and 60 items are bought for £1.50, and 60 items are used in production, the total inventory value is £40 + £90 = £130.

The weighted average would be £130/100 = £1.30 each, so the cost of material would be 60 (items used) × £1.30 = £78. This figure would be used for the costing and showing a reduction in inventory value when an item is used. The problem with this method is that a re-calculation is required whenever the inventory is increased.

To use the example above for FIFO, the items bought first would be the ones costed in, so 40 × £1 = £40 + (20 × £1.50 =) £30, making a total cost of £70.

With standard costing, an estimate would be made of the cost per unit over the coming period and this would be used in costings. For each period, a company would produce a report of the variances from this 'standard' and, if they prove consistently over- or under-budget, the standard is altered.

## LABOUR COSTS

Labour costs are the costs of those making the product or delivering the service, and their time can be measured accurately. It is not quite as simple as it may appear and is the subject of specialist training as a work study engineer. Account needs to be taken of the time taken to complete a task repetitively, machinery breakdowns, natural breaks in the workflow or in the task itself (for example, thread breaks or colour changes for sewing machinists), other allowances such as visits to the bathroom and, last but not least, the rating of the employee. If all employees were paid on the timing basis of the fastest worker, there would be obvious problems! It is measured by means of a 'standard' minute.

The process would be as follows:

- Measure the time taken (observed time) – say, 16 minutes.

- Rate the employee being measured – say, 125 (that is, they are one quarter faster than an 'average' employee).

- Calculate the 'basic' time. This is the observed time × employee rating ÷ standard rating: 16 minutes × 125 ÷ 100 = 20 minutes.

- Add on the relevant allowances for that industry – say, 20%.

- So standard time = 20 minutes + 20% of 20 minutes = 24 minutes.

This figure would be used in the costing of labour for the product after being multiplied by the wage rate.

The use of the 'standard minute' is rarely used in the UK for an individual payment system (known as piecework), but is still prevalent in the low labour cost countries that supply many of our products.

Standard minutes are useful for assessing capacity, production scheduling, giving customers delivery information, costing, and individual and group reward systems.

## DIRECT EXPENSES

Direct expenses, such as royalties, are easily quantified and costed according to the royalty agreement.

## VARIABLE OVERHEADS

Variable overheads, such as consumables, can often be measured but, where this is impracticable, an allowance is made which is often a percentage of the labour or machine cost, on the basis that it will vary in line with the labour or machine cost.

## FIXED OVERHEADS

Fixed overheads are the most difficult to measure and allocate to a product and, whilst the total is easily quantified, this needs to be spread or 'absorbed' equitably across all products by various bases. The simplest way of absorbing the total overheads is by taking the total and dividing it by the number of products planned to be manufactured.

The following example for a company Serro Gory shows the calculation.

**Example**

Serro Gory Ltd manufacture one product, a Riggert, which weighs 50 kg, and which uses the following resources:

- Material A – 30 kg (but they need to use 40kg to produce finished product).

- Material B – 20 kg (no wastage).

- Direct labour – 8 hours.

The cost of material A is £30 per kg and material B is £40 per kg.

They pay the labour @ £60 per hour (including other on costs such as NI and holiday pay).

They expect to sell 2,000 Riggerts this month at a price of £3,000 each, and their overheads are £500,000 per month.

**Questions**

1.  Calculate the total cost of a Riggert.

2.  Do they expect to produce a profit this month, and what would the budgeted income statement look like?

3.  What would be the total cost of a Riggert if they actually sell 2,500 in the month?

**Answers**

| 1) Cost of Materials – | Material A | 40kg (used) @ £30 = | £1,200 |
|---|---|---|---|
| | Material B | 20kg @ £40 = | 800 |
| Total cost of Materials | | | £2,000 |
| Cost of labour | | 8 hrs @ £60 = | £480 |
| Total Direct costs per unit (Prime Costs) | | | £2,480 |
| Overheads are £500,000 spread over 2,000 Riggerts | | 500,000 ÷ 2000= | |
| which gives an average cost per unit of | | | £250 |
| So the total cost of a Riggert is | | £2,480 + £250 = | £2,730 |

| 2) Selling Price is £3,000, which leaves £3,000 – £2,730 = £270 per unit. | | |
|---|---|---|
| Income Statement for month would be 2,000 units @ £3,000 = | | £6,000,000 |
| Less Direct Costs – Materials 2,000 @ £2,000 = | 4,000,000 | |
| Labour 2,000 @ £480 = | 960,000 | 4,960,000 |
| Gross profit | | 1,040,000 |
| Less Overheads | | 500,000 |
| Budgeted Profit (£270 × 2,000) | | £540,000 |

3) If they actually sell 2,500 in the month, the overheads would be spread over more products, so would be 500,000 ÷ 2,500 = £200 per unit.

This brings down the overheads (and total costs) by £50 per unit to £2,680.

The real cost of a unit is therefore totally dependent upon the number of units actually produced and sold, and the relationship of the cost of a unit (based on the budget) to the real cost is that they are only identical if all of the budget factors are met.

This therefore leads into the wisdom, or otherwise, of using the budget as a basis of costing.

What if these £50,000 overheads would support the production of 10,000 units per month and we are budgeting on 2,000? Clearly, a competitor with an overhead base designed to support 2,000–3,000 units would have significantly lower overheads and would therefore be able to sell at a much lower price, as their break-even would be much lower. We therefore need to fix our costings based on a reasonable capacity utilisation (depending upon the industry) rather than what we expect to sell. Where a high level of flexibility of service is offered (for instance, a training company), the capacity utilisation may be budgeted on only 50% of the available weeks. So, if the available weeks are, say, 40 weeks, the overheads of say £50,000 might be budgeted as 50,000 ÷ 40 ÷ 5 = £250 per day. This means that, if the training was sold at £250 per day, the fee would only cover the overheads. A general engineering company might expect an 80% capacity utilisation, so the overheads would be proportionately lower.

With the example above, if the capacity of Serra Gory was for 5,000 Riggerts and they fixed on a capacity utilisation of 80%, the overheads should have been allocated as £500,000 ÷ 4,000 (80% of 5,000 units) = £125 per unit and not £250 per unit. Perhaps they would have sold more if they had correctly allocated the overheads which would have produced a lower price, if indeed their pricing was based on a mark-up on cost rather than market price!

# 9

# Absorption Costing

The reality is that few companies produce only one product or service, and therefore allocating overhead costs equally across different units, when each clearly should absorb a differing amount of overhead, would not be reasonable.

With absorption costing, the intention is to create a mechanism whereby the overall fixed costs are allocated to a cost centre, and are then fully recovered in the process of charging customers for the product or service they receive. This involves the distinction between direct and indirect costs. As was explained earlier, direct costs are those costs which can be allocated to a product. For instance, making a chair will involve materials and the labour of the people making it (such as the upholsterer or machine operator). It may involve traceable expenses, such as a royalty payable to a designer. In the case of pottery manufacture, power would be a direct expense (namely, the electricity cost in heating the kilns). The total direct costs are known as the prime costs.

Many costs are direct but are treated as indirect simply because the cost of tracing the cost could be excessive (for example, the electrical power used by a particular machine tool). The more costs which are traceable and therefore measured the better, as the resultant costing will inevitably be more accurate, with fewer costs apportioned and more actually measured. The total costs of a product are made up of the direct costs for that product plus its share of the overheads allocated to that department.

Indirect costs are all the costs which cannot easily be traced specifically to a product, such as rent, salaries, machine lubricant, or electricity.

## Overhead Allocation

Overheads are usually split between departments according to the usage of each department.

They should be split individually rather than as a total, as the proportional usage by each department of individual overheads will vary. Different overheads will be split utilizing different bases, for example:

| Overhead Cost | Basis of Split |
|---|---|
| Machine maintenance | Cost of machine (or 'directly' if full records were kept) |
| Heating bills | Area or number of radiators |
| Personnel office costs | Number of employees |

Once all the overheads have been allocated to all departments, the service departments can then be re-allocated to the production departments. This will result in an overhead figure for each production department which needs to be recovered or 'absorbed' in the product costings.

For instance, the following overhead costs are to be split between two departments of manufacturing and service, and we have the following information:

| Overheads | Totals |
|---|---|
| Lighting Costs | £3,000 |
| Machine Maintenance | £14,000 |
| Heating | £6,000 |
| Total | £23,000 |

We also have the following information:

| Departments | Manufacturing | Service |
|---|---|---|
| Square Footage | 7,500 | 2,500 |
| No of Radiators | 32 | 8 |
| Value of machinery | £60,000 | £10,000 |

This split is done by, first, deciding what will be the basis of the split, and then apportioning on that basis:

| Overheads | (Method) | Totals | Manufacturing | Service |
|---|---|---|---|---|
| Lighting Costs | (area) | 3,000 | 2,250 | 750 |
| Machine Maintenance | (Value of Machinery) | 14,000 | 12,000 | 2,000 |
| Heating | (No of Radiators) | 6,000 | 4,800 | 1,200 |
| Totals | | 23,000 | 19,050 | 3,950 |

We have decided to split the lighting costs by area, as the greater the area the higher will be the lighting costs. The total overall area is 10,000 square feet and, as the manufacturing occupies 7,500 square feet, it would be allocated as 75% (7,500 ÷ 10,000 × 100) to the manufacturing department and 25% to the service department. Similarly, we would allocate the machine maintenance in proportion to the value of machinery, and the heating in proportion to the number of radiators. There is also a good argument for allocating the heating in proportion to the area.

The result is an overall split of costs to be absorbed by the manufacturing department as £19,050 and the service department as £3,950.

## Absorption Bases

In its simplest form, the overheads are absorbed on the basis of number of units produced. So, if the total overheads to be absorbed are £100,000 and there are budgeted 50,000 units, the overheads are absorbed at £2/unit. This is the absorption rate. The cost of one unit would be materials + labour + £2 for the overheads.

However, other bases may be used, such as materials, labour costs, labour hours, prime costs or machine hours. The main question is which are the 'cost drivers'. In an industry which is very labour intensive, such as clothing manufacture, labour hours or labour cost would be used. In a capital intensive industry such as manufacturing packaging materials, where there are comparatively few employees but very expensive machinery, machine hours would be used.

- The total costs of a product or job are the materials plus the labour plus the allocated overheads.

- The allocated overheads are recovered utilising the most appropriate base for the business.

- The base used for recovery is what is budgeted for the next year; so, if the budget is incorrect, so is the rate for recovery of overheads. For instance, if a company budgeted to produce 30,000 units (base for recovery) and its overheads were £90,000, it would use a rate of £3/unit to recover all of its overheads. If it only achieved 25,000 units, it would only recover £3 × 25,000 = £75,000. It has therefore under-absorbed £15,000 which would mean that, as well as losing the profit on the 5,000 units shortfall, it would have also not recovered £15,000 of the overheads, which would again reduce its profitability.

- Costing is, therefore, an inaccurate process, as it is based on estimated future overheads and estimated future activity in the company.

- The result is that two competing companies can produce different costings and therefore different prices, simply because of their budgets, even though in reality their costs are exactly the same.

**Example**

Budgeted overheads allocated for the year to a factory are £200,000. The budgeted labour costs for the year are £800,000. The company recover or 'absorb' their overheads using labour costs as a base.

The absorption rate is therefore:

- Overheads ÷ Base = 200,000 ÷ 800,000
  = 25p per £1 of labour.
  So, a job with £6 materials, £20 of labour costs would absorb £5 overheads (£20 × 25p).
  The total cost of the job would be £6 + £20 + £5 = £31.

Suppose the company changed to absorbing their overheads based on the budgeted machine hours of 40,000.

If the job required two hours of machining, how would the total cost be affected?

First, we would need to calculate the absorption rate based on the new base of machine hours:

- Overheads ÷ Base = 200,000 ÷ 40,000
  = £5 per machine hour.
  So, a job with £6 materials, £20 of labour costs would absorb £10 overheads (2 hrs × £5).
  The total cost of the job would be £6 + £20 + £10 = £36.

A different base used produces a different overhead recovery, so which is correct?

## Key Points of Absorption Costing

- Materials and labour are easily measured.

- Overheads are definable in total, but need to be spread over a variety of products.

- Absorption base determines the amount of overheads assigned to a product.

- Question arises as to whether the company is bearing a fair amount of overheads in its suppliers' products.

(See further Question 6 in the Appendix.)

# 10

# Activity Based Costing

Activity based costing (or ABC) is a comparatively new approach to absorption costing, in that it recognises that to use simply labour hours or machine hours to recover overheads can be inaccurate. It is not a new concept, but it just requires so much more information gathering that it has become popular since the development of information technology. It recognises that many 'fixed' costs are actually driven by differing types of activity. For instance, packing costs are driven by the number of cartons packed and the size of the carton; production control costs are driven by the number of production runs; and transport costs are by the number and length of journeys and size of products. It would therefore be incorrect to expect to recover all of these costs on machine or labour hour bases. There would therefore need to be a 'cost driver' identified for each cost incurred, and some monitoring and control applied to this to establish the correct recovery rate.

This can therefore become very expensive in terms of both setting up and monitoring costs but, if the exercise is carried out accurately, there can be a significant competitive edge gained in understanding what drives costs, so aiding management decision making and its product mix and pricing policies.

A great benefit of ABC is that it enables a more accurate costing of all the processes within an organisation. When that has been done, it enables a clearer view of the real cost of all the processes and then, by altering the processes, savings can be made. Perhaps this involves removing a process altogether (such as product design) and contracting this out if it only has intermittent demand. This mapping and costing of current processes, and the consequential alteration in processes, is now called 'business process re-engineering' (BPR). This is very much an over-simplification but it covers the principles involved.

## Elements of the ABC Methodology

Primarily, the ABC methodology assigns costs to activities rather than production departments by establishing 'cost pools'. Rather than having, say, three departments such as manufacturing, servicing, and marketing and distribution, there might be 10–15 'cost pools' (the total costs of which all add up to the same total costs of the three departments). The principal 'cost drivers' would be established initially, and these cost drivers would then be used to establish the 'pools'. A cost pool would contain all the costs that have the same cost driver. For instance, a cost driver might be 'area' occupied. The costs that are driven by this driver could be rent, rates, cleaning, building maintenance, heating, and lighting. Another cost driver might be number of 'production runs', and the costs associated with this might, for instance, be machine set-up costs, production scheduling, work-in-progress, and wastage of material. The design costs might be driven by the number of parts in the design. The purchasing costs might be driven by the number of purchase orders, and so on.

A traditional costing system (showing the route of overheads through to the product) would look as follows:

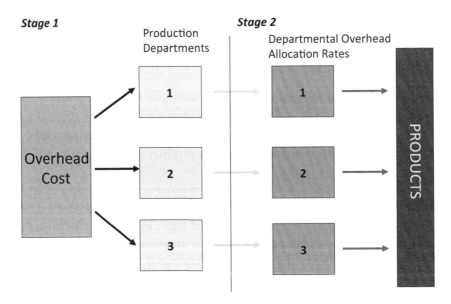

**Figure 10.1   Absorption Costing**

Whereas an activity based system (showing the route of overheads through to the product) would look as follows:

**Stage 1**  Activity Cost Pools           **Stage 2**  Activity Cost Driver Rates

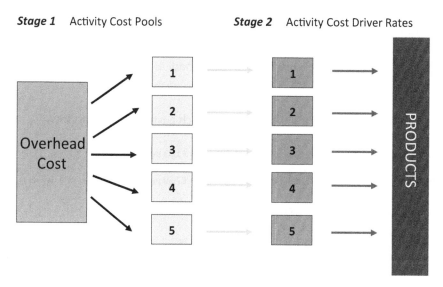

**Figure 10.2    Activity Based Costing**

This clearly shows that there is effectively no difference, except that there are cost pools replacing departments, and cost driver rates replacing absorption rates.

In some ways, this is similar to absorption costing. Rather than being one calculation based on one absorption rate, the overheads allocation comprises several calculations based on the different cost driver rates.

### Example

The overheads for a company are made up as follows:

| | |
|---|---:|
| Administration Costs | 60,000 |
| Production Costs | 75,000 |
| Distribution Costs | 15,000 |
| Total Overheads | £150,000 |

Traditionally, the total overheads were allocated based on total hours budgeted to be worked by the 20 direct labour staff. This was a budget of 1,500 hours per person × 20 = 30,000 hours.

This gave an absorption rate of £150,000 ÷ 30,000 = £5 per labour hour. So a job with 4 labour hours would absorb 4 × £5 = £20 of overheads.

But now suppose that the administration costs had a cost driver of number of total employees (say, 30), the production costs had a cost driver of turnover (say, £500,000), and the distribution costs had a cost driver of number of deliveries (say, 100).

We can now work out a driver rate for each cost element as follows:

| | | |
|---|---|---|
| Administration Costs | £60,000 ÷ 30 ÷ 1,500 | = £1.33 per employee hour for, say, 3 hours |
| Production Costs | £75,000 ÷ 500,000 | = £0.15 per £1 Turnover for, say, £80 |
| Distribution Costs | £15,000 ÷ 2000 | = £7.50 per delivery for, say, one delivery |

This gives a new overhead cost for the job as follows:

| | | |
|---|---|---|
| Administration | 1.33 × 3 | = £4.00 |
| Production | £0.15 × £80 | = £12.00 |
| Distribution | | = £7.50 |
| Total Overhead | | = £23.50 |

compared to £20 using the absorption method.

## Key Points of Activity Based Costing

- Each cost on a supplier's quotation needs to be examined as to whether it is fixed or variable.

- Each cost needs to be examined to determine what is its principal 'cost driver'.

- Your requirement for (or proportion of) that cost needs to be examined and then used in the negotiation process.

(See further Question 7 in the Appendix.)

## Advanced Issues

In order to use ABC as a buyer, it is not necessary to get too deeply involved in ABC calculations, as these can get exceedingly complex and the real benefit is in understanding the negotiation benefits for a buyer.

In order to do this, it is helpful to understand what really drives the supplier's costs and what 'levers' can be used to negotiate prices down.

A good grasp of drivers and levers is extremely useful in a negotiation, as it gives the buyer an edge in overcoming obstacles to lower pricing from the supplier. For instance, a supplier might include in the quotation that the delivery costs are 6% of the selling price. The argument used might be that this reflects the overall delivery costs incurred by the supplier's company, as shown in their accounts. But what actually drives the delivery costs? It is the number of deliveries made by the supplier. You therefore argue a reduction in delivery costs, on the basis of either sharing the deliveries with the supplier by using your own transport (which might have regular trips in the supplier's area anyway) or having only one delivery point at which to drop off the goods.

An example of some of the costs, their drivers and the possible levers that can be used in negotiation are as follows:

| Overhead Costs | Cost Driver | Cost Lever |
| --- | --- | --- |
| Machine Costs | Machine Hours | Change Design or Machine methods |
| Labour | Labour hours and rates | Change Design or Machine methods |
| Set Up | No of Prod Runs/set up times | Less runs |
| Order Handling | No of Purchase Orders | Combine P.O.s |
| Design | Complexity, No of parts | Re-engineer |
| Heating | Area, no of radiators, hours of work | Constantly on? |
| Power | No of Machines, Machine hours | Keep on Capacity |
| Depreciation | No of Components per machine | Higher Volume |
| Packaging | Pack size, materials | Alter Pack size, materials |
| Transport | No of Deliveries, subcontracted? | Share? |

Frequently, the levers are the same as the drivers, as is the case with the set-up costs where the driver is the number of production runs and the lever is obviously less production runs (for example, bulk orders). Similarly, the packaging levers and drivers are the same.

For a major contract, there will usually be a detailed breakdown in the quotation, and a common area of dispute is in the charge for depreciation. A lever for lower depreciation is to have higher volumes being put through a machine or alternatively a cheaper machine. Depreciation is an area where it is not uncommon for excessive charging to take place, based on the depreciation charge possibly being included several times, as follows:

1.   There is a charge included in the 'general' overheads.

2.   Depreciation is also listed separately from general overheads as a charge.

3.     Depreciation is charged on a machine that is being used for the process but is well over specification in the requirement for the job. In other words, it is a very expensive machine to run and well in excess of what is needed for the process.

4.     The machine that is being depreciated has already been fully depreciated in a previous contract with the buyer's company. It is therefore being recovered twice.

5.     The machine is only being run at half its capacity, and the other half is either not being used or it is being used on another client's contract.

The following is a suggested means of combating these supplier methods of being economic with the truth:

1.     Ask for the depreciation charge to be broken out of the general overheads, and then compare the charge as a percentage of the quotation with the depreciation shown in the accounts. For instance, if the charge in the accounts is 5% of the sales for the year and it shows as 15% in the quotation, this should be put to the supplier and ask them to justify it. It might on any given contract be reasonable, but it is up to them to justify it. Perhaps they are using the first year of a reducing balance method to calculate each year's depreciation!

2.     If it is listed separately, ask for a breakdown of the general overheads to ensure it is not also included and, if it is, suggest that the supplier has 'made a mistake'.

3.     If the machine is well over specification, it should be argued that depreciation should be lowered accordingly to reflect the depreciation of an appropriate machine.

4.     It is not easy to identify whether the machine has already been used and depreciated on a previous contract. First, some companies actually keep an asset register of all assets used on supplier's contracts, thus retaining control of this figure. This is a time-consuming process. Secondly, ask the supplier and gauge

the reaction. Thirdly, it is easy to spot if it is a repeat of the same contract. Fourthly, physically check if the machine is new.

5.  How to deal with this problem depends on the type of machine and any agreement with the supplier. If the machine is specialized to your product and has no other use, it is reasonable for the supplier to depreciate it fully as if it was on full capacity, and also to depreciate it fully over the contract life rather than the machine life. In this case, some agreement could be made as to the scrap value at the end of the contract. If the machine is more general purpose, the depreciation should be in proportion to the capacity of the machine used. It should be the supplier's risk to fill the spare capacity of the machine.

# 11

# Costing for Decision Making

## Introduction and the Basic Concept

In this chapter, we examine in more detail the principles surrounding the separation of costs into 'fixed' and 'variable', and how this concept can be used for improved decision making, particularly from the buyer's perspective.

'Marginal costing' is a term used to determine the cost of producing one more item (that is, the marginal item).

If one more unit is manufactured, the total costs of the organisation rise but only some of those costs. These costs which rise are the marginal or 'variable' costs. It is easy to see why certain costs increase. For instance, if you are manufacturing tables and you make one more, the material costs will rise (wood, screws, glue etc). It will also take more labour time to make, there may be design royalties to pay, and there would be more transport and packing costs and sales commission. The total of these costs would be the variable costs. Clearly, the rent and rates would not increase and neither would the managing director's salary. However, what would be the effect if we made 1,000 more tables? Perhaps the factory would not be big enough and so the rent would then increase for the extra space needed. We, therefore, have a situation where some costs may be fixed in the short term but variable in the longer term; so, in any calculation, we must be only concerned with the parameters within which we would operate. This is known as the relevant range (that is, the range within which the cost structure is unchanged).

## Fixed and Variable Costs

Costs are classified into two main headings when assessing cost behaviour: a fixed cost remains unchanged within given output parameters; and a variable cost varies with changes in the level of activity. It can vary proportionately to sales or production. What we are really saying here is that a fixed cost is not totally fixed; it simply means that, if we make more of the product, the cost will not change. Each year, rent and rates may change but they are still fixed costs within this definition.

It is sometimes quite difficult to separate the fixed and variable costs, and some costs are known as semi-variable in that they have one element of each. For instance, a salesperson's salary might be paid partly as a basic (fixed cost) and partly as a commission on sales (variable). There is a simple way of 'decomposing' costs if we assume that only two activity levels will define the variable costs: take the increase in costs, and divide by the increase in activity to arrive at the variable cost per unit. This is because any rise in costs must, by its nature, be a variable cost.

### Example

| Output in Units | 10,000 | 15,000 |
|---|---|---|
| Electricity Costs | £25,000 | £35,000 |

Step 1 – Calculate the variable costs per unit by dividing the increase in costs by the increase in units:

$$(£35,000 - £25,000) \div (15,000 - 10,000) = £2/\text{unit}$$

Step 2 – Take either level of activity (say, 10,000 units) and calculate the total variable costs at that level:

Variable costs are $10,000 \times £2/\text{unit} = £20,000$

Step 3 – Deduce the fixed costs at that level by deducting the total variable costs from the total costs:

Fixed Costs = £25,000 – £20,000 = £5,000 (This may be cross-checked with the other level of output to prove the fixed costs remain the same.)

An alternative is to plot the costs at various levels of output to produce a scattergraph and then draw a line of best fit through it. Where it joins the cost axis (Y axis) would be the fixed costs.

## Contribution Statements

Contribution is a key term in marginal costing, being the difference between the sales value and the variable costs of the product. We say that a product is providing a 'contribution' if this figure is positive. It is 'contributing' towards paying the fixed costs and making a profit.

An income statement may be drawn up for a company and then converted into a 'contribution' statement. For example:

| | |
|---|---:|
| Sales | £1,000 |
| *Less* Cost of Sales | 450 |
| Gross Profit | 550 |
| *Less* Overheads | 450 |
| Net profit | 100 |

### Contribution Statement

| | |
|---|---:|
| Sales | £1,000 |
| *Less* Variable Costs | 400 |
| Contribution | 600 |
| *Less* Fixed Costs | 500 |
| Net profit | 100 |

In each case, the total costs will be the same, but the distribution between variable and fixed costs is not the same as cost of sales and overheads. For instance, factory management costs might be in cost of sales, but they are a fixed cost in a contribution statement.

So what would be the break-even (no profit or loss) for the company?

Instinctively, one looks at the total costs of £900 and says that, if sales are £900, then this is break-even. This is incorrect because, if the sales fall to £900, can you see any costs which would also fall? Obviously, the fixed costs will not change because they are fixed. The variable costs, however, will fall in direct proportion to the sales. This 'direct proportion' is one of the fundamental assumptions we make in utilising the marginal costing concept. As can be seen, the variable costs are 40% of the sales (£400).

So, if the sales fall to £900, the variable costs fall to 40% of £900 = £360.

We would therefore be left with the following contribution statement:

| | |
|---|---:|
| Sales | £900 |
| *Less* Variable Costs | 360 |
| Contribution | 540 |
| *Less* Fixed Costs | 500 |
| Net profit | 40 |

The break-even contribution statement would look as follows:

| | |
|---|---:|
| Sales | £833 |
| *Less* Variable Costs (40%) | 333 |
| Contribution (60%) | 500 |
| *Less* Fixed Costs | 500 |
| Net profit | 0 |

It can now be seen that, if the variable costs are 40% of sales, the contribution is 60%, because it is the difference between sales and variable costs. Similarly, if the variable costs were 72%, the contribution would have been 28%, and so on.

The break-even can be calculated by dividing the fixed costs by the contribution percentage.

So, break-even = 500/60% = 833.

Remember, at break-even, contribution will equal fixed costs.

If contribution is maximised, this will automatically maximise profit, as fixed costs are fixed!

**Example**

| | |
|---|---:|
| Sales | £12,000 |
| Less Variable Costs (75%) | 9,000 |
| Contribution (25%) | 3,000 |
| Less Fixed Costs | 1,500 |
| Net profit | 1,500 |

• The variable costs percentage and contribution percentage remain constant.

• Calculate the profit at sales of £20,000 and the break-even sales.

In order to do this, the best way is to set up a basic skeleton or template of what will not change in the statement. The alternative is to memorise formulae.

The base template would be as follows:

| | |
|---|---:|
| Sales | £X |
| *Less* Variable Costs (75%) | X |
| Contribution (25%) | X |
| *Less* Fixed Costs | 1,500 |
| Net profit | X |

We then just need to fill in the blanks, starting at the top and working downwards, to arrive at the profit:

| | |
|---|---:|
| Sales | £20,000 |
| *Less* Variable Costs (75%) | 15,000 |
| Contribution (25%) | 5,000 |
| *Less* Fixed Costs | 1,500 |
| Net profit | 3,500 |

The variable costs are 75% of the sales, this gives the contribution and then deduct the fixed costs to arrive at the profit.

Working from a known profit (or break-even) is a little more difficult, as we would start at the profit and work upwards:

| | | Order |
|---|---:|---|
| Sales | £6,000 | 4 |
| *Less* Variable Costs (75%) | 4,500 | 5 |
| Contribution (25%) | 1,500 | 3 |
| *Less* Fixed Costs | 1,500 | 2 |
| Net profit | 0 | 1 |

The logic is as follows: if the profit is zero and the fixed costs are £1,500, by simple mathematics the contribution must be £1,500. The contribution is 25% of the sales. Therefore, the sales are the contribution ÷ 25% or £1,500 ÷ 25% = £6,000. This then means the variable costs are £4,500 by a difference. Two things should be noted here. The first is that we go straight from the contribution to the sales and down to the variable costs. (This makes calculations easier.) The second is that, to get from contribution to sales, we divide the contribution by the contribution percentage. Dividing by a percentage is an unnatural act for most people, and the easiest way is to convert the percentage into a decimal. So, 25% is 25 ÷ 100 = .25 as a decimal. You may be thinking, why do we not just multiply the contribution by four?, and you would be right in this case; but, if the contribution percentage was 22.37%, it suddenly becomes a problem trying to take a quick route!

As fixed costs are already assumed to be committed for, they may be ignored for the purpose of making many decisions.

To use marginal costing effectively requires an understanding of the basic assumptions underlying the concept. These are:

- Variable costs, and therefore contribution, are assumed to vary directly proportionately to the activity level (sales or production). Obviously, if sales units are the same as produced units, it has the same effect. In reality, variable costs will not vary directly. For instance, material cost is usually less per item on large orders, as there is less wastage and price discounts are more easily negotiated. Similarly, labour costs usually fall due to the experience of the workforce. This is known as the 'experience' or 'learning' curve.

- Fixed costs remain fixed. In reality, there are jumps in fixed costs with each stage of expansion.

- Other than a change in product mix (such as selling more of a lower contribution item), it is only the buying prices and labour rates or selling prices which affect the variable cost percentage. Higher buying prices result in lower contribution percentage. Higher selling prices result in higher contribution percentage.

- The break-even level of output in value is the (fixed costs ÷ contribution %).

- The break-even level of output in units is (fixed costs ÷ contribution per unit).

- In the example above, break-even is £1,500/25% = £6,000.

If, in the situation above, the products sold at £20 each, the break-even in products would be £1,500/contribution per unit:

The contribution per unit is 25% of £20 = £5.

Break-even is therefore £1,500/£5 = 300 units.

This shows how this concept is used in budgeting either levels of required sales when a required profit is entered or likely profit at a given level of sales. (See further Question 8 in the Appendix.)

## Break-Even Charts

These are used purely to show cost behaviour and are not a practical tool other

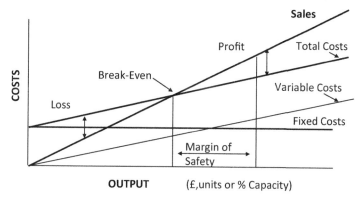

**Figure 11.1    Break-even Chart**

than as a learning aid.

The following example (which shows the point where sales are equal to total costs) indicates the relevant items:

- The break-even chart serves to demonstrate cost behaviour and therefore shows the level of output at which a company attains profitability.

- The variable costs line angle reflects the proportion of variable costs to sales. Therefore, a steep angle indicates a high proportion of variable costs, and a flat angle indicates a low proportion.

- The total costs line is the sum of the variable costs and the fixed costs and is parallel to the variable costs line.

- As the sales price increases, the sales line becomes steeper, and so the profit at a given level of output increases.

- The break-even point is the point where the sales line meets the total costs.

- The margin of safety is the difference between the break-even turnover and the budgeted or current level of turnover, dependent on what is being considered at the time.

- The output can be expressed in number of units, sales value or percentage of capacity.

- It assumes that there is no limit to the relevant range, whereas in practice the range is probably only relevant between plus or minus 20% of the break-even point.

- All break-even charts have a similar appearance. They are easily drawn by inserting the fixed costs line and the break-even point. Then draw two more lines through the break-even point with one starting at zero and the other starting at the fixed costs line on the 'Y' axis.

As has already been mentioned, the fixed costs are only fixed within given output parameters and will actually increase as activity increases but in stages. The first jump might come with an increase in middle management costs, and the second jump might come as the organisation outgrows its premises and needs a bigger building.

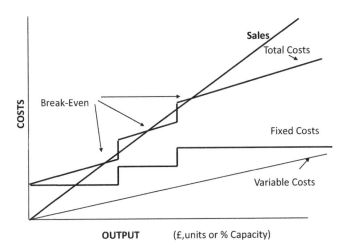

**Figure 11.2    Break-even Chart: Stepped Fixed Costs**

This could be represented by the following figure (which shows multiple break-even points):

Here we can see multiple break-even points, and it becomes fairly clear where the best points are for negotiating with a supplier. If the supplier is just below one of the increases in fixed costs, they are not going to give a particularly good price for a significant order, as they will need to increase their fixed costs in order to supply. On the other hand, if they are on break-even or just above, this means that all their fixed costs are covered, so any further business is pure contribution and profit and so theoretically they could give a competitive price. There would be a similar line of logic when formulating an exit strategy for a supplier. Removing significant work from the supplier would not be such a hardship when they are at a point of high capacity as removing the work when the company is already making a loss or close to break-even. It could even plunge them into liquidation. CSR issues would need to be considered here, as it would not be great PR for a company to be seen to be destroying the biggest employer in a small town, and media intervention could seriously jeopardise the company's image.

So how do we know how near its capacity the supplier is trading?

One way is to ask them. It sounds obvious but it is surprising how good, honest, open questioning will produce useful results. One can also deduce their capacity by examining historical turnover and staffing figures. The best way is to assess the capacity from a survey of their factory. It is not uncommon in large-scale engineering companies, for instance, if the buyer were accompanied by a cost engineer who can quickly take a census of all the machinery and, knowing the capability of each machine, can calculate fairly accurately their total capacity to supply.

## Contribution Analysis

Take a look at the following example:

|                | Totals | Product A | Product B | Product C |
|----------------|--------|-----------|-----------|-----------|
| Sales          | 1,000  | 400       | 300       | 300       |
| Variable Costs | 500    | 250       | 200       | 50        |
| Contribution   | 500    | 150       | 100       | 250       |
| Fixed Costs    | 400    | 100       | 200       | 100       |
| Profit         | 100    | 50        | (100)     | 150       |

If we drop product B, does the profit therefore increase to £200?

The main point is that the fixed costs of £200 borne by product B need to be absorbed by products A and C. As product B is making a contribution to covering these fixed costs, no matter how small, the product should be retained, at least in the short term.

The circumstances in which product B might be dropped are:

1. Some of the fixed costs would also be reduced, since the contribution lost by eliminating the product would be offset by the reduction in fixed costs. These are known as 'specific' fixed costs. In this case, the specific fixed costs would need to be at least £100.

2. The plant is operating at capacity and the contribution lost by dropping B would be made up by an increase in A or B or a new product D. (Note, if product D could produce more contribution, it would not imply that product B was dropped unless there was inadequate capacity.)

3. By dropping product B, the sales of products A and C would automatically increase to create further compensatory contribution (that is, there is an interdependency of products). The reverse is also true, in that dropping product B could adversely affect the sales of products A and C.

Contribution is maximised by concentrating on the product with the highest contribution/unit – in this case, C followed by A. Sometimes it is beneficial to concentrate on the highest contribution percentage if there is a restriction on sales value (for example, selling to a customer with a maximum spend, such as a health authority).

Other aspects affecting the decision would be product life cycles of the lines (it may be beneficial in the long term to drop an old product and bring in a new one), or whether there were any scarce resources such as materials or labour – in this case, rather than concentrating on the highest contribution per unit, emphasis would be put on the product with the highest contribution per scarce resource. For instance, a supermarket's scarce resource would be its shelf space. Therefore, it would concentrate on the product lines that give the highest contribution per square foot of shelf space and not on the products giving the highest contribution per unit.

The decision process in this event would be:

- Calculate contribution per unit of scarce resource (for example, per ounce of material).

- Rank options by contribution.

- Choose the first option which yields highest contribution per unit of scare resource and follow this by the next highest, selling each product up to its market potential.

For what type of decisions is the marginal cost concept used?

- Acceptance of a special order. This refers to selling prices based on marginal costs (for example, when a customer offers to fill a production gap in your factory but will only give an order at a heavily discounted price). This price must be above the variable costs in order to create a contribution and therefore be potentially acceptable.

- Make or buy in product. This is where a product can be bought for a price not just lower than the total costs but lower than the variable costs in making it (such as importing some clothing lines from abroad due to low labour costs). There are other issues raised here, such as control over delivery, quality, price etc. Also, the costs of making a product include some fixed costs. Will these disappear if the products are imported? If not, they need to be added onto the import price to arrive at the total cost.

- Maximising profit by maximising the sales of the product which gives the highest contribution per scarce resource up to its market potential.

- Dropping or bringing in new product lines.

The above provides information towards making a good decision but should not be seen as replacing good commercial sense. For instance, if a low price was accepted for a large order, would this undermine other customer pricing arrangements? What is the overall strategy with regard to dominating the market sector? If a product was dropped, would it allow a competitor to get a foot in the door? If we restrict product lines, how would customers react? Would they buy our other products or move away altogether?

## BUYER PERSPECTIVE

- As some suppliers' costs are fixed, prices are dependent on the order volume, so any change in order volume over quoted volume will affect supplier's pricing. It is not uncommon for a buyer to ask for a quotation from a supplier for, say, 100,000 units and receive a price of £2.30/unit and then finally place an order for 150,000 units. A further quotation should give a better price per unit. Similarly, if a buyer wishes to place an order less than the quoted volume, they should not be surprised if the price per unit is higher.

- Additionally, when negotiating a new order with a supplier, it may be possible to bring the price down to a break-even for the supplier when the supplier is making profit on other orders. In other words, it becomes a product 'bundle', so the supplier will not get order A where there is a £10,000 profit unless they accept order B where there is potentially a loss. As long as the supplier is making a contribution on order B, it would be worthwhile accepting; otherwise, the costs of not accepting would also be the lost contribution on product A. This is a common occurrence where buyers have difficulty in placing orders for parts that are difficult to manufacture and they can use their negotiating power to ensure a price. Also, buyers are increasingly under pressure to reduce their buying costs, and one way is to reduce their number of suppliers.

- Filling a supplier's spare capacity in a quiet period. If a supplier can manufacture 100,000 units per month and is currently on 80,000, there is spare capacity of 20,000 units. Theoretically, any price the supplier received for an order above their variable costs might be acceptable, as it would generate contribution towards their fixed costs which are going to occur whether or not they accept the order. The problem is often not being aware of the supplier's capacity and their current utilisation. The supplier will have to decide whether the spare capacity could be filled in any other way. Also, they would need to consider the commercial considerations of selling at less than their normal price.

- Second-tier suppliers may bring suppliers' costs down. As many large purchasing organisations are seeking to reduce their number of suppliers through the appointment of 'master vendors' or key suppliers, sometimes they are not equipped to manufacture a particular product economically. A buyer may be able to redirect a previous supplier to this master vendor to bring a particular part cost down. For instance, a buyer purchases many parts from supplier A and also one part, component Z, from supplier B. In a supplier reduction process, it decides to purchase only from supplier A. Supplier A could supply component Z for £37 per unit after increasing its fixed costs. However, supplier B was supplying it for £30 per unit. If the buyer directed supplier A to purchase component Z from supplier B and put their 5% management fee on, the purchase would cost £31.50 instead of £37, giving a £5.50 saving. Obviously, this price is more than the original price of £30 but it will satisfy the supply reduction plan and, we assume, it will reduce overall buying costs.

(See Further Question 9 in the Appendix.)

# 12

# Supplier Pricing Options

It is a fallacy to think that supplier's prices are solely driven by cost, because everything is negotiable, and the 'want to' factor is the key aspect of this; that is, how much does the supplier want to sell the product, and how much does the buyer want to buy the product? This will be affected by market conditions.

Some of the factors that affect how a product or service will be priced are as follows:

- level of competition;

- urgency of need;

- stage in the product life cycle;

- supply versus demand;

- certainty of level of service;

- financial year end timing – both the supplier's and buyer's;

- how badly the supplier wants the business;

- seasonality in the service or product;

- whether they are a 'preferred' customer;

- perceived quality ('branding');

- volumes on offer; and

- warranties and service offered.

So, cost is only one (but a major) part in what determines the price at which an item is bought. The product may be a small niche item where there is limited demand but little competition. In this event, the supplier will be taking a 'premium' pricing view but selling fewer items. An alternative approach would be trying to sell more items at a lower price.

That said, there are various standard methods for determining how a supplier would arrive at their selling price.

## Cost Plus Pricing

This method takes the costs in a product or service (as discussed in the chapter on absorption costing) and then a mark-up is added to it. The level of this mark-up depends upon the factors listed above. With high demand and low supply, it is likely that a high mark-up would be applied.

The cost base used for applying the mark-up would be a matter of choice by the supplier. If only the variable costs were used, obviously a higher mark-up would be used than if all the costs were used. Sometimes it is difficult to allocate fixed costs across products, in which case the variable or possibly the production costs would be used.

The method for applying the mark-up would be as follows:

1.  Establish the margin on sales that is required (say, 25%).

2.  Establish the costs to be used as the cost base (say, variable costs of £180 per unit).

3.  Apply the formula Cost ÷ (1 – required margin):

    *   This gives £180 ÷ (1 – 25%) = £180 ÷ 75% = £240

    *   To check this, the margin is £240 – £180 = £60

    *   £60 as a percentage of £240 = £60 ÷ £240 × 100 = 25%.

What this method will do is to give a 'target cost' that theoretically will give enough revenue to cover the costs included in the cost base. However, the margin required will be subject to all the other issues listed above.

Let us suppose that the cost base applied is the variable costs of the product. The decision of how much margin to add would be based on all the other costs required to be covered plus the required profit. The required profit would often be arrived at by taking the capital employed in the organisation and targeting a level of return on that capital.

### Example

Level of return required on capital of £300,000 is 20% or £60,000.

- The number of units expected to be sold are 20,000 units.

- The variable costs of one unit would be £40.

- The total fixed costs are £100,000.

The company therefore need to generate a contribution amounting to the fixed costs plus the profit = £160,000 (£100,000 + £60,000).

This gives a contribution per unit of £160,000 ÷ 20,000 units = £80/unit.

If the contribution is £80 and the variable costs are £40, the selling price needs to be £80 + £40 = £120 per unit. This gives a mark-up of £80 on the variable costs of £40 which equals a 200% mark-up on the variable costs (that is, the selling price is 3 × the variable costs). This is known as a 'target rate of return' pricing which, in this case, is 20%. The weakness, of course, is that demand is usually affected by the price, and so continuous re-calculations are needed to arrive at the 'optimum' price. This is the price at which the overall contribution is maximised.

A major problem with cost plus pricing is that it can distract the seller from controlling the costs and instead take the view that the costs are 'X', so the selling price should be 'Y', without examining whether the costs are too high. Many large government contracts used to be placed at cost plus pricing agreements so that, if a supplier's costs rose, so would the price. The problem with this is that, where there is a preferred supplier, it is in the supplier's interests to keep its costs high, as this would generate a higher profit (for example, if there is a cost plus arrangement of 10% profit on costs and the costs are estimated at £5,000,000, the profit is going to be £500,000). If subsequently, during the contract, the costs rise to £6,000,000, the profit would be £600,000, so where is the incentive for the supplier to keep the costs down? Large contracts are increasingly placed at fixed prices now, with perhaps an allowance for a price alteration based on a commodity price index of a key material.

There is one major advantage of cost plus to the buyer, as the buyer can track the price index of a key commodity included in the product and is able to substantiate a supplier's claim for a price increase or use it to negotiate a lower price if the index falls. Also, a seller may ask for a 10% price increase when the raw materials have increased 10%. If the raw materials in a product account for 25% of the current selling price of £20 per unit, this would mean that the costs have increased by 10% of £5 = 50 pence and not £2 which is the supplier's new suggested price increase based on 10% of £20.

## Marginal Pricing

This is a pricing method which is based on fixing a price which is anything above the variable costs of the product or service. It is a price which generates a contribution but it may not be enough to cover all the fixed costs and required profit.

### Example

|  | Normal Pricing | Marginal Pricing |
|---|---|---|
| Units | 1,000 | 1,000 |
| Sales | 20,000 | 17,500 |
| Variable costs | 15,000 | 15,000 |
| Contribution | 5,000 | 2,500 |
| Fixed Costs | 4,000 | 4,000 |
| Profit | 1,000 | (1,500) |

Here, the normal pricing shows a price that effectively gives £20 per unit with variable costs of £15 per unit. This creates an overall profit of £1,000 after fixed costs of £4,000.

The marginal pricing shows that the price per unit has fallen to £17.50 and this gives an insufficient contribution to cover all the fixed costs, thus producing a loss.

So why should a company price using its marginal cost (variable cost) as its base?

The reasons are not always bad, as one might instinctively think that the supplier is pricing in this way (and so very low) because they have no other work and are effectively buying the work just to keep their business going and that this price is an indicator of impending insolvency. This might be the case, in which event one can only see them as a short-term supplier and certainly should not be a strategic supplier. Provided there is no significant risk if the supplier lets you down, it might be a risk worth accepting if the price is so good. For instance, if the supply could be quickly sourced elsewhere at the right quality, there is a fallback.

Other reasons for suppliers pricing on a marginal basis are as follows:

- The supplier wishes to 'get in' with you. In this event, expect further supplies in the short or medium term to be at a higher price.

- The supplier provides this product as a loss leader in order to make good profits on other products that are supplied. This is typified by printer suppliers who make little profit apparently on the printers but they are sold in order to create large profits on the ink cartridge supplies.

- The supplier has a very quiet period of work and still has to pay the fixed costs. It is therefore a good move financially for the supplier to take any orders, provided they create a contribution to recover some of those fixed costs. This can only be a short-term tactic, as there are clearly other commercial issues involved. For instance, if a retailer, by dint of purchasing at a very favourable price, then retails at an extremely competitive price, this would alert other retail customers (of the supplier) that the supplies have been at a better price than their own, potentially causing a relationship problem for the supplier.

- Optimal pricing. Broadly speaking, a company makes its highest profit when it achieves its highest contribution. This assumes that the fixed costs are indeed fixed. A high contribution can be reached by pricing high on the basis of low sales units. Alternatively, it might price lower on the basis of selling more units. This is demonstrated below:

| Option | A | B |
|---|---|---|
| Units | 500 | 800 |
| Price | £1.50 | £1.40 |
| Sales | £750 | £1,120 |
| Variable Costs (£1/unit) | 500 | 800 |
| Contribution | 250 | 320 |
| Fixed Costs | 100 | 100 |
| Profit | £150 | £220 |

In this case, greater contribution is achieved by pricing lower at £1.25 and selling 60% more units. The problem is knowing how many will be sold at the lower price, and an understanding of demand elasticity is essential in making these types of pricing decision. If demand rises quickly for a small reduction in price, it is said to be highly elastic; and, if there is only a small increase in demand for a material reduction in price, it is said to be inelastic. This information may be available based on historical evidence, knowledge of the market or pure judgment. It becomes very powerful information in the right hands, and a close working relationship between the brand manager (if there is one) and the management accountant can pay great dividends.

## Transfer Pricing

By transfer pricing is meant the price at which goods or services are transferred within a group or divisional structure. For instance, a catering group might own a bakery, and the 'normal' price for subsidiary A (bakery) to sell a standard loaf might be £1.15. Subsidiary B (restaurant) might wish to take a substantial regular order for these loaves, and subsidiary A transfers the loaves at £0.95 instead of the normal £1.15. The transfer price is therefore £0.95.

So what are the issues surrounding this pricing method?

- The bakery will lose profit, as its normal price is much higher.

- The restaurant will appear to gain profit, as it is buying cheaper than the normal price.

- The bakery's normal price might be above the price at which the restaurant could buy it elsewhere.

- The bakery's transfer price might be above the price at which the restaurant could buy elsewhere.

- The bakery might not be able to fill its capacity without the orders from the restaurant.

- If the bakery was in a high tax country and the restaurant was in a low tax area, this would transfer profit from the bakery to the restaurant which would therefore reduce the overall tax bill, although there are laws in many countries preventing this technique abusing international tax intentions.

The methods of transfer pricing would be as follows:

- market price;

- cost price (that is, no profit);

- market price less a percentage;

- cost price plus a percentage; and

- normal price.

The normal price is what the company would normally sell at, using its 'normal' pricing method. This is not necessarily the market price, as it could be higher or lower depending on other factors that influence price. There are some good reasons for transferring at other than the normal price. For instance, there might be significant savings in both selling and marketing costs for the bakery and also credit control costs, therefore reducing administration costs for the bakery. Additionally, if the bakery had little other work, the restaurant's work is acting as a capacity filler and will therefore give an overall improvement in contribution to the group profit situation. In a multinational situation, there would be an improvement in the overall tax paid by the company if profit can effectively be moved from a high tax country to a low tax country. There are, however, limits on price reductions that can be used across borders, and many countries share schemes whereby there are significant penalties for what is effective cross-border subsidy and transfer of profits. Her Majesty's Revenue and Customs (HMRC), the UK tax authority, pursues cases where it believes the price has been set artificially low for tax purposes.

A poor and badly understood pricing policy can cause managers to become severely de-motivated, particularly when faced with having to manage a department or division that is considered to be continually facing a loss situation due to a transfer pricing policy. There could also be a dependence on the restaurant to take a large amount of the capacity of the bakery, and this could cause inefficiencies in the bakery and produce a slackening of marketing and sales effort by them, as they might perceive that all of their capacity is filled. It could also affect their quality if they feel that the restaurant will have to take their products anyway.

Overall, a sensible transfer pricing policy may only enhance group profits where it can generate a contribution level that is not otherwise attainable. However, this needs to be tempered with the possible de-motivational effects and inefficiencies mentioned that may creep in when used as a capacity filler.

**Example**

A company has several divisions that deal with each other. One company, Empire Builders Ltd, lets serviced office space, and the other company, Scrub It Up Ltd, supplies office cleaning services.

Empire Builders can get cleaning services for a cost of effectively 10% of their sales if purchased 'on the open market'.

The accounts of the two look as follows if purchased on the open market:

|  | Totals | Empire Builders | Scrub It Up |
|---|---|---|---|
| Sales | £600,000 | £500,000 | £100,000 |
| Other Variable Costs | 280,000 | (50%) 250,000 | (30%) 30,000 |
| Cleaning Services | 50,000 | 50,000 | 0 |
| Contribution | 270,000 | 200,000 | 70,000 |
| Fixed Costs | 150,000 | 120,000 | 30,000 |
| Profit | £120,000 | £80,000 | £40,000 |

The overall profit for the two divisions is £120,000, with £80,000 profit in Empire Builders Ltd and £40,000 in Scrub It Up Ltd.

Let us now assume that head office have issued a directive that the cleaning services for Empire Builders Ltd must be procured 'internally' if the capability is available. Let us also assume that the internal purchase price would be 20% higher than on the open market at £60,000.

The accounts of the two would now look as follows following internal purchases:

| | Totals | Empire Builders | Scrub It Up |
|---|---|---|---|
| Sales | £660,000 | £500,000 | £160,000 |
| Other Variable Costs | 298,000 | (50%) 250,000 | (30%) 48,000 |
| Cleaning Services | 60,000 | 60,000 | 0 |
| Contribution | 302,000 | 190,000 | 112,000 |
| Fixed Costs | 150,000 | 120,000 | 30,000 |
| Profit | £152,000 | £70,000 | £82,000 |

This shows an overall increase in the profit of £32,000 made up of a decrease in profit for Empire Builders of £10,000 (due to the increase in cleaning service costs) and an increase in profit for Scrub It Up of £42,000 (due to the increase in contribution earned from the extra £60,000 sales to Empire Builders. (Note that, when the figures are 'consolidated', the total sales will be £600,000 and the cleaning services costs would disappear to reflect the removal of inter-company trading.)

In this example, Scrub It Up are more expensive than the open market price (which would irritate the buyers from Empire Builders), but they might in another situation have been cheaper than the open market price, which would 'encourage' large purchases by Empire Builders and may also encourage Empire Builders to sell their own services cheaper due to lower costs. This may or may not be a good thing, depending on market conditions!

The general rules are to set the transfer price equal to marginal cost plus net opportunity cost to the group. In a competitive market, the market price should be used; and, where there is surplus capacity, the marginal cost should be used.

## Market Price and Negotiated Price

Market price is a price based on competitors' prices. The assumption is that of full, shared knowledge between competitors of prices and costs, and it assumes that there is a high enough level of competition to cause a sales reduction if prices were above a certain 'sales band' and, if below this band, a loss would ensue as the price would be uneconomic. However, the full sales offering might be hard to compare when all the other factors (such as service agreements and warranties) are included.

Negotiated price really encompasses some of the other methods previously discussed but essentially is a price negotiated, usually for a large order and frequently based around contribution requirements, depending upon the prevailing pressures on the buying and supplying companies.

# 13

# Cost Modelling

Cost modelling is a tool by which all of the elements of cost are identified for the provision of any goods or services. The broad benefit of being able to identify all of the elements that make up a supplier's quotation is that each element can be compared with what you feel that element should actually cost the supplier. This can then be used in the negotiation process to endeavour to lower the overall price. Suppliers will naturally resist supplying this information, but they may have little option if they wish to work with the customer.

The broad elements of the cost of a product or service are materials, labour, overheads and supplier profit, and being able to get a supplier's quotation submitted against each of these elements can be more of a problem than might at first be thought (and this is dealt with later).

Clearly, cost models may be varied in terms of percentages for a service company as compared to a manufacturing company, as shown here:

|  | Service Company | | Manufacturing Company | |
|---|---|---|---|---|
| Materials | £160 | 10.0% | £640 | 40.0% |
| Labour | £800 | 50.0% | £400 | 25.0% |
| Overheads | £440 | 27.5% | £360 | 22.5% |
| Profit | £200 | 12.5% | £200 | 12.5% |
| Total Cost | £1,600 | 100% | £1,600 | 100% |

Here we can see that the material cost is very low for a service company (such as office cleaning, where it would be made up of chemical cleaning materials) and the labour represents 50% of the overall cost. The manufacturing company has a much higher materials cost (40%) and a lower percentage labour cost. Within these groups, there are very variable cost models for different companies and, for different niche products or services offered, there may be different cost models.

Cost modelling can be an effective process for collecting, analysing and utilising cost information to use during any of the processes of planning, evaluation, negotiation and supplier development, and it moves the approach away from 'price only' comparisons based on alternative quotations to comparisons of 'actual cost' based on unbiased and independent cost information.

It answers the three fundamental questions of

- What drives the supplier's costs?

- What price should be paid?

- Is the current price more than it should be?

It often relies on the sharing of cost information between customer and supplier, and this can create significant tensions. This sharing of cost information is referred to as open book costing (OBC) or cost transparency.

## Open Book Costing and Cost Transparency

The theory behind open book costing (OBC) is that both the customers and the suppliers collaborate to examine supply costs and search for methods to reduce them through joint initiatives, such as shared transport or combining packaging or delivery points. There might be significant savings, and ideally these should be shared between the buyer and seller. If it is a customer-inspired saving, 65% might go to the customer (with 35% to the supplier); and, if it is a supplier-inspired saving, 65% might go to the supplier. It is a one-way process, in that the supplier is opening up his books and giving full disclosure to the customer, but not vice versa.

For instance, Shark Ltd was looking to buy wooden pallets from Minnow Ltd, and Minnow quoted the following unit price for 5,000 pallets:

| | |
|---|---|
| Wood | £1.58 |
| Labour | 2.16 |
| Overheads | 2.40 |
| Profit | 0.90 |
| Total Cost | £7.04 |

A comparison with the cost model shows the 'average' cost breakdown of a pallet as follows:

| Wood | £1.23 |
|------|-------|
| Labour | 2.50 |
| Overheads | 2.00 |
| Profit | 1.00 |
| Total Cost | £6.73 |

The result is that they are clearly showing a low profit and appear to have a high overhead rate and the wood is costing too much. However, the labour is very low. The buyer would need to establish their profit percentage. The next step would be to clarify their sources of supply of wood and perhaps share sources if applicable. The low labour cost might indicate either high efficiency, a mistake in the costing, or perhaps they are paying below the minimum wage or using illegal immigrant labour, which could present CSR issues.

On the other hand, the term that allows full transparency of not only the supplier's cost structure but also the customer's is known as 'cost transparency'. For instance, a food supermarket might wish to buy a coronation chicken sandwich pack to retail at £2.99. They tell the potential supplier that they need at least a 33.33% margin on sales, which means that they cannot pay more than £2.00 for the supply (that is, 2/3 of £2.99). The supplier can then come up with options to suit the customer, having been given a target price. This is a simplified form of cost transparency, as it does not give the supplier an indicator of the customer's costs, only its margin. In this instance, the supplier might well come up with a price exactly on the £2.00 limit rather than a price below that, so full disclosure might not be helpful unless a more detailed breakdown of the costs were provided and the buyer and seller work on these jointly to share ensuing benefits. It would be necessary for the buyer to ensure that the supplier is not too 'comfortable' in relation to likelihood of getting the contract, so as to ensure competitiveness in the quotation. The supplier might find that the current method of display shows only 20 sandwiches per square foot, and the supplier might devise a stand that displays 25 sandwiches per square foot, which could stimulate sales, and both could share in the benefit through the extra sales and the supplier making a greater margin. Alternatively, sharing the distribution methods and costs may help both parties improve overall cost efficiency.

Let us examine the following supplier's cost model:

| | | |
|---|---|---|
| Materials | £700 | 35% |
| Labour | £520 | 26% |
| Overheads | £440 | 22% |
| Profit | £340 | 17% |
| Total Cost | £2,000 | 100% |

This tells us nothing unless we have some way of comparing either the absolute costs for each cost category or the percentage that each category represents of the total cost. It may be that the standard profit in this sector is 10%, in which case this supplier is overloading the profit. However, I would have to ask, 'How often have you seen a supplier show a high profit percentage in a quotation?'. The answer is probably never.

The nature of OBC is that the buyer is forcing, through their power as a buyer, the supplier to part with privileged information. This creates a deal of caginess and economy with the truth, whereas cost transparency theoretically is more collaborative but still instils a level of fear. It is, however, amazing how eager new suppliers are in divulging information to gain orders. Contrast this with asking a supplier for cost breakdowns when, for ten years as a buyer, you have always accepted their quotation, perhaps with a little price negotiation along the way.

One could pose the following three questions about open book costing:

1.   How might the purchasing organisation use the information?

2.   Why might the supplier be worried about disclosing it?

3.   How might suppliers benefit from moving on to OBC?

It is worth giving them some thought for a few minutes before continuing.

## HOW MIGHT THE PURCHASING ORGANISATION USE THE INFORMATION?

- The buyer could generate a cost model from the information and compare it year on year or with other suppliers' quotations.

- The buyer could find areas of excessive cost in a supplier's quotation and use this either for negotiation or, ideally, to advise or help the supplier to reduce this cost area.

- The information could be used to compare with a supplier's actual results in their annual income statements. This can be quite difficult, but it is not usually a case of the buyer telling the supplier what the cost should be, it is more about putting the supplier on the back foot by asking them to justify a given cost; for example, 'Jim, in your accounts, your depreciation figure is 5% of your sales in total, please can you explain to me why the depreciation figure in the quotation is 15% of your total cost?'. It may be reasonable because of specialist machinery or it may not! It should be left up to the supplier to justify this.

- It should undoubtedly help the buyer to work with the supplier on reducing areas of weakness or overcharging in the costing.

- It could be compared with the buyer's own 'should cost' calculations. These could come from two main sources. First, if the buyer's organisation has previously manufactured this product (or supplied this service), there should be significant cost data with which to make a comparison. Secondly, the buyer's organisation may have good technical and research backup, whereby much of the data can be sourced directly. For instance, with the pallets example above, the wood price will be available on a price index (a special index just for pallet wood). It may simply be that the buyer does some basic primary research on elements of the product or service and combines that with a little bit of commercial acumen. For instance, knowing that the packaging cannot be more than £3 per unit, and £6.50 has been put into the quotation.

## WHY MIGHT THE SUPPLIER BE WORRIED ABOUT DISCLOSING IT?

- It could show where the supplier might be overcharging the customer and therefore make it very difficult for the supplier to negotiate such a high price.

- It might damage a relationship based on past charging. For instance, a public sector supplier has been overcharging the organisation for five years and suddenly has to be open with the costing breakdown. How do they deal with this if they are going to be honest about the costings? This brings into play a whole new area of relationship management and ethics and making reparations etc.

- The information could form the basis of specific price reduction negotiations using key areas of known high cost.

- It could enable the customer to use as a baseline price for alternative 'preferred' suppliers.

- The supplier may feel that it is the release of privileged information.

- The customer might have high switching costs and is therefore unable to move suppliers, and releasing costing information could cause more negotiation pressure.

*How might suppliers benefit from moving on to OBC?*

- The action of supplying costing information willingly should improve customer relations if it is handled in the right way and the supplier can gain feedback and would be in a good position to request a cost model from customer on a 'quid pro quo' basis.

- If areas of slack are identified by the customer and, by working with the customer, these can be removed, this should make the supplier more efficient and pass benefit on to their other customer costings.

- It will give a focus on areas of high cost to help the customer give cost saving help. This may develop into the customer freely giving specialist expertise that the supplier may not possess.

- It should, in the long run, help the supplier to retain work from the customer.

- The request from the customer to move to OBC might signal that the customer has high switching costs (and feels tied to the supplier), causing more negotiation pressure but moving the negotiation power to the supplier.

With cost transparency, there are some other issues, such as the supplier seeing the amount of profit being made by the customer and requiring a larger 'slice of the cake'. It can also create a 'cost reduction' culture across both organisations which is highly beneficial, but there are still the fears of what happens to the cost information of both organisations and the effects of it getting into the wrong hands.

The principle of OBC is a reasonable one but a degree of pragmatism needs to be applied. When a supplier gives a full breakdown of the cost structure of a product or service, should the buyer treat this as fact? Suppliers are rarely going to show high levels of profit which therefore means that, if they are making high levels of profit, they are hiding it in some of the other figures and it is necessary to try to 'weed' this out.

The issues of double charging depreciation were discussed in Chapter 10, but there are also many other issues surrounding the way in which different suppliers might allocate costs. Some companies in the engineering world will issue spreadsheets to suppliers to fill in preformed Excel models for their cost breakdowns, which sounds fine in theory but in practice it is fraught with problems. For instance, what does the labour rate cover? It must cover the hourly rate paid to an employee, but does it cover the National Insurance, holiday pay, a standard level of overtime, sickness pay etc? Some companies include other on-costs such as pension costs, a proportion of overhead cost based on area occupied and facilities used, and some do not.

Similarly, when costing is based on a machine hour rate, this rate may cover different things in different companies depending on how they collect their costing information. There is, therefore, no hard and fast set of rules that can be applied. The only thing that buyers can do is to give themselves the knowledge to effectively challenge a figure that appears high and ask the supplier to justify it. For example, if the hourly rate for a particular type of machine operation was significantly different from the 'assumed' standard cost model, this should be challenged. There will always be improvable figures but there are also many provable ones, so some very good 'wins' can be made from the effective challenging of loose costings.

## Using a Cost Model in Negotiations

The first area to be examined is whether a buyer needs to have a cost model to help negotiate a better price. We have discussed open book costing and its use in helping to create information for a cost model, but is cost modelling always appropriate? An example might be when we are buying office furniture and the price will be set on the supplier's buying price from a manufacturer or importer with a level of mark-up. Their money is made out of selling an adequate volume of product at an appropriate mark-up. Other issues such as volumes, capacity utilisation and strategy (as previously discussed) will influence the price more rather than looking for cost savings. We therefore need to look at the categories in the supply positioning model (Chapter 6) for best use of cost modelling and the use of OBC.

The low risk, low spend ('tactical acquisition') quadrant is unlikely to benefit from extensive time in cost modelling and should take up minimal buyer's time. Up-front time is needed by the buyer to arrange a hassle-free contract to minimize time spent by the buyer later. The high risk, low spend ('strategic security') area is unlikely to benefit much from cost modelling. There is little leverage with the supplier and the critical aspect is getting the product/service rather than the price. The low risk, high spend ('tactical profit') can sometimes benefit from cost modelling and OBC, but more often than not the price is controlled by the market, and so, provided the buyer is in very close touch with the market, OBC and cost modelling are not so necessary (although, with the financial sums involved, it would be prudent).

The high risk, high spend ('strategic critical') products are the main area in which cost modelling and OBC can pay dividends, because a close relationship is required, and the benefits will more than outweigh the costs of time and resources. The difficulty is how to apply it, and the principles are examined in the following example:

**Example**

We are purchasing high volume parts for an aerospace engine.

A supplier gives a quotation for the supply of part number X345Z broken down as below:

| | |
|---|---:|
| Materials | £37 |
| Direct Labour | 20 |
| Supervision | 5 |
| Administration | 10 |
| Depreciation | 20 |
| Sundry overheads | 25 |
| Profit | 13 |
| Total cost | £130 |

You have a standard cost model for this part group as follows:

| | Data % |
|---|---:|
| Raw Materials | 25 |
| Direct Labour | 21 |
| Supervision | 2 |
| Administration | 10 |
| Equipment Depreciation | 10 |

| | |
|---|---|
| Overheads | 20 |
| Profit | 12 |
| Total Cost | 100 |

We are also aware that the raw materials actual cost should be £30, and the direct labour cost should be £22, as quoted to us internally if we manufactured it ourselves.

## Questions

- How much profit do you think the supplier is really making?

- Which areas should we negotiate on?

- What should be the target price for this product?

## Answer

The first obvious observation is that the supplier is over-quoting on the material and under-allowing for wages, so one might instinctively challenge the materials figure.

However, the first stage would be to examine the supplier's quotation and develop a cost model from it. Apart from anything else, this will give us a feel for other quotations in the future and perhaps give us an idea of the supplier's normal cost build-up.

This would be done by taking each cost as a percentage of the price quoted. This can then be compared with our own cost model:

| | Quote £ | Quote % | Own Cost Model % |
|---|---|---|---|
| Raw Materials | 37 | 28.46 | 25 |
| Wages | 20 | 15.38 | 21 |
| Supervision | 5 | 3.85 | 2 |
| Administration | 10 | 7.69 | 10 |
| Equipment Depreciation | 20 | 15.38 | 10 |
| Overheads | 25 | 19.23 | 20 |
| Profit | 13 | 10.00 | 12 |
| Total Cost | £130 | | 100 |

It can clearly be seen that the materials percentage is well above our own and the wages percentage is well below. The depreciation is again 50% higher than our own model, but the profit is showing a little less. We could stop here and negotiate on these points alone. It is up to the supplier to prove the buyer's cost model is inappropriate, and this will place the supplier partially on the back foot.

The next stage is to look at what the breakdown of the supplier's quotation would be if our cost model was applied to the price (this is done by applying our cost model percentage to their price to give the 'should cost'):

|  | Quote £ | Quote % | Own Cost Model % | Should Cost |
|---|---|---|---|---|
| Raw Materials | 37 | 28.46 | 25 | 32.50 |
| Wages | 20 | 15.38 | 21 | 27.30 |
| Supervision | 5 | 3.85 | 2 | 2.60 |
| Administration | 10 | 7.69 | 10 | 13.00 |
| Equipment Depreciation | 20 | 15.38 | 10 | 13.00 |
| Overheads | 25 | 19.23 | 20 | 26.00 |
| Profit | 13 | 10.00 | 12 | 15.60 |
| Total Cost | £130 | | 100 | £130.00 |

This table shows in absolute figures the level at what each of the elements should be costed.

We now have further information to put into the mix, namely that of the actual materials and labour figures. If these are put into the 'should cost' column, and the other elements remain the same, the 'difference' in the total must be the supplier's profit:

|  | Quote | Quote % | Own Cost Model % | Should Cost | Actual Costs | |
|---|---|---|---|---|---|---|
| Raw Materials | 37 | 28.46 | 25 | 32.50 | 30.00 | |
| Wages | 20 | 15.38 | 21 | 27.30 | 22.00 | |
| Supervision | 5 | 3.85 | 2 | 2.60 | 2.60 | |
| Administration | 10 | 7.69 | 10 | 13.00 | 13.00 | |
| Equipment Depreciation | 20 | 15.38 | 10 | 13.00 | 13.00 | |
| Overheads | 25 | 19.23 | 20 | 26.00 | 26.00 | |
| Profit | 13 | 10.00 | 12 | 15.60 | 18.40 | 14.72% |
| Total Cost | £130 | | 100 | £130.00 | £125.00 | |

We can now see that the supplier appears to be making £18.40 profit (14.72%) not the £13 (10%) shown in the quotation.

Again, we can stop the calculations here and just negotiate on the larger figures, but we might take this to a final stage, depending on how confident we are in our own cost model. This depends on our sources of supply (covered later).

If we look at the key figures of materials and labour, together they make up £52, which (according to our own cost model) should represent 46% of the price. If this is now inserted into our own cost model, we have the following:

|  | **New**<br>**Should Cost** |
|---|---|
| Raw Materials | 30.00 |
| Wages | 22.00 |
| Supervision | 2.26 |
| Administration | 11.30 |
| Equipment Depreciation | 11.30 |
| Overheads | 22.61 |
| Profit | 13.57 |
| Total Cost | £113.04 |

Step 1 – Insert the Materials and Labour.

Step 2 – Insert the Total Cost – this is £52 ÷ 46% = £113.04.

Step 3 – Insert the remaining figures by their required percentage of the total cost, based on our cost model (namely, the depreciation is 10% of £113.04 = £11.30).

It has to be emphasized that this is not a definitive answer or necessarily what the cost should be. It is purely one method of arriving at a 'should cost' for a product or service that gives a negotiating logic and should put the supplier on the back foot. It is up to the supplier, and not the buyer, to justify the price in their quotation.

We are then faced with using this information, and judgment is needed as to whether our cost model is going to be shared with the supplier and whether we are going to give and take. Many buyers would negotiate on the materials, supervision, depreciation and overheads on the basis that this is where the supplier is above our own estimated costing. If we achieved our own figures, this would save £7, £2.74, £8.70 and £2.39 respectively, giving a new price of £130 – £20.83 = £109.17. This would ignore giving anything back to the supplier on the other items that were under-costed, such as the wages.

Theoretically, if the relationship is as it should be, the wage figure should also be brought into the negotiation. The reason is that the supplier might have information on the mode of manufacture or type of machinery that the buyer is not privy to, and can therefore help to bring the wage cost down. Secondly, the supplier might have a better method of manufacture than we would have assumed. Thirdly, the supplier might have made a mistake. One could take the view that it is their fault and they should therefore carry the can. (This assumes a short-term relationship as, when they eventually find out, they will endeavour to recapture the loss in future work.) Another view is that, in the long term, they will reciprocate any findings that go the other way. A more pressing consideration is that, if the mistake has great financial significance and they could actually fail to supply or go out of business as a result, one must question the wisdom of ignoring it purely for a 'quick win' situation.

A colleague once told me of a supply from an African country that had rampant inflation. He had negotiated a new contract with the country at a fixed price for three years of which he was very proud. He received the goods in the first year but had nothing thereafter as the African state could not afford to supply without going out of business! What was the use of ignoring the supplier's situation unless there were alternative supply sources?

See further Question 10 in the Appendix.

## Advanced Issues – Sources of Information for Developing a Cost Model and Purchase, Price Cost Analysis (PPCA)

The sources of cost model information are:

- direct from the supplier;

- the supplier's quotation;

- the supplier's accounts;

- own internal supply cost history;

- grouping alternative supplier quotations together; and

- consulting on the supplier's premises.

**Direct from the supplier** – This means we ask the supplier directly what is their basis of costing and how are the overheads apportioned. They may or may not part with this information, depending on how they see it being used by the customer.

**The supplier's quotation** – As previously mentioned, the supplier can be asked to quote in pre-specified 'chunks' of cost, and each of these can be expressed as a percentage of the total price to create a model.

**The supplier's accounts** – By examining the published accounts, a basic cost model can be created by viewing the main accounting statements, as in the following example:

### Step 1 from the income statement

| | |
|---|---|
| Sales | 1,000 |
| *Less* Total Costs | 800 |
| Profit | 200 |

### Step 2 from the notes to the accounts

| | |
|---|---|
| Wages and salaries | 200 |

### Step 3 from the cash flow statement or the notes to the accounts

| | |
|---|---|
| Depreciation | 100 |

### Step 4 Calculate the bought in goods and services (BIGS) and other overheads and cost model

| | | £ | % |
|---|---|---|---|
| Total Cost of sales | | 800 | |
| *Less* wages and salaries | 200 | | 20 |
| depreciation | 100 | 300 | 10 |
| Balance must be BIGS + O/H | | 500 | 50 |
| Profit | | 200 | 20 |
| TOTAL | | 1,000 | 100 |

This rudimentary cost model could be further developed if the company publishes its figures on the income statement by nature rather than function, as in this case the materials element may also be separately extracted from the BIGS which is a highly useful percentage. It has to be emphasised that this is only a rudimentary model that would only be useful for a single company (not a group), probably not for a large company and, more often than not, would not show up anything of note (but, on the occasions that it does, the rewards can be sizeable).

**Own internal supply cost history** – This is an excellent source of information, in that, if the buyer's own company has previously supplied the product or service, many of the elements of cost should be known. For instance, if a company has always done its own catering and then decides to contract out the service, all the food costs, wages, machinery, consumables etc will be known. Additional to this, and what is often forgotten, is the buyer's own commercial knowledge of a product or service. The buyer can, without being a specialist, break down the cost of an item just by examining it and looking at the processes in producing it. By applying a 'sense of value' to each element, some interesting bases for challenging a supplier's quotation may arise.

**Grouping alternative supplier quotations together** – This is an excellent way of gaining an approximate cost model. If all the potential suppliers of a contract are requested to quote across standard cost 'chunks', they can be grouped together and an average taken, as in the following example.

The following three quotations were received for the supply of outsourcing the company's IT maintenance over three years:

|  | Supplier A | Supplier B | Supplier C |
|---|---|---|---|
| Consumables | 3,200 | 3,000 | 2,000 |
| Contract Management | 5,000 | 6,000 | 7,500 |
| Software Engineers | 8,000 | 7,000 | 7,000 |
| Hardware Engineers | 15,000 | 12,000 | 16,000 |
| Overheads | 8,000 | 12,000 | 10,000 |
| Profit | 6,000 | 4,000 | 7,000 |
| Total Costs | 45,200 | 44,000 | 49,500 |

The first stage is to calculate each supplier's cost model:

|  | Supplier A | | Supplier B | | Supplier C | |
|---|---|---|---|---|---|---|
| Consumables | 3,200 | 7% | 3,000 | 7% | 2,000 | 4% |
| Contract Management | 5,000 | 11% | 6,000 | 14% | 7,500 | 15% |
| Software Engineers | 8,000 | 18% | 7,000 | 16% | 7,000 | 14% |
| Hardware Engineers | 15,000 | 33% | 12,000 | 27% | 16,000 | 32% |
| Overheads | 8,000 | 18% | 12,000 | 27% | 10,000 | 20% |
| Profit | 6,000 | 13% | 4,000 | 9% | 7,000 | 14% |
| Total Costs | 45,200 | 100% | 44,000 | 100% | 49,500 | 100% |

This immediately tells us that supplier A is heavy on the engineers, supplier B is heavy on the overheads, and supplier C is heavy on the contract management and profit.

If an average is now taken:

| | Totals | Average | |
|---|---|---|---|
| Consumables | 8,200 | 2,733 | 6% |
| Contract Management | 18,500 | 6,167 | 13% |
| Software Engineers | 22,000 | 7,333 | 16% |
| Hardware Engineers | 43,000 | 14,333 | 31% |
| Overheads | 30,000 | 10,000 | 22% |
| Profit | 17,000 | 5,667 | 12% |
| Total Costs | 138,700 | 46,233 | 100% |

The individual quotations can be compared with either the absolute averages or the percentage averages.

If we then decide that the target price should be, say, £43,000, the cost model created from the averages can be applied to this as follows:

| | Target | |
|---|---|---|
| Consumables | 2,542 | 6% |
| Contract Management | 5,735 | 13% |
| Software Engineers | 6,820 | 16% |
| Hardware Engineers | 13,331 | 31% |
| Overheads | 9,301 | 22% |
| Profit | 5,270 | 12% |
| Total Costs | 43,000 | 100% |

If supplier A was the preferred supplier, each item can be examined and negotiated accordingly. In this case, it would be the consumables and engineers to be targeted.

**Consulting on the supplier's premises** – This might be done where there is a very close relationship with the supplier (strategic critical) and the buyer might have specialists (value engineers) within the company who can go to the supplier's premises and analyse their machinery and processes, with a view to recommending a cost model after making line balancing, or machinery improvements to help bring down the costs. This tends to be common practice in the aerospace and motor industries.

## Purchase Price Cost Analysis

This is an expression for a whole process involved in analysing and reducing a supplier's cost base:

- Step 1: Gain a sound understanding of the process of delivering the service or manufactured purchase and then deconstruct the processes into simple steps.

- Step 2: Repeat the previous steps upstream in the supply chain back to the basic raw materials or primary service. Clearly, pragmatism needs to be applied here, so only go back as far as is reasonable in the circumstances.

- Step 3: Identify all of the cost elements, and allocate costs to each based on research or intuition.

- Step 4: Incrementally build up a full cost of the product or service, and then cross-check the data with the supplier in a subtle way.

- Step 5: Compare with others in same business and then prepare the negotiation plan.

Step 1 involves breaking down the product or service supply into its main cost chunks. The standard cost chunks for manufacturing, say, a pressure vessel would be:

- materials – metal sheet, rods, screws, welding consumables;

- labour – machine operators costs;

- overheads – heat, light, tooling, administration etc; and

- profit – percentage mark-up.

A breakdown of a service can be more difficult. The main 'chunks' for a consultancy service might be:

- client management – level, time, rate;

- senior consultants – level, time, rate;

- consultants – level, time, rate;

- expenses – travel, hotel etc;

- equipment – standard or specialist;

- overheads – administration, office costs etc; and

- profit – mark-up.

A critical element is the service level required (a service level agreement is necessary), coupled with time and level of consultant required, as consultancy organisations will often place a higher level of consultants on a contract than are necessary simply to use up the resource.

Steps 3 to 5 are self-explanatory.

The above is a process of cost analysis that links in with the target costing process.

This is the process of working backwards from the price at which your company can sell a product or service to buying this product or service at the right price.

Here there are the five main steps:

1.  Identify the product or service key characteristics. This may necessitate identifying possible suppliers and their early involvement.

2.  Establish the target selling price and consequently the maximum target buying price (to gain the required margin).

3.  Break down the costs to the required level. This may entail researching historic information, obtaining supplier cost data, using cost models, establishing value analysis groups, and opening supplier negotiations.

4.  Identify the activities needed, such as supplier development, and design or process modification. Can we use alternative materials, can the specification be relaxed, is there a change in technology since last costed, what is the required machinery and tooling, what can be traded off between reduced functionality and cost reduction

(would it affect the desirability)? This involves working closely with suppliers to the negotiation conclusions.

5.    Ensure ongoing supplier relationship. The aim is for continuous improvement through managing the supplier relationships, working with them on improvements in value and cost.

## Tear-Down Analysis

This is a method of cost reduction by a detailed examination of a competitor's costs. It is used for analysing a product's materials, functions, features, design, manufacturing processes, assembly time and costs. It was introduced in Japan to the automotive industry and has been developed for other business sectors. A company would purchase a competitor's car and literally pull it to pieces and analyse all the materials, the manufacturing methods used, the patents, machinery etc, the features and added functions. It would then decide which of those it could use itself, which would be prohibitively expensive to incorporate, and which would add value, bearing in mind its market niche. In other words, it would seek to merge the best features of its own product with the best of its competitor's product.

The main applications would be for improving the organisation's competitive position by seeking to innovate or product improvement or product evaluation of a competitor.

The analysis would cover the tooling costs, the manufacturing process, the cost estimates based on materials and the design of components, design features and estimates of direct wage costs and the costs of the finished product.

In conclusion, the overall PPCA process would commence with a supplier selection using a financial sift (that is, is the company financially capable?), dependability and quality, cost and delivery issues. It would be necessary to examine the proposed supplier market/environment and to categorise the supplier in the supply positioning matrix. Their quotation would need to be examined and compared with their latest financial results – again, dependability issues should be reviewed for leverage. Examine areas of excess charging on margin, provisions, wages and overheads by comparing with cost model (open book costing?), and look for second-tier supplier issues before negotiating.

# PART III
# *Managing Resources*

# 14

# Budgetary Process and Budgetary Control – a Buyer's Perspective – Public Sector Issues

## What is Budgetary Control?

Budgetary control is a term used to describe the process of drawing up a plan of how the company is expected to perform in the coming period, usually a year, and then the use of that plan as a measure against which actual performance is judged and the appropriate controlling action taken. There are two key words here, and they are 'plan' and 'control': we draw up a plan, and then control the outcome to ensure that the plan succeeds. A budget is sometimes referred to as the organisation's business plan expressed in financial terms.

## Issues to Consider

There are several key issues involved when we are considering the setting up of a budgetary control system:

- **The need for a goal** – Like any journey by sea to find buried treasure on an island, it is important to first know what you are trying to achieve. In other words, we set a course to steer from our current position. At the beginning of the process, a business plan is produced which covers the whole of the long- and short-term objectives and strategy for attaining them. Setting a budget is purely the financial plan incorporating all of those strategies and actions, and usually it is in detail for just one year.

- **Plan directed to achieving goal** – Clearly, the plan must be drawn up based on a series of actions which, if all of the assumptions are correct, ensure that the goal is achieved.

- **Method of achievement** – We need to consider how we are going to achieve the desired outcome.

- **Resource requirements** – What resources are going to be needed by way of finance, machinery, buildings, labour etc?

- **Human implications** – We need to consider how we are going to implement the budgetary control process from the point of view of the managers and staff who are affected. Will they take readily to it or will they resist the implications?

- **Profit planning – acceptability** – There is an element of profit planning in the budget. Is it acceptable to the relevant parties such as shareholders, stock market analysts, bankers etc?

An improvement on the previous year is always desired, and this may be shown by utilising ratios primarily driven by return on capital and earnings per share.

Break-even analysis may also be used to target profit, sales etc. In the public sector, the primary objective is to give the best possible service for the limited amount of finance available. The plan is to control the finances to within a small margin, say 2%, of the planned expenditure.

## Controlling the Outcome

There is a need not only to monitor what is done but also to control what is done as the operation proceeds. This is done by means of variance analysis, whereby the actual results are compared with the budget to produce a variance report. This is a list of differences or variances from the budget. For example, the following is a report from the sales director for month 3 in the year:

| Current Month – 3 | | | | Cumulative for 3 Months | | |
|---|---|---|---|---|---|---|
| | Budget | Actual | Variance | Budget | Actual | Variance |
| Promotion | 1,000 | 1,100 | (100) | 3,000 | 2,800 | 200 |
| Advertising | 700 | 500 | 200 | 4,000 | 4,700 | (700) |
| Commission | 2,000 | 4,000 | (2,000) | 6,000 | 10,000 | (4,000) |
| Wages | 5,000 | 5,500 | (500) | 15,000 | 16,500 | (1,500) |
| Totals | 8,700 | 11,100 | (2,400) | 28,000 | 34,000 | (6,000) |

In the month, there is an overspend or 'adverse' variance on all but the advertising; but, to properly interpret these figures, the year to date needs to be examined, as one month on its own may not be truly representative of a trend. In the year to date, we can see that the promotion expenses are actually within budget, as it shows a positive or 'favourable' variance overall, and the advertising is £700 over budget when it was under during the month. These reports are known as variance reports or exception reports, in that they sometimes highlight exceptional items automatically by a computer-generated variance, which is outside what would be tolerated. Variances may be adverse (if budgeted profit is decreased as a result of the actual achievement) or favourable (if profit is increased). In other words, if a cost budgeted is exceeded, this would produce an adverse variance. If a sales budget is exceeded, this would produce a favourable variance (and vice versa). A bracket would denote an adverse variance.

These budget reports would be produced by the management accountant each month and given to the person responsible for that section or function. For instance, the sales director receives the sales analysis; the personnel or human resources director receives the personnel analysis, and so on. This is what is known as 'responsibility reporting', where the person responsible reports back on their area of responsibility.

Only the significant variances should be examined (known as management by exception), so as not to waste time examining figures that are close to the budget. *All* significant variances need to be explained, and this includes the favourable ones, as some favourable variances may cause a detrimental effect later. For instance, a favourable advertising variance may show up in a significant reduction in sales the following month! See further Question 11 in the Appendix.

At the monthly board meeting, the directors would each report back on their own areas of responsibility, giving reasons for over- or under-achievement of the budget. If each individual part of the budget is managed successfully, the whole plan should be achieved.

There are many limiting factors which affect the preparation of a budget, such as capacity and size of market, but an example of the way a budget 'cascades' down from the top is as follows (this assumes sales are the only limiting factor and that, normally speaking, sales are the starting point in a budget because they determine many other factors).

Example for a consumer products company:

## 1. SALES BUDGET

These are broken down by product group and geographic area. Decisions are taken on new products and whether to drop old products.

## 2. ADVERTISING BUDGET

To achieve the sales above, an advertising strategy is planned and budgeted.

## 3. FINISHED INVENTORY LEVELS BUDGET

To execute the sales, we need to calculate the inventory required to be available at the end of each month before delivery.

## 4. PRODUCTION BUDGET

To achieve the inventory levels, we need to work out the required monthly production.

## 5. MATERIALS, LABOUR, PLANT CAPACITY AND OVERHEADS

These elements of production all need their own budgets once production requirements are set.

## 6. CASH BUDGET

This financially ties in all the other budgets together, to show the total cash requirements for the period ahead.

## 7. SUMMARY BUDGET

This breaks down the budget across time periods, divisions, subsidiaries etc.

## 8. MASTER BUDGET

This is the one finally adopted when the senior management have adjusted the budget according to what they need to satisfy the investors and other interested parties in the company.

## 9. RESPONSIBILITY REPORTING

The budget is then dispersed to the relevant senior staff whose job it is to control that budget.

Sales may not indeed be the main limiting factor. If a company can sell 5,000 units per month but can only produce 3,500 units per month, the limiting factor would need to be the production capacity. The production budget would therefore be drawn up first, with the sales budget to follow. Similarly, if there was a shortage of an element of production, such as raw materials, the raw materials budget would be drawn up first, followed by the production followed by sales (assuming the company can sell all that it can produce).

# 15

# Corporate Planning and Budgetary Control

## Controlling the Outcome

There are two aspects to controlling the outcome: one is to pinpoint the area of non-performance utilising variance analysis; and the other is to take the corrective action.

## Control through Variances

The interpretation of the variances has already been briefly discussed, but success or failure of the interpretation depends on a number of factors, namely:

1.   The budgeted figures need to be based on *accurate standards*. It is of little use trying to achieve a budget that is unattainable or based on incorrect figures.

2.   *Forecast variances* need to be separated from *performance variances*. By this we mean that, in certain cases, there will be errors in the budget due to inaccurate predictions such as currency exchange rates. This is a forecasting variance, as opposed to a performance variance such as the purchasing of excess material.

3.   *Controllable and non-controllable* costs need to be separated. Managers should not be judged on the part of their budgets over which they have no control. For instance, a warehouse manager cannot control the business rates paid on the warehouse, but the warehouse telephone usage can be controlled.

4.   *Some costs will automatically move in line with activity* (like purchases) and so a fixed budget is not an appropriate control.

## Flexible Budgeting

We have so far been discussing budgets being drawn up which are 'fixed', meaning based on an assumed level of activity. Therefore, if a manager does not achieve the budget, it is deemed to be poor performance. Clearly, a fixed budget is not always appropriate as some costs move in line with activity. Therefore a refinement of the budget setting we have already examined is to budget a price and a number of units that will then be determined in the budget by the number of units actually achieved.

For instance, you might be running a restaurant and your budget for food in the month is £2,000 based on £2 per customer consuming 1,000 meals. Suppose you spend £2,300 but you have served 1,200 customers, what should the variance be? If it was a fixed budget, you have an adverse variance of £300 (budget £2,000 – actual spend £2,300).

A flexible budgeting approach would review the budget on the basis of number of customers up to 1,200 customers @ £2 = £2,400 and so the ensuing variance would be £100 favourable (budget £2,400 – actual £2,300). For some costs, principally variable costs, this approach is sensible.

For an example, see further Question 12 in the Appendix.

## Incremental or 'Zero Based' Budgets

Budgets are usually drawn up based upon the budgeted or actual figures achieved in the previous year, taking into account any expected changes for the following year. This is known as an 'incremental' budget, in that it changes in 'increments' or small movements from the previous year to allow for inflation or known changes in requirements. A problem with this approach is that it will carry forward any weaknesses in the previous year's figures. For instance, if too much has been allowed in the previous year for training costs, the budget may all be spent even if it was not needed. This is where the use of 'zero based' budgeting (ZBB) may be useful. In simple terms, ZBB means that, rather than basing the budget on last year's figures, a completely new budget is drawn up, with each figure being separately justified in minute detail but based on the level of service or number of products required. This is, of course, what would be done in a company's first year of trading when it has no previous year on which to base estimates. By utilising ZBB, it tends to eliminate these carry forward problems, but it is very expensive and time consuming to implement, and companies tend to use it on a different department every year on a rolling basis. For example, the IT department may be subject to a ZBB approach every five years.

## Benefits of a Budgetary Control System

There are many benefits to a well-run budgetary control system:

### 1. MOTIVATION OF STAFF

The staff is motivated to 'beating' the budget assuming that it is realistically set.

### 2. COORDINATION

All members of staff are pulling together with one agreed goal.

### 3. COMMUNICATION

The process aids communication between departments who might otherwise not pass information on or communicate with each other.

### 4. DELEGATION

The process aids delegation of some duties. For instance, the HR manager can delegate the training budget to the training manager.

### 5. PRIORITISATION AND RESOURCE ALLOCATION

The plan will contain clear priority for certain tasks and resources.

### 6. DECISION MAKING

Many decisions are made in advance in the budget, thus making some decision-making during the year easier.

## Criticisms of a Budgetary Control System

There are equally some negative aspects to budgetary control, particularly if the system is not installed well. These are:

## 1. COST

It can be very expensive in time, particularly when standard costing (detailed costing system based on predicted standards) is also included.

## 2. INFLEXIBLE AND LIMITS INITIATIVE

It can encourage a hard line approach which can also lead to an 'unthinking' manager who only does what the budget says.

## 3. DEFENCE MECHANISM

It can be used as a defence for a bad decision. Many budgets are set up a significant period before the year starts, and so the business environment can change and a manager needs to see that, when appropriate, the budget is not adhered to. For instance, if a product is discontinued part way through the year, it would make no sense to follow the original budget in promoting that product.

## 4. CREATES A NEED TO SPEND

If it is not spent this year, it will be reduced for next year. A very common situation with local authority spending and also research or training budgets whereby, if they are not used in a given year, the budget is cut for the following year. This causes a massive spend just before the year end.

## 5. RECRIMINATIONS

Is it fair to use non-performance against a budget as a recriminatory tool? It should be used for improving performance and not for castigating staff.

## 6. PERFORMANCE ASSESSMENT

Is it fair to judge a manager's performance against a budget that was drawn up 18 months ago when the business environment may have been different? Many a good manager can feel under excess pressure when they are managing a poor product line, whereas a poor manager may receive bonus payments when they are managing a product line in a growing market.

The key to successful implementation of a budgetary control system, and to avoid the above problems, is to train the staff involved in the process and to ensure that those charged with the task of managing a budget are involved in the process of formulating the budget in the first place.

## Buyer Perspective

In seeking to draw up a purchasing budget, buyers need to have a close relationship with their own sales department, as the purchases (particularly of materials) will need to be delivered at a time that suits the manufacturing process and, more importantly, the customer. It is therefore important to have a close eye on how the sales are performing to budget to get an idea of how to flex the purchase budget for materials. Additionally, there are many issues besides purchase price that will affect a supplier's ability or desire to sell to our organisation at a given price. These are the same influences affecting our own organisation's sales. These might be, amongst others: sales patterns over previous years; the results of any market research that has been undertaken; seasonal or cyclical variations; the general economic environment; inflation of a key source material; any change in advertising, pricing or promotion undertaken; any changing tastes affecting demand; the level of competition; change in channels of distribution; any new legislation causing demand switch; environmental factors; and any change in product strategy affecting products and markets.

# 16

# Managing Finance – Short Term

## Working Capital Management

'Working capital' is defined as current assets less current liabilities or net current assets. It consists of four key elements – inventory, accounts receivable, accounts payable and bank account – and each of these needs to be managed to ensure there are adequate funds for maintaining the short-term business cycle which is shown in the figure below (demonstrating the conversion process of raw material purchases into cash).

The cycle starts with purchasing raw materials, which then become work-in-progress as labour and overheads are added on the factory floor. They are completed and become finished inventory in the warehouse awaiting despatch. The products are shipped to the customer, where they turn from finished goods

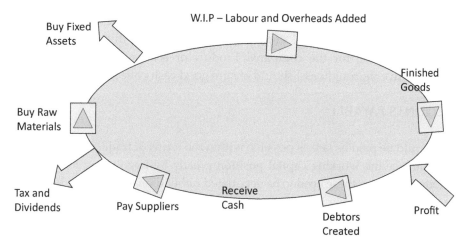

**Figure 16.1    Working Capital Cycle**

at cost price to become accounts receivable (money owed from customers, which now includes profit and VAT). Cash is then received from the suppliers, which refills the bank and this is used to pay suppliers, tax and dividends and also capital investments. Capital investments would be non-current assets and, being a long-term asset, should normally be funded from long-term finance such as loans or shares; but, if there is excess cash in the bank, this may be reasonably used for paying for long-term assets.

Each of these four key items needs managing to ensure there is adequate short-term finance in the company.

## INVENTORY

Raw material inventories should be kept as low as possible, and the buyer should have great influence on this by only ordering materials when needed, taking usage, costs of stockholding, minimum re-order levels and quantities into account. Ideally, goods should be ordered to arrive at the beginning of a month rather than the end of the previous month, as this can aid in payment times being later if settling up is done on a calendar month basis. Similarly, the work-in-progress needs to be minimised, which means a lean and quick production process without bottlenecks. Finished goods needs to be as low as possible (although adequate to service the customer), which means careful inventory requirement planning and distributing as soon as the customer will take them.

## ACCOUNTS RECEIVABLE

Once sold, accounts receivable should be minimised (within the terms of trade), so a competent credit control department is required, as this is the primary source of revenue for the company. Product or service quality, alongside administrative thoroughness, should ensure good cash collection ratios.

## ACCOUNTS PAYABLE

Bills should be paid as late as possible within the terms of trade, and the buyer can influence the working capital position greatly by negotiating long credit periods. However, these need to be negotiated rather than just taken; otherwise, the supplier is unlikely to perform well and could charge excessively for this period of credit but hidden within the costing.

## BANK

The bank should be providing the balance required to run the company during the period of turning raw materials into cash received. Therefore, if it takes four months from initial purchase of raw materials to being paid by the customer, there would need to be a bank facility of approximately four months' total costs (that is, sales less profit). Controlling the bank account should be done by assuming all cheques sent out to suppliers are met immediately by the bank, rather than assuming two to three days for a cheque to clear. This also implies a very close (daily) eye on the 'reconciled' bank account when finance is tight.

There are five main management ratios used to control the working capital:

Overall liquidity is measured by:

- current ratio: current assets/current liabilities:1; and

- acid test (quick ratio): liquid assets/current liabilities:1.

These two are then supported by the detailed ratios of the key working capital elements:

- inventory turnover: cost of sales/value of inventory;

- accounts receivable collection ratio: accounts receivable/sales × 365; and

- accounts payable payment ratio: trade accounts payable/credit purchases × 365.

These ratios are explained fully in Chapter 6.

The buyer can therefore strongly influence the amount of working capital required, by being aware of the customer ordering requirements and the ensuing production requirements. Sourcing the supplier that can best meet these requirements at the right quality, cost and delivery is paramount. Also, the placing of large orders with a supplier can cause great strain on a supplier's working capital finance; so, if their working capital cycle were four months and their total current increase in annual costs from this order were £3,000,000, they would need £3m × 4/13 = £1 million further finance available.

'Overtrading' is a term used to describe a lack of finance behind increasing turnover. If, in the above example, the company took on the order which might give sales of £3,500,000 (leaving a profit of £500,000) but they could only raise finance from their bank for £700,000 (£300,000 short), they would run out of finance despite being profitable. They would need to find ways of financing this work in the short term.

## Sources of Short-term Finance

The broad principles of managing the short-term working capital is to hold as little inventory as possible, get the money in quickly and pay it out slowly. However, there are always trade-offs within these principles.

### INVENTORY

The costs of keeping inventories low can be high ordering costs, cost of stock-outs, such as loss of sales, loss of profits, loss of goodwill and production disruption.

The costs of keeping inventories high might be the cost of tying up cash, storage costs, management costs, obsolescence, deterioration, insurance and protection (that is, security patrols) costs.

### TRADE CREDIT TAKEN (FROM SUPPLIERS)

The cost of not taking credit could be the costs of expensive alternative sources of finance; paying bills on delivery may involve more administration or expense.

The cost of taking credit could be passing up of lower prices or discounts, loss of goodwill if late payment is pushed too far, and administration costs of managing trade creditor records and making payments.

### TRADE CREDIT GIVEN (TO CUSTOMERS)

The cost of giving credit would be administration in managing the debtor, credit collection costs, risk of non-payment, reduced finances in the bank, and increased bank interest on the money outstanding.

The cost of not giving credit would be loss of sales, as customers may go elsewhere simply because they need the credit facility.

## CASH AT BANK

The costs of holding too little cash might be disrupted supplies, loss of discounts from suppliers, inability to cope with emergencies, opportunities missed, higher cost of borrowing, and fall in credit rating.

The costs of holding too much cash in the bank would be loss of interest, and loss of purchasing power as inflation erodes the value of the cash balance.

## Sources of Working Capital Finance

Other than delaying the payment of bills, which helps with cash flow but does not introduce funds to the company, there are several sources of short-term finance:

- **Bank Overdraft** – This may be arranged or extended to a higher facility (limit of borrowing). It is very flexible, and relatively inexpensive to arrange, with a rate of interest that varies with creditworthiness. It is normally unsecured, and company accounts and cash projections will be required. However, it is repayable at call (on demand) so, if the bank become worried about their risk of repayment, they can request that it is immediately paid off.

- **Short-term loan** – This option is quite common for businesses that carry large amounts of finished inventory waiting to be sold, such as an auto dealership. Effectively, the bank loans money secured on the value of the inventory, and this is well used where business is seasonal and the bank can see their money recovered within six months, and they may do the same exercise over the same period the following year. An overdraft would do the same thing but it effectively separates the finance and security for the inventory from the rest of the working capital.

- **Credit factoring** – Similar to the inventory financing, this is where the accounts receivable are effectively 'sold' to a factoring organisation (usually owned by a bank) in return for immediate payment. When a company sells a product to a customer, the customer is invoiced along with a copy of the invoice being sent to the 'factoring' organisation. The customer is instructed to pay the factoring organisation on the due date, and the factoring organisation will pay an agreed percentage of the bill (usually around 75%) immediately to the supplier. The supplier receives the balance of the money (less any fees) from the factor when the factor is paid by the customer. As the debts are assigned to the factor, this will remove some of the bank's security and they may reduce their overdraft facility on account which would negate some of the benefit. The downside to this source of finance is that it can be very expensive, as there are two strands to the fees charged. One is the interest on the money advanced to the supplier (until the factor is paid by the customer). This is usually a fairly competitive interest rate, but the additional strand is a turnover charge of typically 2–5% of the turnover of money factored (which is the sales plus VAT). So, a company with a turnover of £1,000,000 could pay factoring turnover charges of 5% of (£1,000,000 + £200,000) = £60,000. Further costs may ensue if it is required to also insure the debts. There can be a saving in credit control costs, as this is now done by the factor, but other sales administration costs/time might be increased to keep a check on procedures. There are really only three combined situations where this is a worthwhile source. One is that the factor does not usually require personal guarantees by directors, so this keeps personal assets away from the bank. Secondly, there is a good enough margin to easily absorb the turnover charge. Thirdly, where a company is growing and is being stifled by lack of funding, this type of funding for up to two years can make a lot of sense. The difficulty comes in trying to refinance to extract the company from the factoring arrangement, which can be tortuous.

- **Invoice discounting** – This is similar to credit factoring, except that it is confidential (the customer is unaware of the arrangement unlike credit factoring), and the accounts receivable are not assigned to the factoring company. The factoring or discounting company effectively gives a separate overdraft based on an agreed percentage (up to 90%) of all the outstanding accounts receivable. So, if the accounts receivable increase, the loan is increased; and, if the accounts receivable fall, the loan is restricted. Credit control is retained by the supplier, but there is still a turnover charge which is typically 0.5%. The finance provider will only advance money under invoice discounting if the business is well established, profitable and has an effective and professional sales administration system. So it is easier (but much more costly) to obtain finance under a credit factoring arrangement.

## Buyer Perspective

The buyer has two perspectives to which the management of working capital relates. These are how the buyer can work effectively within their own organisation, and how the buyer can improve working relationships with suppliers.

Working internally, it must help to be able to purchase items in economic order quantities at the best times for payment with minimum orders placed and minimum invoices received to improve administration efficiency. However, where 'lean' manufacturing procedures are in place, it is necessary to be ordering in small, more frequent quantities, requiring that a slightly higher price is paid per unit for items. The buyer's job is therefore not always so straightforward. One way to alleviate the price pressure that this causes is by working tightly with sales and production departments, with constant updating of their budgets, so that the buyers can implement better material requirement planning procedures. If these are in place, longer-term orders may be placed with suppliers in confidence, with regulated call-off times, perhaps with a 'trigger' point based on sales volumes. The supplier will then be able to plan their own production and so sharpen production costs. However, this will not cover the increased delivery costs necessitated by more deliveries. Keeping one's own inventory to a minimum is necessary for finance reasons, so a minimum buffer inventory should be kept, depending on the risk aspects (disruption costs) of running out of a given item.

As regards working with suppliers, it is necessary to be aware of key suppliers' financial strengths; sometimes, it is prudent to either avoid suppliers who may struggle with the pressures created by significantly increased orders, or to try to work with them to alleviate the problems. For instance, a relatively risk-free way of helping suppliers' finances is to give them immediate payment. This will mean that they can expand quickly without banking restriction. There are a number of issues surrounding this tactic. First, can the buyer's own company afford to pay immediately and would the financial controller allow it? Is it within allowed buying procedures? Secondly, great discounts can be had by paying suppliers immediately. Frequently, suppliers will give discounts well above the cost of credit finance in order to stay within their banking facility. For instance, if overdraft interest was 12% per annum, this equates to 1% per month. If normal terms are 60 days payment from invoice, if the buyer's company paid instantly for a discount of, say, 5%, this would cost the buyer 2% (2 × 1%) in interest for a saving of 3%, giving a net saving on purchase costs of 3%. This must be significant and will aid the supplier in development. Similarly, the buyer could purchase (and own) the tooling that the supplier may need to purchase for a given contract. This will help the supplier and also tie the supplier in to the buyer more closely.

A big caveat of working capital related to suppliers is if the supplier is debt factoring. This could be a sign of financial instability and indicate increased supplier risk. Many companies' last resort for borrowing is to work with a credit factor and, if they are clearly not expanding, the factoring is another added cost without giving increased financial support. This supplier company may well benefit from longer-term finance, the aspects of which are discussed in the next chapter.

# 17

# Managing Finance –
# Long Term

## Sources of Long-term Finance

There are three principal sources of long-term finance:

- the money supplied by investors or shareholders, called 'share capital';

- the profits the company has made, called 'retained profit'; and

- the money that has been borrowed, principally bank loans.

In other words, it is the money invested, the money made and the money borrowed. The profits made are not a sudden input of finance but accrue over a period of time (see Chapter 3), so this cannot be regarded as a way of 'raising' finance quickly. The details of the other two sources are as follows.

## TYPES OF SHARES

### 'Ordinary' shares

A public sector organisation will not have shareholders, but 'ordinary' shareholders (USA – common stock) represent the risk capital of the business and determine the ownership and control of the organisation. There are two related expressions already described in Chapter 4 that one might encounter – the 'authorised' share capital and the issued share capital – and it is the issued share capital that is shown on the balance sheet and denotes ownership and control. Some aspects are as follows:

- Ordinary shares are high risk, as they are the last to be paid off if the company goes into liquidation, so a high return is expected.

- The returns are potentially unlimited.

- Shareholders have a limited loss liability, so cannot lose more than their investment.

- There is no fixed rate of dividend and no tax relief on dividends paid.

- All of the profits (normally) belong to the ordinary shareholders, so the profit not paid out as dividend should give them growth in their future dividends.

## 'Preference' shares

The basic aspects are as follows:

- They are comparatively rare.

- They cannot be issued without first having ordinary shares that control the company.

- They have a fixed rate of dividend (say, 6%).

- They do not normally share in the profits of the company.

- There is no tax relief on the dividends, making loans often more attractive.

- They are medium risk, in that they are paid off in full before ordinary shareholders; in the event of liquidation, their dividend is paid in full before ordinary shareholders receive any dividend, and the dividend is a fixed rate.

Some of the more complex aspects are as follows:

- They can be redeemable and at a premium – meaning there can be a date set when the shareholders are paid back (say, ten years) and they can receive in excess of their investment.

- They can be cumulative (or non-cumulative) – meaning that, if their dividend is not paid one year (due to low profits), it can be rolled up into the next year.

- They can be convertible – meaning that, upon a special event (such as five years, a level of profits reached, a market flotation or takeover), the preference shares will convert into ordinary shares (for example, one ordinary share for every ten preference shares). This form is often used by venture capital companies who invest in a company and wish to limit their risk but maximise their profit in the event of a takeover.

- They can be part-participative – meaning they can share a little in the profits of the company in their dividend if the profits are above a certain level.

They are relatively uncommon but still a useful form of finance by an investor who wishes to accept a lower level of risk to their investment. An example of one use would be for someone wishing to set money aside, say £16,000, for school fees in five years' time who does not wish or need to have a dividend each year. They could purchase £16,000 of preference shares with zero dividend but redeemable in five years @ £20,000 (the dividend is effectively rolled up in the capital repayment and would represent a 25% undiscounted gain over the period (£4,000 ÷ £16,000 × 100).

For private companies, shares are normally bought and sold by direct contact between the buyer and the seller, and a new share issue for further finance would be a simple agreement of current shareholders to raise further investment in this way. Public companies would raise further finance either by the placing of shares with, for example, an investment bank or, more normally, by a public issue on a stock market. The primary function of a stock market is to raise finance for companies, and its secondary function is to help shareholders trade with each other through brokers. The share price moves with the supply and demand for shares, and on a day-to-day basis is not reflected in the company's balance sheet. However, if a share price loses a high percentage of its value, the company's bankers may well feel increased risk which will affect their lending propensity and so affect the company's ability to expand.

A common method of raising equity finance (that is, ordinary share capital) through a stock market is by a 'rights issue'. A rights issue is a cheap and easy way of raising finance from existing shareholders. It is a promotion to existing shareholders, giving them 'rights' to buy shares in proportion to their current holding at a discount to the current share price. This can be quite significant, and the rights themselves are valuable and can be traded separately. Clearly, in times of stock market volatility, the fixing of the discounted price is both difficult and critical to its success.

## LOANS AND OTHER LONG-TERM SOURCES

There are two types of loans. There is the simple negotiated bank loan, and there are loans traded on a stock market, sometimes referred to as the corporate bond market.

The amount of the loan, its duration, repayment terms and interest rate payable are all open to negotiation and may be tailored to suit the needs of the business. Before making a positive lending decision, a banker will be looking for the two critical aspects of 'security' (collateral) and 'ability to repay the loan'. If the balance sheet looks strong to the banker, the loan may be unsecured. However, if the business is not too stable, the banker would be looking to secure their loan on the assets of the company. This will be done by the signing of a 'debenture trust deed', which sets out the terms and gives the lender the right to seize the secured assets of the company if it is felt that the loan repayment is in jeopardy. With smaller companies, there are often inadequate assets within the company to secure the loan, so the banker will seek to gain security from outside the company, such as personal guarantees by directors secured on their houses. Therefore, in the event of liquidation of the company and a shortfall to the bank, directors may need to sell their houses to pay off the bank from personal assets. For a small company director who has given a personal guarantee, it is therefore in their personal interest to give a company debenture to the bank so that the bank has first charge on the company assets before requiring the director to find the requisite funds out of personal assets.

Buyers should note that debentures are registered at Companies House, and the existence of a debenture on a supplying company, whilst not uncommon, does imply greater risk within that company.

Basic aspects of loans are as follows:

- They are the least costly source of long-term finance.

- Loan interest is tax deductible, unlike dividends, making them even more cost effective.

- They are the least risky to the lender, as they are paid off before shares in the event of liquidation.

- They can be secured.

- They can be redeemable or irredeemable.

- Like preference shares, they can be converted into ordinary shares upon a given event (called convertible loan stock).

It should be noted that, even though loans are theoretically cheaper than shares, unlike with shares and the optional requirement to pay a dividend, there is no option of paying the interest on loans. Excessive loans causing excessive interest will create a very high level of risk to the company's longevity.

There may also be covenants (conditions) on loans giving the lender access to company accounts, restriction on other lending, restriction on dividends and maintenance of agreed levels of liquidity. Breaching any of these could trigger restrictive action by the lender.

## OTHER LONG-TERM SOURCES

**Venture capital** – These are companies specialising in start-up, growth, buy-out or restructuring capital with a view to longer-term company flotation or sale.

**Business angels** – These are individual investors who invest smaller amounts (up to £100,000) in developing companies in return for a shareholding.

**Government** – Grants, matched funding and tax incentives to help specific industries or geographic areas are available.

**Sale and leaseback** – This where an asset previously owned by the company, such as a building, is sold to a lessor company with a right of continued use of the property. This will give an immediate injection of funds but with the obvious loss of ownership of the asset, with ensuing rent reviews and loss of possible capital growth in the asset.

**Finance leases** – These are commonly used where an asset is purchased for the overwhelming majority of the life of the asset and allow the lessee full use of the asset without the financial outlay. For instance, a car may be purchased on a four-year lease. The legal ownership rests with the lessor, although the car will be shown in the lessee's balance sheet under non-current assets (along with outstanding lease payments in the long-term liabilities). It is attractive for medium-term borrowing, as it releases cash flow, the interest tends to be competitive and is tax deductible, the lessee is not tied to ownership, and the lessor has the security of the asset for the lending, making the borrowing comparatively easy.

## Public Sector Finance

Public sector finance starts with how central government raises finance to carry out its objectives of funding public services, such as highways, schools and universities, armed forces, police, local authorities, and the NHS.

Their sources of income fall under the three main headings of taxation, short-term finance, and long-term finance:

- **Taxation** – This falls into two main brackets of direct and indirect taxes. A direct tax is taken off the public and business without any normal means of avoidance, in that it is a tax taken off earned or dividend income or inheritance capital of individuals, or corporation taxes on the profits of companies. Indirect taxes such as VAT can be avoided by not actually purchasing goods or services.

- **Short-term finance** – This is finance raised by the government to fulfil short-term requirements, such as smoothing out tax receipts, most of which come in during December/January and June/July. They would raise loans from the public, such as 91-day Treasury bills.

- **Long-term finance** – This would be raised using government gilt-edged securities (gilts) or National Savings.

Organisations in the public sector do not have shareholders, and their finance comes from a variety of sources in addition to the commercial loans and other non-shareholder sources previously mentioned. They may receive income or finance projects from any mix of the following:

- Voluntary donations, such as to the police or fire services.

- Central government loans.

- Central government grants.

- Fee income derived from charging out their services, such as licensing, or registry fees (for example, births and deaths).

- Fundraising activities such as for hospitals, trusts such as the National Trust, government-funded charities and educational establishments.

- Asset sales, perhaps where assets cease to be utilised or are so out of date that they become obsolete. Sometimes, large buildings or areas of land remain unoccupied, and the money raised from their sale could be the driving force for a new initiative which may save large amounts of finance due to efficiency savings.

- Local government will receive central funding from the rate precept, and income from both domestic and non-domestic council tax, as well as rents received.

- Joint ventures have been increasingly common and were started by John Major's conservative government, but are now coming under scrutiny as partnerships with private enterprise appear to excessively favour the private sector partner, with all the risks being taken by the public sector purse.

- Public private partnerships (PPP) or private finance initiatives (PFI) – A PPP is a general term for any partnership requiring both public and private resources. It can be described as a joint venture between public and private sector partners to provide a public service, which uses the resources and expertise of both partners and shares the risk and rewards. A PFI is one type of PPP in that capital investment is injected by the private partner because of a contract with the government to provide services. The government bears the cost of all or part of the service provision. Types of PPP might be 'design and build' such as a public library or swimming pool, 'operation and maintenance' such as waste disposal, or 'build and operate' such as a hospital or school. A more specific example of a PFI – known as 'design, build, finance, operate' (DBFO) – might be a road scheme awarded in 2009 to

Connect Plus for £6.2 billion. This involved the widening of the M25 in some areas and also its operation and maintenance for 30 years. The benefits are the use of private sector expertise and finance, as well as giving the government 'known' costs throughout the contracting period. However, the level of these costs is increasingly coming into question due to the government apparently taking on most of the risks and being too generous in the contract details, such as giving too high a rental of the completed resource to the private sector organisation where the risks are largely borne by the public sector.

## BUYER PERSPECTIVE

One major aspect for the buyer in the public sector is the cost of the capital behind a project, particularly for a local authority taking out a central government loan. At the time of writing, central government is lending at 0.8% above the gilt rates (recently down from 1% – being the rate that the government borrows from the public). This puts the local authority cost of capital at 4–5%, which is very low compared to the private sector which typically will have a cost of capital of 12–15% (see Part IV). The Local Government Association has been working to reduce this (hence the recent fall of 0.2%) on the grounds of being exceptionally creditworthy and should therefore bear exceptionally low interest rates. A lower interest rate (from the Public Sector Loan Board) would imply projects that are marginally unviable will become viable, and thus increase work activity and so employment and local money supply.

## Investor Ratios – Relevance to the Buying Role

Buyers need to understand not only management ratios in order to assess suppliers but also investment ratios in order to understand the financial pressures that there may be on the supplying company as well as their own company.

For instance, high gross margins would imply that there could be slack in the pricing. Correspondingly, a low dividend cover could imply pressures to increase prices or cut costs, therefore affecting buyers' costs or the service they receive.

There are only a few investor ratios but the most important is earnings per share.

## EARNINGS PER SHARE (EPS)

This is defined as the earnings (profits) after tax ÷ average number of ordinary shares issued during the year.

If there are preference shares, normally paying a dividend, this should be deducted along with tax, as this ratio is concerned with earnings for ordinary shareholders. For example:

Earnings after Tax: £40,000

Preference Dividend: £5,000

No of Ordinary Shares: 50,000

Calculation of EPS (Earnings after tax and Preference Dividend) ÷ No of Shares

= (£40,000 – £5,000) ÷ 50,000 = £0.70 or 70 pence per share.

Making a judgment on this figure alone is fruitless, although it can be compared with the dividend paid per share to arrive at the dividend cover (shown below). It is difficult to compare this figure with other companies unless they are of similar size and share capital structure. If one company has EPS of 70p/share and another has 35p/share, it does not imply from an investor's viewpoint that the investor will get twice the return, as it depends on the number of shares in issue and the price paid for them. It could be that the share with an EPS of 70p cost £3.50 and the share with an EPS of 35p cost £1.40. The more expensive share is giving a return of 70p ÷ £3.50 × 100 = 20%, whereas the lower priced share is giving a return of 35p ÷ £1.40 × 100 = 25%. This is referred to as earnings yield, but is rarely used as the formula is turned the other way up to arrive at the price earnings ratio. This again is covered shortly.

EPS is critically compared with previous years and is, along with return on capital employed (ROCE), one of the key strategic financial ratios, particularly for publicly quoted companies. Many companies target a set percentage growth of, say, 10% in EPS year on year. This effectively enables a 10% growth in dividend/share and a 10% growth in retained profit/share (giving future growth in the dividend). Unfortunately, this ratio is often manipulated in one of two main ways.

First, earnings (for this ratio) are calculated before deducting 'exceptional' items. These are unusual or one-off items, such as large redundancy payments or a loss on the sale of a subsidiary company. However, some companies have ongoing redundancy programmes lasting five or more years and may be inclined to place these 'annual' redundancy costs into exceptional items, thus inflating the earnings for the EPS calculation.

Secondly, a more complex and worrying form of manipulation is where the gearing is altered (and so the interest paid) dependent on the market conditions. The effect is an improvement in the EPS if gearing is increased in a rising market, and also an improvement if gearing is decreased in a falling market. It might be viewed that these are wise decisions anyway in these conditions but, if the decisions are taken purely to manipulate the EPS, it is a very short-term view of the organisation and can cloud strategic decision making.

## PRICE EARNINGS RATIO (PE RATIO)

The PE ratio is used as a measure of confidence that the market has in the future of the company. The calculation is Price/share ÷ Earnings/share, so a high price with comparatively low earnings would imply expected growth (or perhaps a likely takeover). A low price with comparatively high earnings would imply low expectations of the future. Average PE ratios have been about 12 over the last 100 years or so, effectively giving an earnings yield of just over 8%. This average PE will move with general market conditions (as prices move) and also by sector. The average PE in one sector may be 7. This would imply a less attractive sector. The PE ratio can also give a good indicator of the value of a company. So, if the PE in the sector was 7 and the profits (earnings) are £1.5 million, the company could be valued at 7 × £1.5 million = £10.5 million.

Generally, any stock market will accept a higher price PE ratio on a company that has a potential for above-average growth in its profits and dividends.

## DIVIDEND YIELD

This ratio expresses the dividend paid as a percentage of the current price for a share. So, if shares cost £2.50 each and the dividend was 12p/share, the dividend yield would be 12 ÷ 250 × 100 = 4.8%. This could be compared with what an investor may get from other shares or from building society interest. The approximate market average is 3–4% yield, but at a high market this may drop below 2%, and in a market collapse (low share prices) the yield can increase to 8% or more. In the UK, the dividend would be 'grossed up' by 1/9 to show its value before tax, as a 10% (currently) tax credit is assumed when a dividend is received. So, if an investor receives a dividend of, say, £630, the gross dividend would be £630 + (1/9 × £630) = £700. (Note, 10% of £700 is £70 which equates to 1/9 × £630.)

## DIVIDEND COVER

This ratio gives a measure of safety to the receipt of a dividend. It is calculated by taking the earnings per share divided by the dividend per share. The higher the cover, the more likely it is that the dividend is unlikely to fall the following year. If earnings are 40p per share and the dividend is 20p per share, the dividend cover would be 40 ÷ 20 = 2 times. A dividend cover of 2 is not uncommon. This would mean that half the earnings are paid in dividend and half are retained. It is sometimes referred to as the 'payout rate' which, in this case, would be 50% (that is, 50% of the profit is paid out to shareholders). A high dividend with a high dividend cover would be desirable if one is in retirement and living off dividend income.

## BUYER PERSPECTIVE

Buyers should understand some of the pressures on their suppliers, and investor ratios will tell some of that story. For instance, if a supplier's EPS has dropped and its dividend has been maintained, the dividend cover will have fallen, which will mean less retained profits and so limited further investment in the company's assets without finance being raised by loans or a share issue. This might influence the buyer towards another supplier if the supplier is critical and it is desired to increase the inflow of work to them.

## Cash Flow Forecasting and its Effect on the Supplier

The most critical resource is cash, as it does not matter how much profit is made, if the cash resources are not conserved or controlled, the organisation will have a limited life.

## WHAT IS A CASH BUDGET?

A cash budget is a projection (usually monthly, quarterly or annually) of the company's cash position based upon expected income and expenditure over the period. It is the result of all the other budgets (such as sales, production, purchases and wages) expressed in monetary terms as to their effect on the bank balance. It should not be confused with a cash flow statement, which is a part of the historical published accounts, as already explained in Chapter 5.

It is easiest to think of budgeting in one's private capacity and then to turn it into a business situation.

You have, say, £1,000 in the bank on the first of the month but you need to allow for a cheque for £100 which you have issued for a meal which has not cleared your bank. This means you realistically have £900 to spend. Your salary cheque for £2,000 is due in on the third of the month, giving you an expected total of £2,900, but you also have standing orders and direct debits of £1,200 for your mortgage, £500 for your life assurance and another £500 for electricity, rates and sundries. You therefore have an estimated available spending power of £700 in the month. The question is, can it all be used on having fun? The answer is clearly no, because the other bills which you will have to pay fall into two categories. There are those which you have to pay and those which you would like to pay. Those which you would like to pay are called discretionary costs, in that you would only pay them if you have any money spare and they are not necessary. You will have to pay, say, £500 for food and other necessities, leaving £200 spare for non-necessities.

## WHERE IS THE CONTROL EXERCISED HERE?

The answer is that the control over the bank is done by 'flexing' the discretionary payments to ensure that we stay in credit in the bank. It is exactly the same in a company situation. We have an opening position which consists of the three known figures of opening bank balance, opening accounts receivable, and opening accounts payable.

These are the three 'monetary' items which we know reasonably well will come to pass. We then need to superimpose the projected monthly receipts and payments onto this opening position to arrive at the projected monthly bank balance:

|  | Month 1 | Month 2 | Month 3 |
|---|---|---|---|
| Opening Bank | 400 | 500 | 200 |
| Receipts | 600 | 400 | 500 |
|  | 1,000 | 900 | 700 |
| Payments | 500 | 700 | 800 |
| Closing Bank | 500 | 200 | (100) |

Note how the closing bank for month 1 becomes the opening bank for month 2 and so on. Note also that, at the end of month 3, we have gone into 'overdraft' at the bank. If we have no agreement with the bank to borrow money in this period, the bank will not honour our cheques and soon we shall be out of business.

## BROAD BACKGROUND

Cash itself is a commodity which is required to run a business, and it should be treated like any other resource. There needs to be an adequate flow of cash and liquidity in the company for it to survive, and the profitability of the company is one way to achieve this, but of course money can come from outside such as from shareholders or banks.

The main reasons for producing a cash flow forecast are to ascertain whether:

- some action is needed to acquire further cash to ensure the company's financial plans are carried out, or

- there could be a surplus of cash and this could be invested more profitably than just sitting in the bank account.

Cash budgeting itself is of little use without action to follow it up, and a cash budget is usually drawn up twice. The first time is to see what the cash flow would be without certain actions being taken. The second time is to incorporate the results of those actions in the final cash budget.

## BENEFITS OF A CASH BUDGET

- Action can be taken to alleviate problems or re-invest spare cash.

- Sometimes, a seemingly good plan falls apart financially when the cash flow is examined. Action can be taken in advance.

- It is a good communication tool for non-financial staff.

- The act of producing the cash budget, as with all budgets, makes for deeper thought.

- Variances in cash flow can be examined and justified.

## MAJOR FACTORS FOR CONSIDERATION

**Timescale** – Short-term budgets incorporate more detail, and the more pressing the cash flow problems, the shorter the term of the forecasting.

**Classification of costs** – The split of fixed and variable costs and discretionary and non-discretionary costs is important for when the forecast needs adjusting for changes in activity levels.

**Accuracy of forecasts** – The accuracy of the forecasts is critical to management decisions, and the degree of accuracy in the estimations should be clearly stated and 'sensitivity analysis' applied where there are critical assumptions made. (Sensitivity analysis is the testing of the effects of different underlying assumptions.)

## METHOD OF CONSTRUCTION

### Step 1 – Opening position

The first step is to establish the dates at which the cash flow is to commence and cease and the opening position of the bank, accounts receivable and accounts payable. This will give us much of the initial cash flow in the first two months, with the addition of non-credit items such as wages.

### Step 2 – Create a profit forecast

|  | Jan | Feb | Mar | Total |
|---|---|---|---|---|
| INCOME |  |  |  |  |
| Sales Revenue | 3,000 | 4,000 | 5,000 | 12,000 |
| Other |  |  |  | 0 |
| Total Income | 3,000 | 4,000 | 5,000 | 12,000 |
| EXPENDITURE |  |  |  |  |
| Materials | 1,500 | 2,000 | 2,500 | 6,000 |
| Wages | 300 | 300 | 300 | 900 |
| Overheads | 100 | 100 | 100 | 300 |
| Bank Interest | 30 | 30 | 40 | 100 |
| Purchase Fixed Asset |  |  |  | 0 |
| Loan Interest | 30 | 30 | 30 | 90 |
| Total Expenditure | 1,960 | 2,460 | 2,970 | 7,390 |
| Monthly Profit | 1,040 | 1,540 | 2,030 | 4,610 |

This is created based upon all the other budgets created, such as sales, production and labour.

## Step 3 – Cash projection

The cash flow forecast is then created from the information on the profit forecast, making allowance for credit periods, removing non-cash items such as depreciation, and including capital items such as expenditure or capital funds raised such as loans.

| | Jan | Feb | Mar | Total |
|---|---|---|---|---|
| RECEIPTS | | | | |
| Accounts Receivable * | 1,000 | 3,000 | | 400 |
| Sales Revenue | | 3,000 | 4,000 | 7,000 |
| Other | | | 1,000 | 1,000 |
| Total Receipts | 1,000 | 6,000 | 5,000 | 12,000 |
| PAYMENTS | | | | |
| Accounts Payable * | 2,000 | | | 2,000 |
| Materials | | 1,500 | 2,000 | 3,500 |
| Wages | 300 | 300 | 300 | 900 |
| Overheads | 100 | 100 | 100 | 300 |
| Bank Interest | | | 100 | 100 |
| Purchase Fixed Asset | | 2,000 | | 2,000 |
| Loan Repaid | 200 | 200 | 200 | 600 |
| Total Payments | 2,600 | 4,100 | 2,700 | 9,400 |
| Monthly Cash Flow | (1,600) | 1,900 | 2,300 | 2,600 |
| Opening Bank * | (2,500) | (4,100) | (2,200) | (2,500) |
| Closing Bank | (4,100) | (2,200) | 100 | 100 |

* Note opening position

The following should be noted:

- The opening and closing bank are put together at the foot with an extra line added for the monthly cash flow. This line is the difference between the receipts and payments for the month and does, of course, automatically highlight the good and bad months.

- The opening position of bank, accounts receivable and accounts payable. Note that the gap in sales revenue in January is not really a gap, as it is filled by the accounts receivable. Similarly for the accounts payable.

- The sales revenue has been moved one month forward from the profit forecast based on a one month period of credit (as an example). Similarly for the materials.

- Other receipts might be loans, refunds or sale of assets.

- Wages and overheads are as the profit projection, as it is assumed no credit.

- Bank interest is payable quarterly, so that is when it is entered on a cash flow.

- Remember that items go in the profit forecast as they are incurred. They go in the cash flow when they are paid.

- Purchases of non-current assets go in the cash flow but not in the profit forecast. Depreciation would be in the profit forecast but not in the cash flow.

- Loan interest is in the profit forecast, but the interest and the loan repayment would go in the cash flow.

- It shows that we are overdrawn £2,500 at the start, and we finish £100 in credit.

- The totals across and down should be extracted, as they prove the additions before we show the effect on the bank at the bottom.

## Step 4 – Interpretation

The figures are then examined with particular reference to the bank 'facility'. The facility is the maximum that the organisation is allowed to borrow, and this figure should always be kept in mind during the preparation of the cash flow forecast.

If the facility was £3,500 overdraft, clearly it would be exceeded in January, and action would need to be taken, such as delaying payment to accounts payable.

In general, the cause of the problem needs establishing before remedial action. If the problem is lack of short-term funds (working capital) to pay basic bills, there must be a working capital solution (that is, the strategy is to improve collection of debts, pay accounts payable slower, reduce the inventory or raise the bank facility). If the problem is caused by the purchase of a fixed asset, this is a long-term asset and should be funded by long-term finance such as a bank loan, leasing or share issue. Alternatively, delay the purchase or arrange extended credit. What should not be done is to use precious short-term finance (bank current account) to fund long-term assets.

See further Question 13 in the Appendix.

## BUYER PERSPECTIVE

A buyer can improve the cash flow of their own organisation by a range of actions, such as buying economically and making sure the timing is such that items bought are to be used immediately and not sitting in inventory, tying up funds. Agreeing either good settlement or credit terms is another part of the negotiation process that should not be ignored.

However, what is often forgotten is the effect of a buyer's actions on a supplier's cash position. Delaying payment to a supplier will almost certainly affect the supplier's ability to service the buyer effectively and might mean that the supplier puts other customers first. The buyer needs to ensure that their principal suppliers are properly paid on the due date, and are not subject to payment manipulation by the finance department, or else a vital negotiation lever can be removed. Many buyers in large organisations assume that their suppliers are being paid on time, and only find out from the supplier when they come to negotiate the next year's supply requirements. It can be very embarrassing.

Another aspect is the importance of understanding suppliers' cash flow issues when large orders are placed with them. Suppose the buyer's company pays in 60 days and the normal inload to the supplier has just been doubled; the cash flow before the increased order might be as follows:

|                        | April  | May    | June   | July   | August | September | October |
|------------------------|--------|--------|--------|--------|--------|-----------|---------|
| Supplier's Sales Income | 10,000 | 10,000 | 10,000 | 10,000 | 10,000 | 10,000    | 10,000  |
| Materials              | 5,000  | 5,000  | 5,000  | 5,000  | 5,000  | 5,000     | 5,000   |
| Wages                  | 3,000  | 3,000  | 3,000  | 3,000  | 3,000  | 3,000     | 3,000   |
| Fixed Costs            | 1,000  | 1,000  | 1,000  | 1,000  | 1,000  | 1,000     | 1,000   |
| Cash Flow              | 1,000  | 1,000  | 1,000  | 1,000  | 1,000  | 1,000     | 1,000   |
| Cumulative Cash Flow   | 1,000  | 2,000  | 3,000  | 4,000  | 5,000  | 6,000     | 7,000   |

This shows the ongoing cash flow situation, with a £7,000 cash flow gain over the seven months.

Note now the effect of doubling the orders in April (that is, start manufacturing in April for first delivery in May, paid in 60 days):

|                          | April   | May     | June     | July     | August   | September |
|--------------------------|---------|---------|----------|----------|----------|-----------|
| Supplier's Sales Income  | 10,000  | 10,000  | 10,000   | 20,000   | 20,000   | 20,000    |
| Materials                | 5,000   | 10,000  | 10,000   | 10,000   | 10,000   | 10,000    |
| Wages                    | 6,000   | 6,000   | 6,000    | 6,000    | 6,000    | 6,000     |
| Fixed Costs              | 1,000   | 1,000   | 1,000    | 1,000    | 1,000    | 1,000     |
| Cash Flow                | (2,000) | (7,000) | (7,000)  | 3,000    | 3,000    | 3,000     |
| Cumulative Cash Flow     | (2,000) | (9,000) | (16,000) | (13,000) | (10,000) | (7,000)   |

Whilst there is good profit for the supplier in the orders (monthly profit increased from £1,000 to £3,000), their cash flow after three months is £19,000 worse off! That is, it was £3,000 and is now –£16,000). This assumes that materials are on one month credit and wages are as incurred. The supplier might have additional capital expenditure to fund on top of this. Whilst it is most certainly the supplier's responsibility to finance their own company adequately, the buyer should be anticipating their problems, and a good examination of the balance sheet and income statement will give an indication of their ability to borrow more funds (that is, security and ability to repay loans).

## International Issues

There are extra issues facing a buyer when trading internationally which can be summarised under the following headings of extra costs, currency risk and corporate social responsibility.

### EXTRA COSTS

These fall into three main areas:

- management costs;

- insurance; and

- disruption costs.

### Management costs

There are increased management costs in handling a supplier from another country. These principally include travel costs and the additional time needed to work with a foreign supplier. Some forms of contracting may take ten times the management time for a foreign supplier as compared to a UK supplier, so it is necessary to balance what might be, on the face of it, a much lower price with the additional costs relating to time, travel, language difficulty, seasonal weather situations, political or economic instability etc.

## Insurance

Critical supplier failure insurance is a relatively new concept, where a business can insure against the damage caused by supplier failure. The premiums are expensive, and the insurance company may restrict the use of certain necessary suppliers.

## Disruption costs

Being aware of the potential disruption costs, in the event of a supplier failing in its supply obligations, will at least help in reducing the damage caused. The ultimate problem is loss of sales, both immediate and future, so mitigation of these needs to be thought out beforehand. There can be disruptions in the manufacturing, so alternative suppliers might be needed in the short term at a higher cost. With a foreign supplier, the costs of prevention might be significantly higher. For instance, quality issues could be prevented by on-site quality assurance. Delivery issues can occur due to shipping issues, such as transport or port strikes. This may mean shipping supplies earlier, to reduce the risk, which will mean extra finance costs and warehousing costs. Alternatively, a performance bond may be used (as it is with the UK) to tie down the supplier to an agreed level of performance.

## CURRENCY RISK

When purchasing in a foreign currency, there is added risk due to the volatility of exchange rates. If purchasing from the UK an item for $1,000 from the USA, say the exchange rate at the time of purchase was £0.62 to the dollar, it might be assumed the costs to be $1,000 × 0.62 = £620. However, suppose that the dollar exchange rate changed to £0.68 to the dollar at the time that the goods needed to be paid for. One would now have to purchase $1,000 to pay for the goods, which would cost £680, making a currency loss on the original deal of £60. The dollar had 'strengthened' against the pound, and it would be necessary to avoid this risk by buying $1,000 ahead at the time of the product purchase, to protect the rate of exchange and therefore the price. This is known as a forward contract. One might think it worth the risk of waiting, if the dollar was weakening; but, if it was really known that the dollar would continue to fall, everyone would be millionaires by betting on the currency! There are also significant transaction costs in converting currencies so, in a situation where the buying company based in the UK is purchasing in dollars from the USA and it is also selling (and receiving currency) in dollars, it may well be useful to retain a dollar account (without converting all sales income back into UK pounds) and use this to pay suppliers in dollars, thus saving both currency translation costs and transaction costs. Another way of mitigating the volatility of exchange rates adversely affecting sales income is to turn loans into the foreign currency of the income. So, if receipts were in Euros from sales and it is thought that the Euro might weaken, either the Euros could be sold ahead of receipt (a futures contract), or else a Eurobond (a loan in a currency not native to the country where issued) could be taken out. Therefore, the loan in Euros would be paid back in Euros so, if the Euro weakened against the pound, reduced sales income in Euros (after translation) would be offset by reduced loan repayment costs in Euros.

There are two instruments commonly used for purchasing from foreign sources:

1.  **Bill of exchange** – This is similar to being paid by cheque and is usually drawn on a bank, but with a promise to pay the required sum at three months in the future. It is not a guarantee of payment as, like a cheque, the bank may only honour it if the company has the requisite funds.

2.  **Letter of credit** – This again is a promise to pay, but the buyer's bank guarantees that, if the company does not have the funds, the bank will cover it. The supplier will not receive payment from their bank until it gives proof of shipping to the buyer's bank, thus ensuring the goods have been despatched. It is therefore a much safer way of doing business with an unknown supplier.

Open account trading would only be used for paying tried and trusted suppliers.

Another risk, similar to the currency risk, would be the risk of commodity price changes. Forward contracts can be placed in these, very similar to currency, so that the current price is secured for a future transaction. Unfortunately, when enough people purchase future contracts, it has the effect of driving prices up further, and this can create panic buying and stocking, causing a global shortage of sometimes essential commodities like food, where the total developing country food import bill rose from about $191 billion in 2006 to $254 billion in 2007 due to high prices.

## CORPORATE SOCIAL RESPONSIBILITY (CSR)

There is an impact on costs from CSR policies within the company (for instance, the purchase of goods from a non-ethical source, such as one that uses child labour or appalling labour conditions or wage rates). It is a buyer's duty in these circumstances to check out the suppliers through a full audit of the supply chain. This would need not just the supplier being audited but also the supplier's principal suppliers. This will increase the costs of sourcing abroad, but should pay off in the long term and will support the company's ethical stance and image.

## BUYER ISSUES

Overall, the buyer issues are clear and, in assessing the costs of disruption, management and failed CSR policies, the principal risk factors need to be considered. Both the impact of the events and the probability of their occurrence need to be kept in mind.

# PART IV

# *Long-term Capital and Revenue Purchasing Decisions and Techniques*

# 18

# What is Capital Investment Appraisal?

In general, a company has to commit a great deal of capital to a project without getting an immediate return from the 'investment'. It is therefore necessary to have some way of determining, first, whether an 'investment' in this project is worthwhile or feasible on its own and, secondly, if there is a choice of two or more projects, which would be the best project.

The former is determined essentially by whether the total money invested in the project is recovered during the life of the project. The latter is determined by a series of 'ranking' methods depending on which appraisal technique is chosen.

However, before looking at methods of appraisal, it is worthwhile examining the differences between, and implications of, making a capital purchase decision or a revenue purchase decision.

Capital purchase decisions are made on high-cost items such as business takeovers, purchases of land and buildings, machinery and motor vehicles. These are non-current assets and will have a life of more than one year. They will usually require specific authorisation from a senior manager dependent on the level of cost. Being high cost, that will tie up finite funds of the organisation and will also be subject to specific accounting policies and rules, such as depreciation and amortisation (depreciation on intangible assets). The decision whether or not to proceed with the capital investment decision will usually be determined by the complex nature, requiring both financial projections and non-financial benefits and costs, together with the internal political requirements of the company.

Revenue purchase decisions tend to relate to the income statement, in the sense that they might be purchases of consumables, services or office supplies, they tend to be lower unit costs, and they are all consumed in the short term. They are subject to buying policies within the organisation, and the buying decision is straightforward. They will be treated in the accounts using standard accounting policies and rules, such as being consumed or written off in the year of purchase.

# 19

# Steps in Investment Appraisal

The following steps are required:

- The total project requirements need to be ascertained over the relevant number of years. For instance, a corner shop might only be looking over a six-month period, and a large corporation might be looking over five to ten years, or even a 20-year period.

- The sum total of all the possible projects is then computed over the time period, and it is compared with the available capital. Most often, there is a shortfall as the capital is restricted or 'rationed' for a whole variety of reasons (for example, desire of business owner to stay within a certain size, shortage of cash, inability to raise the finance from the bank or shareholders, caution, or decision to invest only out of previous years' profits).

- The projects then have to be ranked alongside each other, to establish which gives the best rate of return based on their 'relative' (see later) benefits and costs.

Strangely, it is not always the project which gives the highest return which is approved. When a sum of money is set aside for investing in capital projects, one large project might use less of that sum of money than two small projects. For instance, suppose there was £100,000 available to be spent on capital projects and there are three possible projects all independent of one another (that is, pursuing one project does not invalidate any of the others):

- Project 1 costs £80,000 and yields 12% per annum.

- Project 2 costs £60,000 and yields 11% per annum.

• Project 3 costs £40,000 and yields 10% per annum.

We also assume any spare capital not used is invested at 4%.

On the face of it, Project 1 is the most lucrative, as this will net 12% or £9,600 per annum, plus it will give 4% on the remaining £20,000 (that is, £800). This gives a total of £10,400.

However, if we select Project 2, we have enough capital left to also select Project 3. We would therefore earn as follows:

| | | |
|---|---|---|
| Project 2 | 11% of £60,000 | £6,600 |
| Project 3 | 10% of £40,000 | £4,000 |
| | Total | £10,600 |

which gives a better overall return on the capital.

This is relevant for independent 'projects' but projects can also be 'mutually exclusive'. Here, the acceptance of one project immediately excludes the commencement of another (for instance, the purchase of an IT system, where one might be looking to purchase only one system out of a choice of three suppliers).

A method is therefore needed to rank projects against each other, and the most common techniques are set out in the next chapter.

# 20

# Techniques of Appraisal

There are four techniques most commonly used in organisations, although variants on all of them may be used:

- payback;

- accounting rate of return;

- discounted cash flow methods – net present value; and

- internal rate of return.

## Payback

This method assesses how quickly the capital outlay is recouped from the project.

For instance, you wish to purchase a machine costing £8,000 and it will save you £2,000 per annum in reduced wastage. The capital should be divided by the annual savings to get the payback. In this case it is four years.

We should normally talk about the 'cash flows' generated by a project rather than the profit, as we are looking at the real payback of cash and not an accounting concept such as profit. Therefore, when assessing the running costs of the machine, we should ignore depreciation, as the cash flow is unaffected by it. Note also, in assessing cash flows from a project, they can be savings made as well as revenue created.

Alternatively, the cash flows from a project may be uneven, in which case a cumulative approach to the cash flows should be adopted. In other words, add up the cash flows until the capital outlay is reached.

For example, the company above spends £8,000 on a new machine, but the cash flows over four years are £2,000, £3,000, £2,000, £4,000 and so on. What would the payback time be?

**Answer**

| | Cash Flow £ | Cumulative Cash Flow £ |
|---|---|---|
| Year 1 | 2,000 | 2,000 |
| Year 2 | 3,000 | 5,000 |
| Year 3 | 2,000 | 7,000 |
| Year 4 | 4,000 | 11,000 |

The payback of the £8,000 is not reached until the fourth year. However, by assuming that the cash flows come in evenly, it can be calculated more precisely.

Year 4 has a cash flow of £4,000, and £1,000 is required out of this at the end of year 3 to reach payback. The proportion of £1,000 ÷ £4,000 or ¼ can be used to arrive at ¼ through the fourth year. In other words, payback is reached after 3 years and 3 months. So, take the shortfall in the year before the year of payback, divide it by the cash flow in the year of payback, and multiply by 12 (months) to arrive at what stage full payback occurs through the payback year.

The shorter the time period of returning the initial outlay, the less risk there is. Not only is the capital at risk for less time, but also the ability to predict benefits in the future significantly decreases the further into the future we go.

This is the most commonly used form of appraisal, mainly because it is the easiest understood without much training. It does have its weaknesses, and the greatest is that it does not assess the return after the payback period. However, many large companies use payback on the basis that, provided there is an ongoing return after the payback period, that is often so far into the future that, so long as the money has been paid back quickly, all the rest is a bonus. It is not sophisticated but it does work. The most common use is as a 'hurdle rate', such as 'we shall not consider any project which gives less than a three-year payback'. This has the effect of filtering the number of projects and then another, more complex form of appraisal is used afterwards. It also does not address the time value of money (covered later).

- When companies reach a cash flow problem, they will often set the payback period as low as two years or even one year!

- In order to rank a project with this method, one clearly chooses the one with the quickest payback.

- Sometimes, companies will use payback as a percentage over a period of time such as, what percentage payback is there over five years? One project may yield 110% and another may yield 125% so, provided both projects meet the hurdle rate of, say, three years, the 125% payback project would be selected.

See further Question 14 in the Appendix.

## BUYER PERSPECTIVE

It is not only used for assessing capital projects, as it can usefully be used in deciding between changing a source of supply. For instance:

| Current Supplier | Year 1 | Year 2 | Year 3 | Year 4 | Year 5 |
|---|---|---|---|---|---|
| Cash Flows (current) | £1,000 | £1,000 | £1,000 | £1,000 | £1,000 |
| Alternative Supplier | £1,500 | £800 | £800 | £800 | £800 |

The alternative supplier will cost more in year 1 because of extra tooling etc, but then make savings on costs. To assess the payback, first the cumulative change in cash flows of each alternative supply source would be calculated, and the point where it becomes positive would be the payback.

In this case, the cumulative figures would be:

| | Year 1 | Year 2 | Year 3 | Year 4 | Year 5 | |
|---|---|---|---|---|---|---|
| Change in Cash Flows | −£500 | £200 | £200 | £200 | £200 | (current less alternative) |
| Cumulative change | −£500 | −£300 | −£100 | £100 | £300 | |

So, the payback occurs after 3 years and 6 months (3 years + 100 ÷ 200 × 12). If there was a payback requirement on projects of four years or less, this would be considered.

## Accounting Rate of Return (ARR)

It is, quite simply, a calculation of the average annual return from a project during its life that is assessed against the average capital employed. It is, therefore, very like looking at the return from a building society or bank over several years.

For instance, a capital outlay of £21,000 on a machine yields profits after depreciation of £3,000, £5,000, £2,000 and £2,000 over its four-year life. Total profits are £12,000, or £3,000 per year.

If we assume the value of the machine is £3,000 at the end of the project, the average capital employed is (opening capital + closing capital)/2 = (£21,000 + £3,000)/2 = £12,000.

£3,000 as a percentage of £12,000 gives 25%, which may be compared either with the cost of the source of capital (such as a bank or the overall cost of capital – covered in the section below) or with another project, and the one with the highest return is picked.

This method was commonly used to assess projects in the days before computer spreadsheets could recalculate discounted cash flow at the touch of a button. We also recalculate the project profits to allow for a write-off of the equipment of £18,000 over its life down to £3,000. The profits are arrived at after writing off the equipment by £18,000 but, if the capital was totally written down to zero, the profits would have been £9,000 (£3,000 extra depreciation), or £2,250 per year on average. The average capital would now be £10,500 {(£21,000 + 0)/2}, giving an ARR of £2,250 ÷ £10,500 × 100 = 21.43%.

If a total write-off of capital is assumed, which is common, we now have a simplified ARR calculation as follows:

(Total profit before depreciation less capital cost) ÷ No of Years × 100

Capital Outlay ÷ 2

This method is commonly used by small businesses for a quick and simple percentage return, but it has one major drawback: it makes no allowance for the time value of money, as discussed in the section on discounted cash flow below.

See further Question 15 in the Appendix.

## COST OF CAPITAL

Before moving on to the discounted cash flow techniques, it is necessary to explore more deeply the meaning of the term 'cost of capital'.

When computing cash flows for a project, they should exclude all financing costs, as the cost of finance is used as a benchmark against which projects are measured. If one borrows money from a bank at 12% to invest in a project, it is necessary that the return is greater than 12%, or else the project is making a loss.

If one borrows half the money from a bank at 12% and half the money at 8%, the average cost of capital is (12% + 8%) ÷ 2 = 10%.

However, capital in a company is made up of several elements, such as ordinary shares, preference shares, bank loans and overdraft.

Each element has a cost. With a bank, it is the interest, but what about the ordinary shares? Do they really have a cost, as we only normally pay a dividend when a profit is made and, even then, there is no commitment to paying it?

The cost of ordinary share capital is twofold. First, growth is offered in the share price and, if that is not achieved in the long term as a quoted company, it will cease to exist. Secondly, a dividend with growth is offered, which is also a long-term commitment to the shareholders, even though it is not a contractual one.

The cost of ordinary shares is therefore the dividend plus growth, expressed in percentage terms. In other words, it is the dividend yield plus the expected percentage growth. If the expected growth is 10% and the dividend yield is 4%, the overall cost of the ordinary shares would be 14%.

The capital in a company therefore has a cost overall and in its different parts. The overall cost is known as the weighted average cost of capital (WACC) and, whilst the buyer would not be expected to calculate this figure, it is useful to understand where this figure came from. It is not uncommon for even a large company to calculate this figure one year and then use that figure for project evaluation year after year, even when the capital structure (and therefore cost of capital) within the company has changed. A figure would normally be given to the buyer from the finance department, and this figure would be updated each year after a review of the calculation.

## Example

| | |
|---|---:|
| Ordinary share capital (500,000 shares at market price of £3 per share) | £1,500,000 |
| Bank loans | 500,000 |
| Total Capital Employed | £2,000,000 |

If the bank loans were attracting interest of 7% and the dividend was being paid at 9p/share and the growth expected was 8% (perhaps based on historical growth although it should be based on planned growth), calculate the overall cost of capital.

First, the cost of each constituent part needs to be calculated.

Ordinary shares cost calculation is the dividend yield plus growth.

Dividend yield = dividend per share ÷ share price × 100 = 9 ÷ 300 × 100 = 3% + 8% growth = 11% (note, market price for the shares is used for calculating both the capital and cost of capital).

The weighted average calculation can now be completed:

| | Capital | % cost | Element cost |
|---|---|---|---|
| Ordinary share capital | £1,500,000 | 11% | £165,000 |
| Bank loans | 500,000 | 7% | 35,000 |
| Totals | £2,000,000 | | £200,000 |

So, the WACC would be £200,000 ÷ £2,000,000 × 100 = 10%, and this would be the benchmark against which all projects are judged.

A buyer needs to be aware that the source of the finance could affect the viability of the project. For instance, when assessing a project relating to changing suppliers, this essentially means a source of finance related to working capital. It might be reasonable therefore to take the cost of capital as just being the marginal cost (that is, the cost of that extra capital needed for just that project, rather than the total cost of capital based on the overall capital structure of the company). In this case, it might just be bank loan interest of 7% rather than the weighted average cost of capital which we have calculated at 10%.

The marginal cost should only be used for smaller projects, unless the project is so big that it will drastically alter the capital structure in the company, in which case either the new WACC should be used, or the old WACC if there is a commitment to retain the same capital structure. In other words, if the WACC is 12% but we are raising £2,000,000 by 8% bank loans to put into a project (for example, a takeover), the company may well have taken its gearing above an acceptable level and would rectify this by an issue of shares, thus retaining the WACC at its former level. This therefore necessitates the cost of capital percentages to be available to buyers when making a judgement – the marginal cost and the weighted average cost. Many large organisations do not like this, as it can create a degree of confusion, and so they often choose to judge all projects based on the weighted average cost of capital.

## Discounted Cash Flow – Net Present Value Method (NPV)

This method has become increasingly popular in the last 20 years or so, not least because of the development of information technology. As it is more complex, it requires a great many calculations that are, of course, easily done with a spreadsheet. The basic principle is that, when a business expends money today and tries to relate it to money received in several years' time, there is a comparison of 'unlike' units. For instance, would you rather receive £1,000 today or in one year's time? If you receive £1,000 now, you could invest it at, say, 10% and it is worth £1,100 in a year. This therefore means that £1,100 received in one year has a 'present value' of £1,000. £1,000 received today would be worth £1,210 in two years' time (compound interest of 10%). So the present value of £1,210 received in two years is £1,000, and so on. Discounted cash flow is therefore the reverse of compound interest.

### Example

We wish to invest in a project which costs £3,000, and the cash flows from the project are £1,000 per year for four years. If we invest, that capital will cost us, say, 10%, which is the rate at which the bank is lending the money. The project, therefore, must yield greater than 10% to be worthwhile.

To work out if it is feasible, we must lay it out as follows to arrive at the present values of all the cash flows:

| Year | Cash Flows | Discount Factor | Present Values |
|------|-----------|-----------------|----------------|
| 1 | £1,000 | | 909 |
| 2 | £1,000 | | 826 |
| 3 | £1,000 | | 751 |
| 4 | £1,000 | | 683 |

The present values are arrived at by finding for, say, year 1 what would be needed to be invested at 10% to give £1,000. The answer is £910 because £909 + 10% of £909 = £1,000. For year 2, it is £826 + 10% of £826 + 10% of the result. In other words, we have taken 10% twice, as in compound interest. Whereas compound interest is straightforward, here we are using the principle in reverse which is not so straightforward. In order to add on 10% we need to multiply by $110 \div 100$. The reverse is also true in that, if we are to get at the present value of a cash flow received in one year's time, we multiply by $100 \div 110 = 0.909$. We can therefore say that the 'discount factor' for one year at a 10% cost of capital is 0.909. Similarly, for year 2 we would arrive at a factor which is $0.909 \times 0.909 = 0.826$, and for year 3 it would be $0.909 \times 0.909 \times 0.909 = 0.751$. In other words, it would be 0.909 to the power of the year or $0.909^3$. If preferred, discount tables can be used to look up the factor corresponding to the year and cost of capital percentage.

The table could therefore be completed as follows:

| Year | Cash Flows | Discount Factor | Present Values |
|------|-----------|-----------------|----------------|
| 1 | £1,000 | 0.909 | 909 |
| 2 | £1,000 | 0.826 | 826 |
| 3 | £1,000 | 0.751 | 751 |
| 4 | £1,000 | 0.683 | 683 |

We now have the present values for each cash flow and can add them up and compare with the initial cost as follows:

| Year | Cash Flows | Discount Factor | Present Values (£) |
|------|-----------|-----------------|--------------------|
| 1 | £1,000 | 0.909 | 909 |
| 2 | £1,000 | 0.826 | 826 |
| 3 | £1,000 | 0.751 | 751 |
| 4 | £1,000 | 0.683 | 683 |
| | | Total Present Values | 3,169 |
| | | Less Initial Cost | 3,000 |
| | | Net Present Value (Surplus) | 169 |

As the net present value (NPV) is a surplus, this must imply that the project is yielding more than the cost of the borrowed capital (in other words, > 10%). If the NPV was negative (a deficiency), it would mean that the project was yielding less than the cost of the money and so was unviable.

Tip. Where, as in this case, the cash flows are the same, there is a useful shortcut that can be applied to quicken a manual calculation. If all the discount factors are added together for the requisite number of years and multiplied by the yearly cash flow, the same total present values will be achieved: (0.909 + 0.826 + 0.751 + 0.683) = 3.169 × £1,000 = £3,169.

We can develop this model somewhat and ask, what if the cash flows were received half in year 3 and half in year 4?

| Year | Cash Flows | Discount Factor | Present Values (£) |
|---|---|---|---|
| 1 | 0 | 0.909 | 0 |
| 2 | 0 | 0.826 | 0 |
| 3 | £2,000 | 0.751 | 1,502 |
| 4 | £2,000 | 0.683 | 1,366 |
| | | Total Present Values | 2,868 |
| | | *Less* Initial Cost | 3,000 |
| | | Net Present Value (Deficiency) | (132) |

The project is now unviable. Using ARR would not have highlighted this issue.

In order to judge one project against another, we can use a ranking method called the profitability index (PI). Whereas the NPV = present values – cost, the PI = present values ÷ cost

which in the surplus case above is £3,169 ÷ £3,000 = 1.056.

To be viable, a project must have a PI greater than or equal to 1.

An alternative method of ranking is to calculate the NPV/£1 of capital. Again, in the case above, it would be 169 ÷ 3,000 = £0.056. The highest NPV/£1 of capital would be the first choice.

Both methods are used to rank, but difficulties come where the capital payments are spread. In this case, all the capital outlay which is not in the first year needs to be converted back to present value.

Due to this problem, many companies often rank by the highest NPV rather than the highest NPV/£1 of capital, which will result in a more efficient use of capital. The problem is then extended into what is capital and what is revenue in a project! For instance, tooling, dependent on its significance, can be classified in either.

A further development is to introduce a year 0 which is undiscounted:

| Year | Cash Flows | Discount Factor | Present Values (£) |
|------|-----------|-----------------|--------------------|
| 0 | (£3,000) | 1.0 | (3,000) |
| 1 | £1,000 | 0.909 | 909 |
| 2 | £1,000 | 0.826 | 826 |
| 3 | £1,000 | 0.751 | 751 |
| 4 | £1,000 | 0.683 | 683 |
| | | Net Present Value (Surplus) | 169 |

If the capital is spread, there will be an increasing benefit in the present values, which of course is the reverse if the revenues are spread over a longer period.

If the NPV works out at exactly zero, this means that the project is yielding exactly the same as the rate of the borrowed money (that is, 10%). So, if a discount rate was used in a project that gives an NPV of zero, this is known as the internal rate of return (IRR). This is the effective percentage rate that the project is yielding.

**Example**

You wish to set up a new manufacturing company for a key source of supply and you need to establish how much you can afford to spend.

The following purchase demand is forecast over five years in value as:

| | |
|--------|------------|
| Year 1 | £5 million |
| Year 2 | £7 million |
| Year 3 | £3 million |
| Year 4 | £2 million |
| Year 5 | £1 million |

You expect to make 20% savings on these costs in each year, and the cost of capital is 12%.

What is the most that can be spent on setting up the company?

**Answer**

The first stage is to establish the cash flows for the project. These would be 20% of the purchase demand. These are then discounted by the factors for 12% cost of capital, as follows:

**Manufacturing Co Spend**

| | | | | | | | |
|---|---|---|---|---|---|---|---|
| Discount Rate | 12% | | | | | | |
| Purchases (£ million) | | £5.00 | £7.00 | £3.00 | £2.00 | £1.00 | |
| Year | 0 | 1 | 2 | 3 | 4 | 5 | |
| Cash Flows (20% of purchases) | 0.00 | 1,000,000 | 1,400,000 | 600,000 | 400,000 | 200,000 | |
| Factor | 1.00 | 0.8929 | 0.7972 | 0.7118 | 0.6355 | 0.5674 | |
| DCF | 0 | 892,857 | 1,116,071 | 427,068 | 254,207 | 113,485 | |
| Net Present Value | £2,803,689 | | | | | | |

The sum of the discounted cash flows (DCF), amounting to £2,803,689, represents the most that the company can afford to spend on the project.

See further Question 16 in the Appendix.

## Internal Rate of Return

The internal rate of return is the average annual return that a project is yielding through its life. It can also be described as the break-even rate that produces a zero NPV when using that rate for discounting. It can be arrived at by an iterative process of constantly changing the discount rate until the NPV comes to zero. The benefit of also calculating the IRR is that you get an idea about how far above the cost of capital the project is, and so it gives some idea as to the riskiness of the project being unprofitable. Needless to say, spreadsheets calculate the IRR instantly (as they do the NPV), so long drawn-out calculations are not necessary.

Excel uses the function =IRR(A2:E2) where A2 to D2 are years 0, 1, 2, 3 and 4.

There is a manual method for calculating the IRR that revolves around making two guesses.

This consists of taking a best guess at what the IRR might be. The NPV calculation is then worked out and, if the result is a surplus, this means that the IRR must be higher than the first guess. A second guess is then made of a much higher rate in order to calculate an NPV which is negative. This will prove that the IRR is between the two guesses. It is necessary to have two guesses which span the real rate.

Now the formula can be applied:

$$IRR = a + (b \div c \times d)$$

where 'a' is the guess of the lower interest rate; 'b' is the surplus from applying the lower rate; 'c' is the spread of the surplus and deficiency from the two rates (for example, if there was a surplus of 3,500 on guess 1 and a deficiency of 1,200 on guess 2, 'c' would be 4,700); and 'd' is the difference between the interest rates (for example, if guess 1 was 7% and guess 2 was 12%, 'd' would be 12% − 7% = 5%).

So it would be calculated as follows:

IRR = 7% + (3,500 ÷ 4,700 × 5%) = 10.72%

The accuracy is increased if there is a narrow spread of interest rate guesses, and also the rate calculated should always be tested as the discount rate to produce close to zero in a NPV calculation; this is because, where there are large tranches of capital investment producing a mixture of positive and negative cash flows, some odd results can follow, giving a mathematical possibility of more than one rate! In practice, the spreadsheet function mentioned would always be used.

It is a useful tool to have alongside an NPV calculation, as it gives a 'rate' of return in percentage as well as an absolute return.

## Contrasting NPV and IRR Techniques

- NPV gives an absolute figure, whereas IRR gives a percentage.

- IRR gives no indication of size of the project or actual profitability.

- IRR can be used to compare with the cost of capital percentage – so, if the cost of capital was 14% and the IRR of the project was 17%, it would be worthwhile proceeding with the project.

- NPV needs to be recalculated when the cost of capital changes.

- Both assume the cash flows occur exactly 365 days apart, because they effectively apply a whole discount factor (a year's worth) to the cash flow when it is spread throughout the year.

- Both assume that, when cash is received, it is reinvested at either the discount rate for NPV or the IRR rate for IRR. This is unlikely, and it is more likely just to be reinvested at bank interest or overdraft rate.

- They do not necessarily give the same answer when choosing projects. A small project may have a high rate of return (IRR) but a low NPV, as compared with a large project producing a high NPV but a lower rate of return.

- In practice, it is good to use both methods together, as an actual return (NPV) alongside a percentage return (IRR) gives the best of both worlds. If two projects show a similar NPV but one gives a significantly higher IRR, the project with the higher IRR should be chosen.

## Discounted Payback

This is a hybrid of discounted cash flow (DCF) and payback, and simply means how long it takes to get the initial capital back after discounting against the cost of capital. It is basically a more refined version of payback which makes allowance for the time value of money.

**Example**

Capital cost £15,000

Cash flows per year are £3,000 p.a., so normal payback would be in five years.

If the cost of capital is 8%, the payback would be as follows:

| Year | 0 | 1 | 2 | 3 | 4 | 5 | 6 | 7 |
|------|---|---|---|---|---|---|---|---|
| Cash Flows | −15,000 | 3,000 | 3,000 | 3,000 | 3,000 | 3,000 | 3,000 | 3,000 |
| Factor | 1 | 0.9259 | 0.8573 | 0.7938 | 0.7350 | 0.6806 | 0.6302 | 0.5835 |
| DCF | −15,000 | 2,778 | 2,572 | 2,381 | 2,205 | 2,042 | 1,891 | 1,750 |
| Payback | −15,000 | −12,222 | −9,650 | −7,269 | −5,064 | −3,022 | −1,131 | 619 |

The discounted payback would therefore be 6 years plus $1{,}131 \div 1{,}750 = 6.65$ years, which is significantly different.

See further Question 17 in the Appendix.

## Relative Benefits and Costs

When cash flows are projected for a project, it is common to only use the profit from that project, rather than using what should be the *changes* in the cash flows from proceeding with the project. The cash flows may change due to increased revenues as a result of the project or reduced costs (such as less wastage). If a new vending machine was expected to produce £1,800 per year cash flows, this could be compared with the initial cost of £3,600 and so produce a payback of two years. However, if there was already an old vending machine in place giving cash flows of £600 per annum, the 'benefit' of the new machine would only be £1,200 p.a. (£1,800 – £600). Therefore, although the new machine generates £1,200 p.a., its net benefit is £600 p.a. The payback would now move to £3,600 ÷ £1,200 = three years.

A further example shows other issues that affect relevant cash flows.

**Example**

Dig 'em Up Prospecting Co only considered projects which gave them a *three-year payback* or less on their initial costs. After a geological survey costing £2 million, there was an opportunity to open a gold mine which would yield £10 *million* p.a. in gold. The mining rights would cost £10 *million.*

In order to accept this project, Dig 'em Up would need to close down their silver mine which yielded £5.5 *million* in silver, as it could not finance new equipment and machinery for the gold mine.

Both mines cost £4 *million* in running costs. Additionally, Dig 'em Up's parent company, Grab it All, required £1 *million* contribution to their current head office costs out of all new projects.

*Taxation* is to be assumed at one third of profit and payable the following year.

Should the project be considered?

**Answer discussion**

Running through the *italic* figures one by one:

- The three-year payback is the 'hurdle' rate that the company applies to sift out its projects, so the cumulative cash flows need to be positive within three years.

- The geological survey of £2 million has already been spent. It is a 'sunk' cost and cannot be recovered. Therefore, it should not be considered relevant in making a calculation of payback, as it has happened whether or not the project goes ahead. Politically, it might be a different matter as, if a manager had authorised the spend of £2 million on a survey, they would have a strong vested interest in the project going ahead, as they might feel a little foolish having spent £2 million of Dig 'em Up's money.

- The yield of £10 million in gold is clearly a relevant benefit.

- The mining rights costing £10 million are effectively the capital outlay upfront, and this sum would again be a relevant cost. It is what needs to be recouped in the payback period of three years.

- The silver mine would lose its £5.5 million income if the gold mine was opened up. It must therefore be considered a 'cost' of opening the gold mine. It is known as an opportunity cost in that, to open the gold mine, they are forgoing the opportunity of the sales on the silver mine.

- Both mines cost £4.4 million so could be considered irrelevant as they are both the same. However, for the purpose of the calculations below, they are included as if the costs were different; either the change in costs would be included, or the total costs in each mine calculation.

- Grab it All required £1 million p.a. contribution. This is a philosophical debating issue. First, it is assumed that the head office costs do not increase as a result of this project. The issue is whether it is the duty of a subsidiary's management to maximise the profits of the group or of the subsidiary. It should be the former, as shareholder wealth improvement would be a critical objective. In this case, the contribution to head office would be irrelevant, as it would be out of one pocket (subsidiary) and into another (holding company head office). That would be the basis of the answer below. However, as a manager of a subsidiary that was autonomously run, the manager would only take on projects that satisfied investment criteria and, if there were costs going to head office, these would in all likelihood be deducted in arriving at cash flows, and the transfer would then be deemed relevant.

- Taxation would be relevant, as it would be the increased tax based on the increased profit and payable the following year.

### Answer

The gold mine would yield £10 million with running costs of £4 million, giving a net of £6 million p.a.

It would forgo the opportunity of the silver mine contribution of income £5.5 million less costs of £4 million = £1.5 million per annum.

Therefore, increase in net profit before tax is £6 – £1.5 = £4.5 million.

| Cash flow | Year 1 | Year 2 | Year 3 | Total |
|-----------|--------|--------|--------|-------|
| Profit    | 4.5    | 4.5    | 4.5    | 13.5  |
| Tax       |        | 1.5    | 1.5    | 3.0   |
| Cash Flow | 4.5    | 3.0    | 3.0    | 10.5  |

The project should therefore be considered, as survey costs are not are 'relevant' and it is questionable whether head office costs should affect the decision.

We could define a relevant cost as one which can be avoided if the project did not proceed. The opportunity cost is the benefit forgone by choosing one project over another. Sunk costs can never be relevant. Fixed costs are usually irrelevant, and variable costs are usually relevant.

## Buyer Perspective – Long-term Purchase Agreements

Another use for discounted cash flow (DCF) is during the negotiation process of placing a value on concessions given in long-term purchase agreements.

In a four-year agreement, suppose there is a supplier who gives a price today for 100 parts per annum at £1,000 per part, but with a 10% price increase year on year. You need to assess whether this is a better deal than a price now of £1,150 held for three years. The cost of capital is 12%. (The assumption is that the initial price is good for the first 12 months.)

This can be done by discounting the yearly costs against the cost of capital. For example:

| Quote 1 | Year 1 | Year 2 | Year 3 | Year 4 |
|---|---|---|---|---|
| Costs | 100,000 | 110,000 | 121,000 | 133,100 |
| Discount factor | 1.0 | 0.893 | 0.797 | 0.751 |
| DCF | 100,000 | 98,230 | 96,440 | 99,958 |
| NPV | 394,628 | | | |

| Quote 2 | Year 1 | Year 2 | Year 3 | Year 4 |
|---|---|---|---|---|
| Costs | 115,000 | 115,000 | 115,000 | 115,000 |
| Discount factor | 1.0 | 0.893 | 0.797 | 0.751 |
| DCF | 115,000 | 102,700 | 91,700 | 86,363 |
| NPV | 395,765 | | | |

So, quote 1 is marginally better (a lower 'today' cost), even though quote 2 costs far less in year 4. *If this was a five-year agreement, quote 2 would be better!!*

The broad principle is quite straightforward, in that the cash flows are multiplied by the appropriate discount factor to arrive at the discounted cash flow for each year. Each year's discounted cash flows are then added together, to arrive at the net present value. The real difficulty, once the principle is understood, is in compiling realistic cash flow projections.

## Impact of 'Total Cost of Ownership' (TCO) on Purchase Decisions

When purchasing any product or service, in some cases its initial purchase price might be a fraction of its overall cost to the company or user. For instance, a consumer buying a washing machine may spend time on the internet searching for possible suppliers, travel to a supplier and park the car, spend time choosing a model, negotiate a price, decide on a warranty period, return home, await delivery on the due date, pay to have the old machine taken away, pay to have the new machine installed. Then there are the running costs of the machine in electricity, water usage, any maintenance costs that fall outside the warranty and, finally, costs of having the machine sent for disposal at the end of its life. The buyer should be aware of its 'total cost of ownership', whether it be a capital or a revenue item, although this usually refers to long-term assets. This expression is also referred to as 'total cost of acquisition' or 'life-cycle costing' or 'whole life costing'. The purchaser tracks costs throughout its life, from before the purchase to sometimes long after it has been used or written off in the books. The total cost of ownership is a method for calculating the whole cost of an asset throughout its life.

There are five main stages:

1.  **Pre-purchase costs** – These might be research costs into the supply
    and travel costs to the supplier. It would also include negotiation
    time and travel time which, for certain purchases, could mean
    travel across the world and continue over many months.

2.  **Costs of acquiring** – These would include the basic price of the
    purchase, expediting the order, any delivery or commissioning
    costs, costs of initial spares, and costs of any lost production whilst
    the new asset is being installed.

3.  **Costs of owning** – These might be costs of training the operators to
    use the asset, warranty and financing costs.

4.  **Operation and maintenance costs** – These would include the costs
    of labour to use the machinery, the maintenance costs including
    consumables, the cost of the power for the installed equipment, the
    cost of change over time on jobs and machinery set-up, and the
    costs of spares and storage.

5.  **Disposal or decommissioning costs** – For some assets, these can
    be minimal, and for others they can be prohibitive. For instance,
    the cheapest electricity in the UK would certainly be generated by
    nuclear power stations. However, the cost of decommissioning a
    nuclear power station is so high, and to some extent unquantifiable,
    that it raises serious doubts as to the economy of nuclear power
    generation. There could be legal and environmental costs to take
    into consideration, as well as the cost of actually selling or disposing
    of the asset. Against that, there could be significant sale proceeds.

A major problem in organisations is that different departments will be
responsible, and have support funding, for the separate stages of the asset
acquisition, so no single department or person would have the incentive to
apply all the analysis principles of total cost of ownership. It is by its nature
a long-term approach to costing, and therefore can hold up decision making.

There are several benefits of TCO analysis, not least being able to compare
differing purchase options over their whole life and so get a better long-term
accuracy of cost and comparison. Also, this allows a better projection of costs,
their profiles and what concessions should be made in order to get a clear

purchase decision in a competing situation. These benefits apply to service contracts in just the same way as capital purchases. Sometimes, a piece of equipment may be much cheaper but require four operators, whereas a more expensive piece of kit may only require three operators.

## Example

Machine 1 costs £3.5 million and needs four operators at £25,000 p.a. each. It would have no decommissioning costs.

Machine 2 costs £3.6 million and needs three operators at £25,000 p.a. each. It would cost £100,000 to decommission.

Both machines will last eight years, and both produce the same output.

## Answer

The TCO of machine 1 would be £3.5 million plus eight years × £100,000 p.a. (4 × £25,000) = £4.3 million.

The TCO of machine 2 would be £3.6 million plus eight years × £75,000 p.a. = £4.25 million.

Therefore, machine 2 would appear to be the better choice, although a DCF calculation on the cash flows should be done to prove this, as follows (assuming a cost of capital of 12%):

| Cost of Capital | 12% | | | (£'000) | | | | | | |
|---|---|---|---|---|---|---|---|---|---|---|
| Years | 0 | 1 | 2 | 3 | 4 | 5 | 6 | 7 | 8 | Totals |
| Machine 1 | −3,500 | −100 | −100 | −100 | −100 | −100 | −100 | −100 | −100 | −4,300 |
| NPV | −£3,997 | | | | | | | | | |
| Machine 2 | −3,650 | −62.5 | −62.5 | −62.5 | −62.5 | −62.5 | −62.5 | −62.5 | −162.5 | −4,250 |
| NPV | −£4,001 | | | | | | | | | |

This shows that the total cash flows from machine 2 are £4,250,000 and from machine 1 are £4,300,000. However, the calculations after applying discount factors would imply machine 1 now has a lower TCO after discounting, as machine 2 gives an NPV of £4,001,000 and machine 1 gives £3,997,000, bringing them much closer after discounting, but just favouring machine 1 in this case.

See further Question 18 in the Appendix.

## Minimising Risk in Investment Decisions

Investment decisions are by their nature risky, as they rely almost totally on projections of the future, which are estimates based on some sort of judgment. The figures and examples we have examined so far are assumed to happen. In other words, they are decisions based on conditions of certainty. In reality, decisions are taken under conditions of risk and uncertainty. *Risk* identifies a number of possible events and perhaps the probability of their occurrence without being sure which, if any, will occur. *Uncertainty* describes the state of being unable to identify all the possible events. Those statements do not really help us deal with risk and uncertainty, but may help to clarify their separate meanings.

The level of risk should be judged on the following two key criteria: impact on the organisation; and probability of occurrence. Impact could be judged on the effect on profitability – such as high, medium, or low – if it cannot easily be quantified, such as a loss of reputation resulting from a chemical leak. Where there are both high impact and probability of occurrence, that situation is much better avoided altogether, unless action can be taken to reduce the probability and its impact.

It can be represented diagrammatically as follows (showing the mapping of probability of occurrence against its business impact):

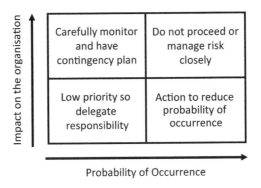

**Figure 20.1     Impact Assessment**

There are many types of risk, from strategic to operational, to project and financial risk; and, in the supply chain, there are four key areas of risk:

- **Financial risk** – This is the risk that a supplier causes the firm to suffer additional cost. This can be because the supplier under-quotes on a contract and may risk going into liquidation, and therefore there could be a failure to supply. It could be due to raw material price increases beyond the supplier's control or the buyer's poor estimates of inflation or exchange rates.

- **Performance risk** – This is the risk that a supplier does not fulfil its obligations on delivery, quality, and so on, therefore causing a knock-on effect in supply efficiency, perhaps causing the triggering of a penalty clause on the buyer's organisation.

- **Product risk** – This is the risk that a supplier's product causes damage or injury, such as breakage that causes fire or other damage. This could be mitigated by product liability insurance.

- **Environmental risk** – This is the risk that a supplier's actions may adversely affect the environment during the life of the product supplied or that their product may cause environmental damage. This could be caused by a regulatory issue, such as changes in the law.

The buyer therefore needs to try to cover these areas of risk and, if they cannot easily be insured against (such as supplier failure), there are techniques that can help towards reducing risk in a purchasing decision, such as:

- **Least cost** – If two projects have similar returns, then, if all else is the same (which it rarely is!), go for the project that costs the least, as there is less money at risk.

- **Payback** – Whether discounted or not, this technique puts the accent on receiving returns quickly and therefore reduces the risk of projections further into the future adversely affecting the project returns.

- **Sensitivity analysis** – This describes the 'flexing' of key assumptions in the project proposal, such as material prices, level of wages, sales volumes, and oil price inflation. It tests the sensitivity of changes in individual assumptions so that either individual assumptions can be tested by fixed percentage movements as to their effect on a project's viability, or each assumption can be tested as to how big an adverse movement can be before the project becomes unviable. A base case is created, like one of the previous examples under conditions of certainty, then each assumption is flexed and returned back to its original base value before the next assumption is tested. If three or more assumptions are flexed together, it becomes a little unwieldy for decision making.

### Example: Discounted cash flow – net present value (production line)

You wish to set up a production line, and you need to establish the viability of a tentative quotation for the supply and installation of the equipment for £2,650,000.

You have the following projected sales per annum over five years for part number RB37432:

| Year 1 | £5 million |
| Year 2 | £7 million |
| Year 3 | £3 million |
| Year 4 | £2 million |
| Year 5 | £1 million |

You expect to make a 20% gross profit from the sales in each year, and the cost of capital is 12%.

Is this project viable, and which are the principal assumptions to be flexed to show their sensitivity?

### Answer

**Step 1.** The first step is to establish the 'base case' and whether the project is viable. In other words, is the NPV positive or the IRR greater than 12%?

| Discount Rate | 12% | | Gross Profit % | 20% | | |
|---|---|---|---|---|---|---|
| Sales(£ million) | | £5.00 | £7.00 | £3.00 | £2.00 | £1.00 |
| Year | 0 | 1 | 2 | 3 | 4 | 5 |
| Cash Flows | −2,650,000 | 1,000,000 | 1,400,000 | 600,000 | 400,000 | 200,000 |
| Factor | 1.00 | 0.8929 | 0.7972 | 0.7118 | 0.6355 | 0.5674 |
| DCF | −2,650,000 | 892,857 | 1,116,071 | 427,068 | 254,207 | 113,485 |
| NPV | | £153,689 | | | | |
| IRR | | 15% | | | | |

This shows that, taking the gross profit as the net benefit (cash flows are 20% of the sales), the project is viable at this quotation level, as the NPV is £153,689 and the IRR is 15% (that is, 3% greater than the cost of capital).

**Step 2.** Decide on the principal assumptions. These might be the following – level of sales, gross profit percentage, cost of capital percentage, supplier's quotation – although, in practice, there may be many more, such as the elements of cost deducted in arriving at the gross profit.

**Step 3.** Test each assumption for its level of fall until it reaches a zero NPV.

## LEVEL OF SALES

| Discount Rate | 12% | | | Gross Profit % | 20% | | |
|---|---|---|---|---|---|---|---|
| Sales(£ million) | | £4.73 | £6.62 | £2.84 | £1.89 | £0.95 | |
| Year | 0 | 1 | 2 | 3 | 4 | 5 | |
| Cash Flows | −2,650,000 | 945,183 | 1,323,256 | 567,110 | 378,073 | 189,037 | |
| Factor | 1.00 | 0.8929 | 0.7972 | 0.7118 | 0.6355 | 0.5674 | |
| DCF | −2,650,000 | 843,914 | 1,054,892 | 403,658 | 240,272 | 107,264 | |
| NPV | | £0 | | | | | |
| IRR | | 12% | | | | | |

This shows that the level of sales could fall to close to 95% of their original value before the project becomes unviable. (You can use the 'goal seek' function in Excel to easily find this with feeder cell starting at 100% and the sales shown above being the product of this feeder cell and another base sales row of cells.)

Now set the sales back to their base case.

## LEVEL OF GROSS PROFIT PERCENTAGE

| Discount Rate | 12% | | | Gross Profit % | 19% | | |
|---|---|---|---|---|---|---|---|
| Sales(£ million) | | £5.00 | £7.00 | £3.00 | £2.00 | £1.00 | |
| Year | 0 | 1 | 2 | 3 | 4 | 5 | |
| Cash Flows | −2,650,000 | 945,183 | 1,323,256 | 567,110 | 378,073 | 189,037 | |
| Factor | 1.00 | 0.8929 | 0.7972 | 0.7118 | 0.6355 | 0.5674 | |
| DCF | −2,650,000 | 843,914 | 1,054,892 | 403,658 | 240,272 | 107,264 | |
| NPV | | £0 | | | | | |
| IRR | | 12% | | | | | |

This shows that the gross profit percentage can only fall to approximately 19% before reaching zero NPV.

Now set the sales back to their base case.

## LEVEL OF COST OF CAPITAL PERCENTAGE

| Discount Rate | 15% | | Gross Profit % | 20% | | |
|---|---|---|---|---|---|---|
| Sales(£ million) | | £5.00 | £7.00 | £3.00 | £2.00 | £1.00 |
| Year | 0 | 1 | 2 | 3 | 4 | 5 |
| Cash Flows | −2,650,000 | 1,000,000 | 1,400,000 | 600,000 | 400,000 | 200,000 |
| Factor | 1.00 | 0.8696 | 0.7561 | 0.6575 | 0.5718 | 0.4972 |
| DCF | −2,650,000 | 869,565 | 1,058,601 | 394,510 | 228,701 | 99,435 |
| NPV | | £813 | | | | |
| IRR | | 15% | | | | |

This shows, not surprisingly, that the zero NPV is reached when setting the cost of capital to the IRR, which is 15%. In other words, the cost of capital could rise to 15% (perhaps by more equity funding than loan) and still be viable.

Now set the sales back to their base case.

## SUPPLIER QUOTATION

| Discount Rate | 12% | | Gross Profit % | 20% | | |
|---|---|---|---|---|---|---|
| Sales(£ million) | | £5.00 | £7.00 | £3.00 | £2.00 | £1.00 |
| Year | 0 | 1 | 2 | 3 | 4 | 5 |
| Cash Flows | −2,803,689 | 1,000,000 | 1,400,000 | 600,000 | 400,000 | 200,000 |
| Factor | 1.00 | 0.8929 | 0.7972 | 0.7118 | 0.6355 | 0.5674 |
| DCF | −2,803,689 | 892,857 | 1,116,071 | 427,068 | 254,207 | 113,485 |
| NPV | | £0 | | | | |
| IRR | | 12% | | | | |

This shows that the supplier's quotation could be as high as £2,803,689 before the project became unviable. Note also that many capital projects are not just in the first year.

Now set the sales back to their base case.

**Step 4.** List all the assumptions, with their base case values and their zero NPV values:

| Assumption | Base Value | Sensitivity | Judgment |
|---|---|---|---|
| Sales level | 100% | 95% | Possible |
| Gross Profit % | 20% | 19% | Likely |
| Cost of Capital | 12% | 15% | Unlikely |
| Supplier Quotation | £2,650,000 | £2,803,689 | Critical |

This shows the areas of risk that need to be managed (particularly the gross profit and the supplier quotation) if the project is to be a success after we proceed. If too many of the judgment areas show a likely occurrence, a further decision would be needed as to whether it is even worth the risk.

- **Probability** – There is sometimes little point in flexing principal assumptions without some idea of their likelihood of occurrence. Assuming that a fall in volume of only 10% renders a project unprofitable, and therefore highly sensitive to volume changes, it would not be realistic to proceed if, for instance, it was a government-guaranteed contract and more likely to increase than fall. The probability of reducing by more than 10% could be less than 1%. This is further developed in the section on 'expected value' below.

- **Scenario planning** – This describes the effect on all of a project's principal assumptions upon a given event. For example, an oil exploration company might be drilling in a politically unstable country, so it might create a 'scenario' whereby there was a military coup and in which assumptions might change as a result, such as the cost of drilling licences, increased security, wage inflation, interest rates and exchange rates. Another scenario, with its effects and costs, would be a large oil spillage, such as happened to BP in the Gulf of Mexico. This technique is regularly used in the oil exploration sector.

- **Invest in *known* returns** – If there is a choice of two machines, and machine A is a brand new model from a new supplier supposedly processing 30 units per minute, and machine B is a well-established model from a known supplier with proven volume of 28 units per minute, it minimises risk by purchasing machine B, as machine A may produce 30 units per minute but may also produce 25 units per minute. This is why many takeovers occur, because the time and risk of unknown factors in setting up a new business is high risk (although potentially higher returns) as compared to purchasing a company with a known track record.

- **WACC + % for risk** – If the weighted average cost of capital (WACC) is, say, 14% and therefore the yardstick against which a project is measured, it may be that, where there is a choice of two or more projects, the risks of one project are perceived to be significantly higher, perhaps due to potential climate issues or terrorist threats affecting business. In this case, the riskier project may be assessed against a higher WACC of, say, 17% (applying a risk premium of 3%).

## Example

There is a choice of two projects, both lasting four years. WACC is 14%.

Project A costs £2,000 and has positive cash flows of £800, £1,000, £700, £400.

Project B costs £2,500 and has positive cash flows of £1,000, £1,200, £800, £600.

A like-for-like calculation would show as follows:

| Cost of Capital | 14% | | | | |
|---|---|---|---|---|---|
| Years | 0 | 1 | 2 | 3 | 4 |
| Project A | −2,000 | 800 | 1,000 | 700 | 400 |
| NPV | £181 | | | | |
| Project B | −2,500 | 1,000.0 | 1,200.0 | 800.0 | 600.0 |
| NPV | £196 | | | | |

In this case, project B shows the higher NPV. However, if we assume there is a significantly higher set of risks associated with project B, we might choose to compare project A discounted at a WACC of 14% with project B discounted at rate reflecting the added risk and so adding a premium of 3%. We now have:

| Cost of Capital | 17% | | | | |
|---|---|---|---|---|---|
| Project B | −2,500 | 1,000.0 | 1,200.0 | 800.0 | 600.0 |
| NPV | £51 | | | | |

This shows a reduced NPV of £51, which is now less than project A of £181, and so project A would be chosen.

There is clearly much subjective judgment in what level of risk premium is included in the WACC, but it must be better than not addressing the issue of risk at all.

## Balanced portfolio

This is about the holding of a portfolio of investments in order to reduce risk. From a corporate viewpoint, it relates to different projects spreading the risk.

It is like betting on two horses to win a race rather than one. The probability of the highest returns is reduced, but so is the probability of the lowest.

**Example**

A company has £4 million to invest and can invest it all in Teddy Bear manufacture or all in Dolly manufacture. The potential profit or loss outcome percentages and their probabilities are as follows:

| Project | % on Capital Outcomes | Probability |
|---|---|---|
| Teddy Bears | +15% | 0.5 |
| | −10% | 0.5 |
| Dollies | +15% | 0.5 |
| | −10% | 0.5 |

If all of the £4 million is invested in either project, there would be two possible outcomes: either +£600,000 (15% of £4 million) or − £400,000 (−10% of £4 million). There would be a 0.5 probability of each outcome. In other words, there is a 50% chance of making a loss.

If half is now invested in each project, what are the possible results and probabilities?

| £2 million in Teddy Bears @ +15% | gives | £300,000 | @ 0.5 |
|---|---|---|---|
| £2 million in Teddy Bears @ −10% | gives | −£200,000 | @ 0.5 |
| £2 million in Dollies @ +15% | gives | £300,000 | @ 0.5 |
| £2 million in Dollies @ −10% | gives | −£200,000 | @ 0.5 |

This now gives four possible outcomes, therefore reducing the probability of each combination, as the probabilities of each outcome must be multiplied together:

| £2 million in Teddy Bears @ +15% and £2 million in Dollies @ +15% | gives | £600,000 | @ 0.25 |
|---|---|---|---|
| £2 million in Teddy Bears @ +15% and £2 million in Dollies @ −10% | gives | £100,000 | @ 0.25 |
| £2 million in Teddy Bears @ −10% and £2 million in Dollies @ +15% | gives | £100,000 | @ 0.25 |
| £2 million in Teddy Bears @ −10% and £2 million in Dollies @ −10% | gives | −£400,000 | @ 0.25 |

This now shows there is only a 25% chance of making a loss, although the likelihood of a £600,000 profit has fallen to 25% from 50%.

From a buyer's perspective, this would imply spreading the supply risk across more suppliers, but perhaps not getting the best possible price as supply sources are spread. This would go against large company trends in cutting the supply base, which shows the importance of proper risk analysis before embarking on this exercise.

## Concept of 'Expected Value' using Probability

A common way of applying probability factors to project outcomes is by the use of a weighted average of the best case, 'normal' case and worst case, after applying probability factors to each of these values. With probabilities, the sum of all possible outcomes must be a certainty and should therefore add up to 1 (100% certain). Probabilities are usually expressed as a decimal (say, 0.3) rather than as a percentage (say, 30%).

### Example

Suppose that, as a buyer, you are trying to assess the likely purchase price of a unit, and previous history of sales shows that demand might be 900 units, 1,000 units or 1,100 units, with probabilities of 0.2, 0.5 and 0.3 respectively. If the contribution per unit is £4, the range of possible outcomes is as follows:

a)    £4 × 900 = £3,600 with a 0.2 probability

b)    £4 × 1,000 = £4,000 with a 0.5 probability

c)    £4 × 1,100 = £4,400 with a 0.3 probability

The range is therefore between £3,600 and £4,400.

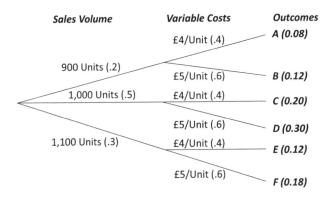

**Figure 20.2    Contribution Outcomes based on Differing Purchase Costs**

The example is now complicated to a step nearer realism, and the notion is introduced of a range of variable costs (material purchases) of either £4/unit (original basis) or £5/unit, with probabilities of occurrence of 0.4 and 0.6 respectively.

This now gives not three contribution outcomes but 3 × 2 = 6 outcomes where, at each level of sales, there are two outcomes based on differing purchase costs.

These outcomes may usefully be represented by the following diagram:

We can now apply the concept of 'expected value' by taking a weighted average of all of the possible outcomes:

|   | Contribution | Prob | Weight | |
|---|---|---|---|---|
| A | 3,600 | 0.08 | 288 | (900 units × £4 contribution/unit) |
| B | 2,700 | 0.12 | 324 | {900 units at £3 (£1 higher variable costs) cont/unit} |
| C | 4,000 | 0.20 | 800 | |
| D | 3,000 | 0.30 | 900 | |
| E | 4,400 | 0.12 | 528 | |
| F | 3,300 | 0.18 | 594 | |
| | | Expected Value | £3,434 | |

This would be the expected contribution after assessing all outcomes.

A less complex approach would be involved when drawing up a purchase budget for a project, perhaps several months in advance. You obtain three quotes for the raw materials from three sources. The best quotation is £78,000, the worst price is £94,000 and the third quotation is for £85,000. You might just be tempted to take an average of the three, giving you £85,667. However, historically, the probabilities have been best case achieved 0.1, worst case achieved 0.3 and middle (normal) quotation 0.6, so the expected value concept can be applied:

|  | Quotation | Probability | Weight |
|---|---|---|---|
| Best Case | £78,000 | 0.1 | £7,800 |
| Worst Case | £94,000 | 0.3 | £28,200 |
| Normal Case | £85,000 | 0.6 | £51,000 |
| Expected Value | | | £87,000 |

Because of the probabilities, the weighting has therefore swung towards the worst case, and £87,000 would be the figure used in the budget.

There are several problems with this method. First, it relies on having the data from which to draw conclusions as to the probability factors applied to each case. One can apply subjective judgment as to the probability factors, but this is very unreliable. One way around this is to apply a simple program evaluation and review technique (PERT) approach. This is a technique for estimation that uses a weighted average of the three cases to arrive at the expected value.

- The pessimistic (P) case would be when everything has gone wrong (say, £1,000).

- The normal (N) case would be with normal (expected) problems and gains (£700).

- The optimistic (O) case would be where everything has gone right (£600).

The final 'PERT' estimate is calculated as (P + 4N + O)/6. This is the 'weighted average', as the most likely (expected) estimate is weighted four times the other two. This estimate is weighted nearer the optimistic or pessimistic value, depending on which one is furthest from the most likely. In this case, it would be (£1,000 + 4 × £700 + £600)/6 = £733 as the 'P' is more pessimistic than the 'O' is optimistic. It is effectively using the previous expected value calculation, but with the probabilities of 0.167, 0.667 and 0.167 ($1/6$, $4/6$ and $1/6$). It is not perfect, but it is better than not acknowledging the best and worst possibilities at all.

The other major problem is that these models ignore the possibility of all the values in between the best and worst case outside the three estimates, and how those values might be distributed. There would be an almost infinite number of possibilities in between. This would be an extremely complex calculation to do manually and even with a spreadsheet. Several programmes exist (such as Oracle's spreadsheet-based Crystal Ball) which simulate all the possibilities, and the type of distribution pattern could be entered (such as normal or flat or Poisson). This type of programme is used in aerospace, construction and financial services, where a history of estimates creates enormous probability information, so increasing the forecasting accuracy.

See further Question 19 in the Appendix.

# Public Sector Approach to Investment Decisions

There are three main differences between public and private sector investment decisions: the cost of capital; the fact that projects might proceed, even with a negative NPV; and many of the benefits are unquantifiable.

## COST OF CAPITAL

As mentioned in Chapter 17, the cost of capital in the public sector is based on 0.8% plus the cost of central government borrowing and gilts (government bonds). If the gilt rate is 3%, the cost of capital is 3.8%. This is extremely low, as there are no shareholders needed to be satisfied by dividends and growth. This therefore results in a greater propensity to accept marginal projects because of a lower cost of capital, as compared with the private sector which may be at 12–15%.

## NEGATIVE NPV AND UNQUANTIFIABLE BENEFITS

These two issues are closely linked. We have assumed to date that the project must yield a surplus to be viable. In other words, it is giving a return greater than its cost of capital. In actual fact, many projects might proceed that give less than the rate of the cost of capital. Many public sector projects might proceed where some of the benefits are unquantifiable, such as social benefits. For instance, a council wishes to build a municipal golf course and has two possible project suppliers. Both will ultimately cause a negative NPV because the net revenue will not give enough benefit to compensate for the financing costs of the original development. The council would go ahead with the least negative NPV in this case (all other things being equal). Other instances of projects proceeding with negative NPV could be environmental projects, highways projects, legally enforceable projects (such as having to fit a system on chimneys to filter out hazardous waste), and quality improvement projects. Sometimes, projects go ahead simply because the CEO has a vision of an end result that cannot always be expressed in money terms.

## COST BENEFIT ANALYSIS (CBA)

In the case of a public sector project, the term 'cost benefit analysis' is usually used in place of an investment appraisal exercise or capital appraisal justification. The two are similar except the CBA will also include justification of all costs and consequences, whether they are quantifiable of not. Because of this difficulty in evaluation of the many benefits in the public sector, 'market' or 'shadow' prices can be used. Many books have been written on quantifying the unquantifiable using shadow prices.

For instance, let us say that constructing a local swimming pool and health club complex was estimated to save 200 burglaries per year. This would be based on lower crime rates in areas where local amenities and services were significantly better, and a swimming pool would fit this category. There would be explicit research to arrive at the figures. Also, research has been done to arrive at the cost of a burglary in a given area. This cost would include costs relating to police time and travel, victim support costs, building damage, loss of property or insurance costs. Suppose this average figure amounted to £4,000, we can now calculate the saving by putting in a swimming pool complex as 200 burglaries × £4,000 = £800,000 per annum. This gives a large additional annual 'shadow' income or benefit to justify the expense.

Another example might be the construction of a new highway. A shadow or 'market' cost saving would be the time saved by motorists getting to work quicker and so saving, say, 30 minutes per day. If they work for five days/week for 46 weeks/year, that would compute to 30 ÷ 60 × 5 × 46 = 115 hours of extra work done. If they are paid on average £20,000/year for a seven-hour day, that would represent approximately £12/hour. Therefore, each person would generate an extra 115 hrs × £12 = £1,380 in value of work per year. If 10,000 different motorists use the road, there would be a 'shadow' cost saving of £13,800,000 per annum. There are many problems and assumptions in making these calculations. For instance, there is an assumption that people will get to work quicker. In fact, they will probably just stay at home to have a longer breakfast!

Sometimes, no 'market' prices exist such as for environmental benefits, in which case they need to be recorded but will fall outside any financial calculations. Again, consider the tangible and intangible benefits of a police division procuring a new IT system. How do you put a value on speed of information?

There are other approaches to evaluation of costs and benefits:

- **Identify inputs and outputs** – This is simply a list of benefits and costs of a given project without quantification.

- **Performance indicators** – Here the benefit might be an improvement in the detection rate of burglaries by a change in the police communication system (for example, the rate is expected to rise from 53% to 61%).

- **Cost analysis** – This revolves around which is the cheapest. It should include the full total cost of ownership.

- **Value for money (VFM) analysis** – This requires the maximum output for a given level of resource (for example, putting £1 million into a drug rehabilitation project could be compared with the value of putting £1 million into finding parents who do not pay alimony). Comparing the two for value would not be a simple task but would revolve around which would improve the current situation the most.

- **Cost effectiveness analysis** – This would be measured as input cost per unit of output (for instance, cost per child at school, or cost per hospital patient).

- **Cost consequence analysis** – Costs and consequences are listed but not summarised. This is similar to the first approach but would include longer-term ramifications of the project, both good and bad. (Reference: Geoff Heath, 'Economic Analysis and the Evaluation of Police Service Projects; Clarification and Critique', *Police Research & Management*, Vol. 6/1 (2003)).

## Example

## COUNTY COUNCIL

### Cost Benefit Analysis – Pool and Gymnasium

Your council currently operates a public swimming baths which is in a location close to the town centre. It was originally built in 1935, is a listed building and has building maintenance costs of £45,000 p.a., and it does not really have either the capacity or atmosphere of a modern leisure and fitness centre. Its gross revenue is £100,000 p.a. and the running costs (excluding building maintenance costs) are £151,000 p.a.

You also operate a gymnasium with similar ageing problems. It has building maintenance costs of £36,000 p.a. and is poorly located and inadequate facilities for the disabled, as well as being very costly on lighting. It has a revenue of £175,000 with running costs of £183,000 (excluding building maintenance).

Both sites are poorly serviced by car parking, with poorly parked vehicles causing severe congestion down side roads. This causes many parking tickets to be issued, cars towed away and police resources wasted, and leads to many irate users of the gymnasium and swimming pool.

## PROPOSED NEW SCHEME

There is the possibility of developing a new site (unused and currently owned by the council) which could house both operations. This would be close to an existing council car parking which is not over-used, close enough to the town centre and would provide an ideal modern building to take these services forward for the next 30 or so years.

This new development would cost £26 million and the building is estimated to cost £10,000 p.a. in building maintenance for the foreseeable future.

It is also estimated there would be savings in the following combined costs:

- heating: £55,000; and

- wages (security and admin): 38,000.

Revenue for the pool is expected to increase by 50% and for the gymnasium by 20%.

Additionally, the two current sites could be sold for much-needed low-cost housing development. The swimming pool should sell for £11 million and the gymnasium for £13 million. Cost of loans (principal and interest) to fund the development would be 10%.

Produce a cost benefit analysis of both financial and non-financial benefits and disadvantages of proceeding with the deal.

## Answer

## COUNTY COUNCIL

## Cost Benefit Analysis – Pool and Gymnasium

## Financial effects

| Effect | Pool, Gym or Combined (P, G or C) | Cost change | Benefit |
|---|---|---|---|
| Maintenance | C | £10,000 p.a. | |
| Maintenance | P | | £45,000 p.a. |
| Maintenance | G | | £36,000 p.a. |
| Revenue Increase | P | | £50,000 p.a. |
| Revenue Increase | G | | £35,000 p.a. |
| Heating | C | | £55,000 p.a. |
| Wages | C | | £38,000 p.a. |
| Totals | | £10,000 p.a. | £259,000 p.a. |
| | | | |
| Sale of Site | P | | £11 million |
| Sale of Site | G | | £13 million |
| Development Cost | C | £26 million | |

Overall net annual benefit: £249,000.

Net cost of site is £2 million (£26 million – £24 million) at 10% loan cost, giving £200,000 p.a.

Therefore, the net annual surplus (undiscounted) is £49,000.

## Non-financial effects

| Effect | Benefit | Cost |
|---|---|---|
| Capacity Improvement | C | |
| Building Risk | C | |
| Maintenance | G | |
| Lighting (Environmental) | G | |
| Car Parking – Congestion, Police | C | |
| Local public Image | C | |
| Unused Site | C | |
| Car Parking Revenue | C | |
| Social Housing | C | |
| Listed Building demolition | | P |
| Timing and certainty of property deals | | C |
| Loss of Income (closure) | | C |
| Improved Social Amenity | C | |
| Cost Inaccuracy | | C |
| Disability Access Improvement | G | |
| Income Projection Risk | | C |
| Peripheral Costs (applic and appeal) | | |

APPENDIX

# *Further Questions and Answers*

## FURTHER QUESTIONS

## Question 1

### STAKEHOLDERS

You are a project manager for a UK supermarket chain 'Cost Grubbers' and have researched a new large site that you wish to develop close by a small country town. It will mean levelling an area which includes some rare wildlife habitats and is also very close to a primary school. It will generate about 200 jobs during the construction phase and 50 permanent jobs thereafter, and will be expected to attract many customers from outlying areas. There is a well-run local newspaper which is owned by Harry Blofeld, the same person who also owns two local food and delicatessen shops, and he is also on the local council.

Who are the key stakeholders, and how could stakeholder mapping aid the management of any potential issues?

## Question 2

### WEB DESIGNS LTD

Re-arrange the following into an income statement:

| | |
|---|---|
| Opening stock | 65,000 |
| Sales | 250,000 |
| Motor Expenses | 7,000 |
| Salaries | 45,000 |
| Depreciation | 12,000 |
| Loan Interest Paid | 4,000 |
| Taxation | 4,000 |
| Closing Stock | 70,000 |
| Dividend Declared | 3,500 |
| Sundry Overheads | 25,000 |
| Direct Wages | 10,000 |
| Materials | 140,000 |

# Question 3

## BOLIVIA LTD

Convert into a balance sheet:

| | |
|---|---|
| Cash at Bank | 1,000 |
| Shares | 20,000 |
| Land & Buildings | 50,000 |
| Other Accounts Payable | 6,000 |
| Plant & Machinery | 20,000 |
| Reserves (Retained Profits) | 46,000 |
| Inventory | 20,000 |
| Accounts Receivable | 14,000 |
| Trade Accounts Payable | 8,000 |
| Fixtures | 5,000 |
| Loans (Long-term) | 30,000 |

# Question 4

## CERVINIA LTD

Create a cash flow statement for Cervinia Ltd from the following two years' balance sheets (assume the profit for the year is the movement in the retained profits):

| | Year 1 | Year 2 |
|---|---|---|
| Land & Buildings | 34,000 | 26,000 |
| Plant & Machinery | 5,000 | 7,000 |
| Inventory | 6,000 | 3,000 |
| Accounts Receivable | 12,000 | 17,000 |
| Bank (In Credit) | 0 | 3,000 |
| Total Assets | 57,000 | 56,000 |
| | | |
| Accounts Payable | 15,000 | 9,000 |
| Bank (overdraft) | 4,000 | 0 |
| Loans | 20,000 | 25,000 |
| Shares | 4,000 | 4,000 |
| Reserves (Retained Profits) | 14,000 | 18,000 |
| Total Equity & Liabilities | 57,000 | 56,000 |

# Question 5

## PRESTIGE KITCHEN COMPANY LTD

The Prestige Kitchen Co Ltd trades as a kitchen manufacturer. They have always judged themselves on their return on capital and seem to think that they have improved the shareholders' position.

You are interested in re-assessing them for your approved suppliers' list, and you need to further clarify the position as you have further orders to place. They have given you the following information for your analysis for the last two years.

You are required to prepare a presentation to their board of directors lasting no more than five minutes as to where they might have gone wrong.

**Income Statements**

|  | Year 1 | Year 2 |
|---|---|---|
| SALES | 13,000 | 15,000 |
|  |  |  |
| Materials | 5,000 | 5,700 |
| Direct Wages | 3,000 | 4,000 |
| Gross Profit | 5,000 | 5,300 |
|  |  |  |
| OVERHEADS |  |  |
| Sales & Admin | 300 | 250 |
| Transport & Warehouse | 300 | 900 |
| Salaries | 400 | 500 |
| Total Overheads | 1,000 | 1,650 |
| Operating Profit | 4,000 | 3,650 |
| Loan Interest | 1,200 | 900 |
| Net Profit (Pre-tax) | 2,800 | 2,750 |
| Corporation Tax | 1,100 | 900 |
| Net Profit after Tax | 1,700 | 1,850 |
|  |  |  |
| Ordinary Dividend | 850 | 750 |
| Retained Profit for year | 850 | 1,100 |

*Notes*

|  | Year 1 | Year 2 |
|---|---|---|
| Average Employees per year | 150 | 195 |
| Cash Sales | 2,000 | 500 |
| Finished Inventory | 500 | 3,000 |
| Turnover with Your Company | £4,000 | £7,000 |

**Balance Sheets**                    **(£'000s)**

|  | Year 1 | Year 2 |
|---|---|---|
| ASSETS | | |
| NON-CURRENT ASSETS | | |
| Tangibles | 9,000 | 5,000 |
| Investments | 4,000 | 4,000 |
| Total Non-current Assets | 13,000 | 9,000 |
| | | |
| CURRENT ASSETS | | |
| Inventory & WIP | 3,500 | 7,500 |
| Investments | 1,000 | 0 |
| Accounts Receivable | 4,000 | 6,400 |
| Bank | 1,500 | 0 |
| Total Current Assets | 10,000 | 13,900 |
| TOTAL ASSETS | **23,000** | **22,900** |
| | | |
| MEMBERS EQUITY & LIABILITIES | | |
| MEMBERS EQUITY | | |
| Ordinary Share Capital | 6,000 | 6,000 |
| Revenue Reserves | 2,200 | 3,300 |
| Shareholders' Funds | 8,200 | 9,300 |
| | | |
| NON-CURRENT LIABILITIES | | |
| Loan Capital | 12,000 | 8,000 |
| | | |
| CURRENT LIABILITIES | | |
| Trade Accounts Payable | 800 | 1,500 |
| Other Accounts Payable | 2,000 | 2,100 |
| Bank Overdraft | 0 | 2,000 |
| | | |
| Total Current Liabilities | 2,800 | 5,600 |
| Members Equity and Liabilities | **23,000** | **22,900** |

**CASH FLOW STATEMENT Prestige Kitchen Company**

| | | |
|---|---|---|
| Net income | 3,650 | |
| Add depreciation | 100 | |
| Working capital provided by operations | | 3,750 |
| Decrease (Increase) in inventories | | −4,000 |
| Decrease (Increase) in accounts receivable | | −2,400 |
| Increase (Decrease) in accounts payable & accruals | | 1,100 |
| Sale of Investments | | 1,000 |
| Net Cash Outflow from Operating Activities | | −550 |
| Interest Paid/ Received | | −900 |
| Taxation | | −1,100 |
| Sale of Tangibles | | 3,900 |
| Net Cash Inflow before Financing | | 1,350 |
| Financing – Loans Repaid | −4,000 | |
|      – Dividend | −850 | −4,850 |
| Movement in Cash in Year | | −3,500 |
| Cash at bank at beginning of Year | 1,500 | |
| Cash at Bank at End of Year | −2,000 | |
| Movement in Cash equivalents | | −3,500 |

## Question 6

### GNESHT & FRIMBUS

Gnesht & Frimbus Engineering Ltd offers specialist engineering services to the aerospace industry. It has two production departments – machining and finishing – and a service department which maintains both departments' machinery. Expected costs for the following year are:

| | |
|---|---:|
| Rent | 27,600 |
| Build Insurance | 6,600 |
| Insurance of Machinery | 8,500 |
| Light/heating | 18,600 |
| Depreciation of machinery | 100,000 |
| Supervisor Salaries | 150,000 |
| Maintenance Wages | 50,000 |
| Factory Cleaning | 24,000 |
| *Consumable Materials* | |
| – Machining | 120,000 |
| – Finishing | 10,000 |
| Total | £515,300 |

You ascertain the following information:

| | Machining | Finishing | Maintenance |
|---|---|---|---|
| Floor Area (sq metres) | 600 | 400 | 200 |
| No of Employees | 70 | 25 | 5 |
| Value of Machinery | £800,000 | £200,000 | |
| Budgeted Machine Hrs (for question 4 only) | 35,000 | | |

The factory works a 40-hour week for 47 weeks per year.

You are required to:

1. Prepare an analysis of overheads showing the basis of apportionment and allocation to the three departments. Then re-allocate the service department overheads to the production departments on the basis of value of machinery.

2. Calculate an overhead absorption rate based on direct labour hours for each of the two departments (NB – rounded to pence).

3. Calculate the cost of a job which has the following costs:

|                          | Machining Dept | Finishing Dept |
|--------------------------|----------------|----------------|
| Direct Materials         | £300           | £50            |
| Labour                   | 5 hours        | 4 hours        |
| Wage rates               | £6 per hour    | £3.75 per hour |
| Machine Time (Part 4)    | 2 hours        |                |

4.  Re-calculate the cost of the job if overheads in the machining department recovered overheads on the basis of machine hours. What is the implication?

## Question 7

### ACTIVITY BASED COSTING (NOTY BRAIL)

Cabinet makers Noty Brail Ltd assemble two cabinets from rough bought-in components – Crotpests and Wrats.

Details of manufacture are:

|                            | Crotpests | Wrats    |
|----------------------------|-----------|----------|
| Component Material cost (£) | 6.00      | 4.50     |
| Output in Units            | 5,000     | 10,000   |
| Component numbers          | 6         | 3        |
| Number of production runs  | 250       | 40       |
| Machine Hours per 100 units| 3         | 6        |
| Items packed in cartons    | 5 units   | 40 units |

The output of Crotpests is smaller but, with double the components, is produced in frequent production runs in small numbers and is packed in small carton capacity.

Overhead costs are budgeted at:

|                                  | £        |
|----------------------------------|----------|
| Component purchasing & handling  | 20,000   |
| Production Control               | 16,000   |
| Machine Set-up costs             | 20,000   |
| Machine running costs            | 60,000   |
| Packing                          | 20,000   |
| Total Costs                      | £146,000 |

Calculate the cost of manufacture of Crotpests and Wrats.

## Question 8

### CONTRIBUTION – GOTHAM CITY

Gotham City Council had a severe shortage of Batmobiles (due to Robin's Saturday night drunken revelries) and have placed an initial order with Joker Fabrications Ltd for ten new Batmobiles at a price of £4,000 each.

1.  Calculate the profit for Joker Fabrications Ltd on this order, given that the fixed costs are £21,600 and the variable costs are 40% of the sales. They have no other orders.

2.  Calculate the break-even number of Batmobiles and the maximum profit achievable, given an overall plant capacity of 15 units.

3.  If the sales price of the contract for the ten Batmobiles is fixed, to what percentage must the variable costs be reduced in order to give a 10% return on sales?

## Question 9

### DECISION-MAKING EXERCISES

### (A) Dropping a Product

If a company has a range of products, one of which is deemed to be unprofitable, it may consider dropping the item from its range.

**Example**

A company produces three products for which the following operating statement has been produced:

|  | Product A | Product B | Product C | Total |
|---|---|---|---|---|
|  | £ | £ | £ | £ |
| Sales | 60,000 | 48,000 | 40,000 | 148,000 |
| Total Costs | 45,000 | 60,000 | 35,000 | 140,000 |
| Profit/(Loss) | £15,000 | (£12,000) | £5,000 | £8,000 |

The total costs comprise two-thirds variable and one-third fixed.

The directors consider that, as product B shows a loss, it should be discontinued.

Based on the above cost, should product B be dropped, and what other factors should be considered?

## (B) Acceptance of a Special Order

By this is meant accepting or rejecting an order which utilises spare capacity, but which is only available if a lower than normal price is quoted. The following example shows the problem:

### Example

Good Boy Ltd manufactures a pet food which they sell for 40p per can. Current output is 800,000 cans per month, which represent 80% of capacity. They have the opportunity to utilise their excess capacity by selling their product at 26p per can to a store chain who will sell it as their own label.

Total costs for the last month were £224,000, of which £64,000 were fixed costs. This represented a total cost of 28p per can.

Should Good Boy accept the supermarket offer, and what commercial aspects should be considered?

## (C) Make or Buy

Management regularly need to decide whether to produce a product themselves or to buy it in, perhaps from abroad.

Generally, the choice is between the marginal cost of production and the buying-in cost, unless the fixed costs associated with the production cannot be transferred or eliminated.

### Example

A company manufactures a product, and the current costs for the production of required units are:

|  | Cost/Unit (£) |
|---|---|
| Materials | 5.50 |
| Labour | 6.45 |
| Variable overheads | 2.05 |
| Fixed overheads | 4.00 |
| Total cost | £18.00 |

This product could be bought in for £15.20 and, if this were done, the present production capacity would not be utilised.

Should this product be bought in, and what other commercial considerations might there be?

## Question 10

### COST MODELLING

Your company decides to contract out its catering arrangements and the quotation per year for a three-year contract from a prospective contractor is as follows:

|  | Quote |
|---|---|
| Contract Management | 10,000 |
| Food | 20,000 |
| Supervision | 15,000 |
| Catering Staff | 60,000 |
| Equipment Depreciation | 10,000 |
| Overheads | 15,000 |
| Profit | 12,000 |
| Total Cost | £142,000 |

Your own cost model from supplying the catering is as follows:

|  | Own Cost Model % |
|---|---|
| Contract Management | 4.00% |
| Food | 21.00% |
| Supervision | 6.00% |
| Catering Staff | 36.00% |
| Equipment Depreciation | 15.00% |
| Overheads | 8.00% |
| Profit | 10.00% |
| Total Cost | 100.00% |

You also determine that the actual cost for the contract management should be 25% of an annual contract manager's wage of £28,000, and that the catering staff would be three full-time equivalent staff of £15,000 each.

The questions are as follows:

- How would you use your cost model to estimate the profit the supplier would really be making?

- Which areas would you negotiate on?

- What do you think the price breakdown should be, using the 'known' costs as a basis for calculation?

## Question 11

FIXED BUDGET

*Chic Designs Ltd (1)*

Budgetary Control Question

As the manager of the design department of Chic Designs Ltd, you have been asked to draw up the new budget for the year ahead.

You ascertain the following:

| | |
|---|---|
| Salaries | 200,000 |
| Pensions | 20,000 |
| Entertaining | 200,000 |
| Training Costs | 5,000 |
| Drawing Office Materials | 50,000 |
| Photocopy Leasing Costs | 50,000 |
| Motor Expenses | 80,000 |
| Telephone | 10,000 |
| Total Costs | £615,000 |

You expect inflation of 10% next year.

However, (ignoring inflation on the following) you intend to reduce entertaining not surprisingly to £100,000 and increase your training expenditure to £40,000. You also intend to take on an extra designer at £20,000 p.a. half way through the year that will also put an *annual* increase on your motor expenses of £4,000.

Additional expected increased workload means you budget for double the usage of drawing office materials, and you intend to rent a computer to help your design performance at a cost of £10,000 p.a.

You are required to draw up the new budget, and place the figures in the budget column below.

### Chic Designs Ltd (2)

Time has now passed and you find, at the end of the year, that you have spent the following:

| | **Budget** | **Actual** | **Variances** |
|---|---|---|---|
| Salaries | | 210,000 | |
| Pensions | | 22,000 | |
| Entertaining | | 104,000 | |
| Training Costs | | 25,000 | |
| Drawing Office Materials | | 140,000 | |
| Photocopy Leasing Costs | | 53,000 | |
| Motor Expenses | | 103,000 | |
| Telephone | | 12,000 | |
| Computer Costs | | 10,000 | |
| Total Costs | | £679,000 | |

Calculate and explain the possible reasons for the variances, and suggest action to be taken.

## Question 12

### GRIMSBY BOROUGH COUNCIL

Grimsby Borough Council's municipal baths operates a small restaurant, for which the following budget report has been prepared.

Rewrite in a more useful form to management:

**Flexed Budgeting**
**y/e 31 March 2012**

| | per meal | Budget | Actual | Variance (−ve = Adverse) |
|---|---|---|---|---|
| Number of Meals | | 20,000 | 24,000 | |
| | | | | |
| *Expenditure* | *per meal* | £ | £ | £ |
| Provisions | | 28,000 | 32,000 | −4,000 |
| Labour | | | | |
| − Supervisor[1] | | 22,000 | 22,500 | −500 |
| − Staff[1] | | 20,000 | 21,000 | −1,000 |
| Heat & Light[2] | | 5,000 | 7,000 | −2,000 |
| Administration[3] | | 5,000 | 5,500 | −500 |
| Depreciation | | 4,000 | 4,000 | 0 |
| Central Support | | 10,000 | 15,000 | −5,000 |
| Total Expenditure | | 94,000 | 107,000 | −13,000 |
| | | | | |
| *Income* | 5 | 100,000 | 120,000 | 20,000 |
| | | | | |
| *Surplus* | | 6,000 | 13,000 | 7,000 |

*Notes*
1. Supervisor's salary is a fixed cost. There are two catering staff, each budgeted to cost £5,000 p.a., plus a rate based on the number of meals sold.
2. Heat and light are a fixed cost.
3. Admin costs are semi-variable, with a fixed element amounting to £3,000.

# Question 13

## CASH FLOW FORECASTING

Action Stations Ltd are projecting their future cash requirements from 31.12.0X and have the following information:

1. Debtors at 31.12.0X are £60,000, two-thirds of which is payable within 30 days and the balance within 60 days.

2. Creditors at 31.12.0X are £50,000, payable within 30 days.

3. Opening unreconciled bank balance is £40,000 overdrawn, but there are unpresented cheques to suppliers of £10,000.

4. Sales run at £30,000 per month, payable in 60 days from invoice.

5.   Purchases run at £20,000 per month, payable in 30 days from invoice.

6.   Overheads are £2,000 per month, payable monthly.

7.   Capital equipment is to be purchased in February for £10,000 on one month's credit.

8.   There is a refund of corporation tax due in April of £10,000.

9.   Wages and salaries are £5,000 per month.

10.  Depreciation for the year is £12,000.

11.  The overdraft facility is £64,000, and the bank wish to reduce this.

Present a case to the bank, using the template below:

**Cash Flow Forecast Action Stations**

| Receipts | Jan | Feb | Mar | Apr | May | Jun | Total |
|---|---|---|---|---|---|---|---|
| Debtors | | | | | | | |
| Sales | | | | | | | |
| Tax Refund | | | | | | | |
| Total Receipts | | | | | | | |
| Payments | | | | | | | |
| Creditors | | | | | | | |
| Purchases | | | | | | | |
| Wages | | | | | | | |
| Overheads | | | | | | | |
| Capital | | | | | | | |
| Total Payments | | | | | | | |
| Cash Flow | | | | | | | |
| Opening Bank | | | | | | | |
| Closing Bank | | | | | | | |

# Question 14

## PAYBACK

You have a choice of laying down one of two production lines to satisfy an expected demand for motor scooters:

- Line 1 will cost £850,000 and the annual cash flows from the project would be £150,000.

- Line 2 will cost £750,000 and the annual cash flows from the project would be £120,000.

Which has the best payback, and would both projects be considered if the minimum payback hurdle is six years?

## Question 15

### ACCOUNTING RATE OF RETURN

Taking the same figures as above, but with the cash flows ceasing after seven years and the plant fully written off, we have:

- Line 1 will cost £850,000 and the annual cash flows from the project would be £150,000.

- Line 2 will cost £750,000 and the annual cash flows from the project would be £120,000.

Which has the best ARR, and would both projects be considered if the minimum ARR is 5%?

## Question 16

### NET PRESENT VALUE – OIL WELLS

You wish to sink an oil well where there is an outlay for initial equipment with expected income from oil revenues over the following five years (all figures are in £000s).

You have a choice of equipment, where supplier Cheap & Slick have quoted £3,800, and supplier JR Associates have quoted £5,300.

Due to the extraction qualities of the machineries, the expected revenues are as follows:

|        | Cheap & Slick | JR Associates |
|--------|---------------|---------------|
| Year 1 | 1,500         | 1,000         |
| Year 2 | 2,000         | 2,500         |
| Year 3 | 2,000         | 2,000         |
| Year 4 | 1,000         | 2,500         |
| Year 5 | 1,000         | 1,500         |

The cost of capital is 15%, and the discount factors for this rate are as follows:

|        | Factor |
|--------|--------|
| Year 1 | 0.8696 |
| Year 2 | 0.7561 |
| Year 3 | 0.6575 |
| Year 4 | 0.5718 |
| Year 5 | 0.4972 |

Evaluate the best project.

# Question 17

## DISCOUNTED PAYBACK

If the cost of a new photocopying machine is £7,000 and it is estimated to produce savings of £2,000 per year, what is the payback time? What is the discounted payback time if the cost of capital is 12%, giving discount factors in year 1 of 0.8929, year 2 of 0.7972, year 3 of 0.7118, year 4 of 0.6355, and year 5 of 0.5674? What are the implications if a four-year payback time was required for all new projects?

# Question 18

## TOTAL COST OF OWNERSHIP – SOLAR HEATING PANELS

The current electricity for heating is generated by solar panels in the roof converting the solar energy into heat. The solar panels are beginning to lose their effectiveness and even cease working altogether, and the company is working on a replacement of the panels on an 'as and when' basis.

There are 30 panels on the roof and they are being replaced at the rate of five per year, at a cost of £2,000 per panel, so each panel is lasting approximately six years.

If all the panels were replaced at once, it would cost £1,500 per panel and they would all be expected to last six years before needing replacement. Additionally, it would be expected that the electricity savings would be £750 per year as against the current situation due to efficiencies not lost due to the maintenance process.

The questions are as follows:

- Is it worthwhile replacing the panels all at once?

- What are the other issues involved?

## Question 19

### EXPECTED VALUE

You are a buyer trying to estimate the number of parts you need of product ZZAAJJD for placing with a supplier next year. You have estimates of demand from your marketing department of best case 3,000,000, worst case 2,000,000 and normal case 2,750,000. The marketing department have been extremely optimistic in the past and have only produced their best case 10% of the time, their worst case 30% of the time and normal case 60% of the time.

What should you give to the supplier for their budgeted number of parts?

## Question 20

### DISCOUNTED CASH FLOW – NET PRESENT VALUE (ALTERNATIVE MACHINES)

You are getting a significant number of rejects (costing 5% of the sales value in reworks) due to the age of machinery being used on a given project and now wish to replace that machinery.

The projected sales per annum for this project are:

| | | | |
|---|---|---|---|
| Year 1 | £2 million | Year 4 | £3 million |
| Year 2 | £3 million | Year 5 | £2 million |
| Year 3 | £4 million | | |

You have a choice of two machines to replace your current one:

- Machine A costs £300,000 and expects to eliminate ½ of the rework costs.

- Machine B costs £400,000 and expects to eliminate ¾ of the rework costs.

The cost of capital is based on the target capital structure of 50% equity and 50% loans, where the cost of equity is 12% and loans 4%.

The questions are as follows:

- Which is the best deal?

- What if the funding for this particular project was expected to be 10% equity and 90% loans?

- In projecting these savings, you are aware that machine A has the following best case savings of 72% and worst case of 48%. Machine B, on the other hand, has much greater downside risk, and the best case savings are 77% and worst case of 60%. Historically, your projections have shown a 20% probability of the best case, 50% of the 'normal' case and 30% of the worst case scenario. Might this alter your decision?

## ANSWERS TO FURTHER QUESTIONS

## Answer 1

### STAKEHOLDERS

The stakeholders would first need to be grouped by their power or influence against their interest in the project. We could use the four permutations as discussed in Mendelow's Matrix to group these.

- **High power / high interest** – Cost Grubbers' Directors, local planning authority, Harry Blofeld, traffic authorities, construction company.

- **High power / low interest** – Shareholders, bank, police, central government, national press.

- **Low power / high interest** – Local residents, local business competitors, more distant shoppers, parents of local schoolchildren, environmental lobbyists, local potential employees, potential managers within Cost Grubbers, current purchasing managers for Cost Grubbers.

- **Low power / low interest** – More distant residents.

## High power / high interest

These would need to be on board with the project from the beginning, with the biggest threat coming from Harry Blofeld, who not only has a lot of power (as he is on the council), but he can also stir up the local residents and effectively turn their high interest / low power into high interest / high power when they act together. Additionally, he has a lot to lose, as his businesses would suffer, so he will be well motivated to thwart any planning moves. A solution might be to purchase his businesses at a very favourable price or allow him some kind of in-store concession as, without his agreement, the planning could be very difficult. Traffic authorities would need satisfaction that both the parking and road plans were adequate, and the construction company (whilst having little power before gaining a contract) would have high power after its award, so would need to be treated as such. All of these would need constant inclusion in plans and ideas, and advice should also be sought from them before proceeding to the next stage.

## High power / low interest

This group needs to be kept in this quadrant and should not develop a high interest. This means furnishing them with all the relevant information. Any stories that come out in the local press would need to be of comparatively little importance so that the national press was uninterested. For instance, the issue of local wildlife would need to be dealt with sensitively.

## Low power / high interest

It is necessary to keep them as low power, which means 'divide and conquer'. Each stakeholder should be dealt with and questions answered separately, and 'group' meetings should be avoided where possible until the more inflammatory issues have been dealt with. Local parents would be interested from a health and safety aspect with regard to the traffic, so this should be an essential part of the planning. Current purchasing managers in Cost Grubbers would be interested, as this could affect their negotiations with suppliers, but the potentially problematic area would be the environmental lobby, and perhaps the creation of an alternative habitat should be costed into the exercise.

### Low power / low interest

Minimal effort with basic information should be issued.

The overall principle would be to 'sell' the benefits of the new supermarket to the local residents, such as lower food costs with greater choice, good parking, and bringing jobs and wealth to the area.

## Answer 2

## WEB DESIGNS LTD

| Income Statement | | |
|---|---|---|
| Sales | | 250,000 |
| *Less* Cost of Sales | | |
| Opening stock | 65,000 | |
| Materials | 140,000 | |
| | 205,000 | |
| Less Closing Stock | 70,000 | |
| | 135,000 | |
| Direct Wages | 10,000 | |
| | | 145,000 |
| Gross Profit | | 105,000 |
| *Less* Overheads | | |
| Motor Expenses | 7,000 | |
| Salaries | 45,000 | |
| Depreciation | 12,000 | |
| Sundry Overheads | 25,000 | |
| | | 89,000 |
| PBIT | | 16,000 |
| Loan Interest Paid | | 4,000 |
| | | 12,000 |
| Taxation | | 4,000 |
| | | 8,000 |
| Dividend Declared | | 3,500 |
| Retained Profit for Year | | 4,500 |

## Answer 3

### BOLIVIA LTD

**Non-current Assets**

| | | |
|---|---|---|
| Land & Buildings | 50,000 | |
| Plant & M/C | 20,000 | |
| Fixtures | 5,000 | |
| | 75,000 | |

**Current Assets**

| | | |
|---|---|---|
| Inventory | 20,000 | |
| Accounts Receivable | 14,000 | |
| Cash at Bank | 1,000 | |
| | 35,000 | |
| TOTAL ASSETS | 110,000 | |

**Members Equity**

| | | |
|---|---|---|
| Shares | 20,000 | |
| Reserves | 46,000 | |
| | 66,000 | |
| | | |
| Loans | 30,000 | |

**Current Liabilities**

| | | |
|---|---|---|
| Trade Accounts Payable | 8,000 | |
| Other Accounts Payable | 6,000 | |
| Total Current Liabilities | 14,000 | |
| TOTAL EQUITY AND LIABILITIES | 110,000 | |

## Answer 4

### CERVINIA LTD

Cash flow statement for Cervinia Ltd:

| | | |
|---|---|---|
| Profit for the year | | 4,000 |
| *Add* Sources | | |
| Sale of Land & Buildings | 8,000 | |
| Inventory Reduction | 3,000 | |
| Loan Increase | 5,000 | 16,000 |
| *Less* Uses | | |
| Purchase of Plant | 2,000 | |
| Increase in Accounts Receivable | 5,000 | |
| Reduction in Accounts Payable | 6,000 | (13,000) |
| Net Movement in Bank | | 7,000 |

# Answer 5

## PRESTIGE KITCHEN COMPANY LTD

| | Year 1 | Year 2 | IND Ave |
|---|---|---|---|
| **Profitability** | | | |
| ROCE | 20% | 21% | 23% |
| AUR | 0.64 | 0.87 | 0.60 |
| Gross Profit | 38.46% | 35.33% | 40.00% |
| Mats/Sales | 38.46% | 38.00% | 37.00% |
| Wages/Sales | 23.08% | 26.67% | 23.00% |
| | | | |
| Salaries & Admin/Sales | 2.31% | 1.67% | 3.00% |
| Salaries/Sales | 3.08% | 3.33% | 3.00% |
| | | | |
| **Financial Status** | | | |
| Current | 3.57 | 2.48 | 2.00 |
| Acid Test | 1.96 | 1.14 | 0.90 |
| Gearing 2 | 146.34% | 86.02% | 67.00% |
| Interest Cover | 3.33 | 4.06 | 8.00 |
| | | | |
| **Activity** | | | |
| Sales/Fin Inventory | 26 | 5 | 20 |
| Inventory T/o (Times) | 2.7 | 2.2 | 3.0 |
| Inventory Days | 137 | 169 | |
| Accounts Receivable T/O (Days) | 132.73 | 161.10 | 90 |
| Accounts Payable T/O (Days) | 66.36 | 109.50 | 60 |
| Work Cap (Days) | 203.24 | 220.93 | 55 |
| Fixed Asset T/O | 1.44 | 3.00 | 3 |
| | | | |
| **Other Ratios** | | | |
| Sales/Employee | 86,666.7 | 76,923.1 | 90,000 |
| Profit/Employee | 26,666.7 | 18,717.9 | 28,000 |
| Dividend Cover | 2.0 | 2.5 | |

## SUMMARY OF PRESTIGE KITCHEN CO LTD

### Own Company Work

This grew by 75% in year 2 and accounted for all of their growth. Their work with other companies must have reduced.

### Profitability

ROCE improved marginally but still below industrial average.

ROS has fallen dramatically by 7%, and is 3% below average.

Gross profit has fallen 3%, due principally to a rise in wage costs and is overall 5% below average.

Selling costs very low.

Transport costs doubled.

Overall profitability is well down as percentage of sales, and actual profit down even though ROCE is up. This is due to paying off long-term loans by using bank overdraft facilities and liquidating investments. Change in depreciation policy has helped figures.

## Financial Status

- Short-term – Current and acid test falling although still satisfactory.

- Long-term – Gearing down but still high. Interest cover down and well under industry average.

## Activity

Inventory turn is very poor and falling.

Accounts receivable collection time is worsening to five months.

Accounts payable payment time increased to 109 days.

Bank moved from credit to overdraft.

Reduction in tangible assets has caused improvement in fixed asset turnover. Does this mean a lack of adequate replacement of assets, or selling assets to stay solvent?

## Overall

Profit is down and cash position suffering, with poor control of working capital. Growth in sales has not been followed by growth in either operating or net profit, and the reduction in long-term loans by using short-term finance is potentially disastrous.

Company is stable but needs close watching the following year.

## Answer 6

## GNESHT & FRIMBUS

1)

| Cost | Total | Machine | Finish | Maint | |
|---|---|---|---|---|---|
| Rent | 27,600 | 13,800 | 9,200 | 4,600 | |
| Build Ins | 6,600 | 3,300 | 2,200 | 1,100 | |
| Ins M/C | 8,500 | 6,800 | 1,700 | 0 | |
| Light/heating | 18,600 | 9,300 | 6,200 | 3,100 | |
| Depreciation | 100,000 | 80,000 | 20,000 | 0 | |
| Salaries | 150000 | 105,000 | 37,500 | 7,500 | |
| Maint Wages | 50,000 | | | 50,000 | |
| Fact Clean | 24,000 | 12,000 | 8,000 | 4,000 | |
| Materials | 130,000 | 120,000 | 10,000 | 0 | |
| Totals | 515,300 | 350,200 | 94,800 | 70,300 | |
| Reallocate | 0 | 56,240 | 14,060 | (70,300) | |
| Totals | 515,300 | 406,440 | 108,860 | 0 | |

2) Hours worked are 40 × 47 = 1,880 hrs/employee.

- Total hours machining 70 × 1,880 = 131,600 giving rate of 406,440 ÷ 131,600 = £3.09

- Total hours finishing 25 × 1,880 = 47,000 giving rate of 108,860 ÷ 47,000 = £2.32.

3)

| Cost of job | M/C | Finishing | Total |
|---|---|---|---|
| Materials | 300 | 50 | 350 |
| Labour | 30 | 15 | 45 |
| Overheads* | 15.45 | 9.28 | 24.73 |
| Total | 345.45 | 74.28 | 419.73 |

* M/c £3.09 × 5 = 15.45, Finish £2.32 × 4 = 9.28

4) Reworked cost for machining department.

Materials and labour stay at £330 total. Overheads now recovered on machine hours basis.

Machine hour absorption rate is 406,440 ÷ 35,000 = £11.61/hour

2 hours for this job therefore covers £11.61 × 2 = £23.22 overheads.

Costs for machining department are therefore £330 + £23.22 = £353.22 (an increase of £7.77)!

## Answer 7

ACTIVITY BASED COSTING (NOTY BRAIL)

*Step 1. Calculate the overhead rates.*

Identify all the costs which are driven by one cost driver. This is the 'cost pool'.

In this case, there is only one cost per cost driver, with the exception of production control and machine set-up costs.

*Component purchasing and handling (driver – component numbers)*

$$\frac{£20,000}{(6 \times 5,000 + 3 \times 10,000)} = 67\text{p per component.}$$

*Production control and machine set-up costs (driver – production runs)*

$$\frac{£16,000 + £20,000}{250 + 40} = £124 \text{ per production run}$$

(The above two represent one cost pool)

*Machine running costs (driver – machine hours)*

$$\frac{£60,000}{(3 \times 50 + 6 \times 100)} = £80 \text{ per machine hour}$$

*Packing (driver – no of cartons packed)*

$$\frac{£20,000}{1,000 + 250} = £16 \text{ per carton}$$

*Step 2. Apply the overhead rates to the relevant usage by each product to calculate the cost of manufacture of each item.*

|  | Crotpests | Wrats |
|---|---|---|
|  | £ | £ |
| Material cost | 6.00 | 4.50 |
| Purchasing & Handling | 0.40 | 0.20 |
| Production control and M/c set-up (1) | 6.20 | 0.50 |
| Machine running (2) | 2.40 | 4.80 |
| Packing (3) | 3.30 | 0.40 |
| Total | 18.30 | 10.40 |

*Notes* (Crotpests)
1. 5,000/250 = 20 made per run, so cost per item = £124/20 = £6.20
2. 3/100 units × £80 = £2.40
3. 5 units in carton therefore cost is £16/5 = £3.30

This example shows that short runs drive overheads more than the long runs.

# Answer 8

## CONTRIBUTION – GOTHAM CITY

|  | a) profit | b) Break-even |
|---|---|---|
| Units | 10 | 9 |
| Sales | 40,000 | 36,000 |
| Variable Costs (40%) | 16,000 | 14,400 |
| Contribution | 24,000 | 21,600 |
| Fixed Costs | 21,600 | 21,600 |
| Profit | £2,400 | 0 |

|  | b) max profit | c) |  |
|---|---|---|---|
| Units | 15 | 10 |  |
| Sales | 60,000 | 40,000 |  |
| Variable Costs (40%) | 24,000 | 14,400 | (36%) |
| Contribution | 36,000 | 25,600 |  |
| Fixed Costs | 21,600 | 21,600 |  |
| Profit | £14,400 | £4,000 |  |

This shows that the variable costs need to fall to £14,400 or 36% of the sales. This represents a cost cut of £1,600 (£16,000–£14,400).

The memo that might be issued to the buyers would therefore be to ensure a cost cut of 10%.

## Answer 9

### DECISION-MAKING EXERCISES

### *(A) Dropping a Product*

The variable costs of product B are two-thirds of the total or £40,000. Deducting this from the sales of £48,000, there remains a contribution of £8,000. The product should therefore be retained unless this would restrict the sale of any other products or dropping it would remove 'specific' fixed costs to the value of at least the contribution lost of £8,000.

### *(B) Acceptance of a Special Order*

If 800,000 cans are sold for 40p/can, this gives £320,000 sales value.

If £64,000 were the fixed costs last month, £160,000 were variable costs or 50% of the sales value or 20p per can. As this is less than the 26p/can offered, the order would generate a contribution of 6p/can or 6p × 200,000 cans = £12,000 that would not otherwise be earned. These lower prices could affect other orders, and the company would forgo the opportunity of earning more if sold at the correct price, as there is no more capacity. To generate the same contribution at the original price of 40p, the company would need to sell only £12,000 ÷ 20p per can contribution = 60,000 cans.

### *(C) Make or Buy*

The current variable costs are as follows:

| | |
|---|---|
| Materials | 5.50 |
| Labour | 6.45 |
| Variable overheads | 2.05 |
| Total Variable Costs | 14.00 |

This figure is less than the cost of buying in of £15.20, and so the product should not be bought in unless at least £1.20 (excess of variable cost per unit £15.20 – £14) × the number of units could be saved by a reduction in the overall fixed overheads.

## Answer 10

## COST MODELLING

| | Quote | Quote % | Own Cost Model % | Should Cost | Actual Costs |
|---|---|---|---|---|---|
| Contract Management | 10,000 | 7.04% | 4.00% | 5,680 | 7,000 |
| Food | 20,000 | 14.08% | 21.00% | 29,820 | 29,820 |
| Supervision | 15,000 | 10.56% | 6.00% | 8,520 | 8,520 |
| Catering Staff | 60,000 | 42.25% | 36.00% | 51,120 | 45,000 |
| Equipment Depreciation | 10,000 | 7.04% | 15.00% | 21,300 | 21,300 |
| Overheads | 15,000 | 10.56% | 8.00% | 11,360 | 11,360 |
| Profit | 12,000 | 8.45% | 10.00% | 14,200 | 19,000  13.38% |
| Total Cost | £142,000 | | 100.00% | £142,000 | £142,000 |

- First, the supplier's cost model should be calculated and compared with our own cost model. This shows some large differences on the staffing and the food.

- Secondly, we calculate the cost breakdown using our cost model percentage but the supplier cost price.

- Thirdly, by using our cost model and inserting the 'known' figures for contract management (25% of £28,000) and catering staff (3 × £15,000), we can establish that the supplier is making £19,000 (13.38%) profit, and not £12,000 as per the quotation.

If we now produce a new 'should cost' breakdown using our cost model plus the known figures, we arrive at the following:

| | New Should Cost |
|---|---|
| Contract Management | **7,000** |
| Food | 27,300 |
| Supervision | 7,800 |
| Catering Staff | **45,000** |
| Equipment Depreciation | 19,500 |
| Overheads | 10,400 |
| Profit | 13,000 |
| Total Cost | £130,000 |

This shows that the new cost should be in the region of £130,000, calculated by assuming that the known figures of contract management and catering wages together amount to £52,000 and should represent (according to our cost model) 40% of the price (£52,000 ÷ 40% = £130,000).

They have clearly over-quoted on the catering staff as well as the contract management, supervision and overheads, and the food is worryingly low, which might well reflect on the quality of food being used or excessively harsh portion control. Additionally, the equipment depreciation is very low, again leaving the thought that inferior equipment might be planned.

## Answer 11

### FIXED BUDGET

*Chic Designs Ltd:*

|  | Budget | Actual | Variances |
|---|---|---|---|
| Salaries | 230,000 | 210,000 | 20,000 |
| Pensions | 22,000 | 22,000 | 0 |
| Entertaining | 100,000 | 104,000 | (4,000) |
| Training Costs | 40,000 | 25,000 | 15,000 |
| Drawing Office Materials | 110,000 | 140,000 | (30,000) |
| Photocopy Leasing Costs | 55,000 | 53,000 | 2,000 |
| Motor Expenses | 90,000 | 103,000 | (13,000) |
| Telephone | 11,000 | 12,000 | (1,000) |
| Computer Costs | 10,000 | 10,000 | 0 |
| Total Costs | £668,000 | £679,000 | (11,000) |

Possible reasons:

- Salaries – under budget – did not recruit extra, did not pay bonuses, did not work overtime.

- Pensions – n/a.

- Entertaining – over budget but good effort at reduction so keep it tighter.

- Training – under budget – not done training, new staff were recruited who did not need it, supplier not invoiced us!, robbing Peter to pay Paul, meaning that training has been cut just to save money.

- Drawing office – over budget (note double usage plus inflation) – causes, inefficiency, inaccurate prediction of workload, theft!

- Leasing – under budget, but not significant.

- Motor – over budget – old vehicles requiring maintenance, fuel prices, private mileage!

- Telephone – over budget by 10% – any number of reasons.

- Computer – n/a.

## Answer 12

### GRIMSBY BOROUGH COUNCIL

*Workings*

1. Provisions VC/Unit = 28,000/20,000 = £1.40

2. Staff = (£20,000 – 10,000)/20,000 = £0.50/unit

3. Admin = (£5,000 – £3,000)/20,000 = £0.10/unit

4. Income = £100,000/20,000 = £5/unit

| | Budget | Actual | Variance |
|---|---|---|---|
| **Flexed Budgeting** | | | (−ve = Adverse) |
| Number of Meals | 24,000 | 24,000 | |
| | | | |
| *Expenditure* | £ | £ | £ |
| Provisions | 33,600 | 32,000 | 1,600 |
| *Labour* | | | |
| – Supervisor | 22,000 | 22,500 | −500 |
| – Staff | 22,000 | 21,000 | 1,000 |
| Heat & Light | 5,000 | 7,000 | −2,000 |
| Administration | 5,400 | 5,500 | −100 |
| | | | |
| Controllable Costs | 88,000 | 88,000 | 0 |
| | | | |
| *Income* | 120,000 | 120,000 | 0 |
| | | | |
| *Surplus Before UC Costs* | 32,000 | 32,000 | 0 |
| | | | |
| UC Costs (Depn & Central) | 14,000 | 19,000 | −5,000 |
| | | | |
| Overall Surplus | 18,000 | 13,000 | −5,000 |

*Notes*
- Budget flexed to reflect increase in activity producing zero variances before uncontrollable costs.
- Uncontrollable costs (UC) separated later.
- Most of adverse expenditure removed as well as income.
- Some cost variances now favourable, but adverse need investigation despite good achievement by the management to increase activity level over budget.

# Answer 13

## CASH FLOW FORECASTING

| **Cash Flow Forecast** | | | **Action Stations** | | | | |
|---|---|---|---|---|---|---|---|
| *Receipts* | *Jan* | *Feb* | *Mar* | *Apr* | *May* | *Jun* | *Total* |
| | | | | | | | 0 |
| Debtors | 40,000 | 20,000 | | | | | 60,000 |
| Sales | | | 30,000 | 30,000 | 30,000 | 30,000 | 120,000 |
| Tax Refund | | | | 10,000 | | | 10,000 |
| | | | | | | | 0 |
| | | | | | | | 0 |
| Total Receipts | 40,000 | 20,000 | 30,000 | 40,000 | 30,000 | 30,000 | 190,000 |
| *Payments* | | | | | | | |
| Creditors | 50,000 | | | | | | 50,000 |
| Purchases | | 20,000 | 20,000 | 20,000 | 20,000 | 20,000 | 100,000 |
| Wages | 5,000 | 5,000 | 5,000 | 5,000 | 5,000 | 5,000 | 30,000 |
| Overheads | 2,000 | 2,000 | 2,000 | 2,000 | 2,000 | 2,000 | 12,000 |
| Capital | | | 10,000 | | | | 10,000 |
| | | | | | | | 0 |
| | | | | | | | 0 |
| | | | | | | | 0 |
| Total Payments | 57,000 | 27,000 | 37,000 | 27,000 | 27,000 | 27,000 | 202,000 |
| Cash Flow | −17,000 | −7,000 | −7,000 | 13,000 | 3,000 | 3,000 | −12,000 |
| Opening Bank | −50,000 | −67,000 | −74,000 | −81,000 | −68,000 | −65,000 | −50,000 |
| Closing Bank | −67,000 | −74,000 | −81,000 | −68,000 | −65,000 | −62,000 | −62,000 |

*Notes*

The bank facility has been exceeded from the first month to the last but is within the facility by the end. There are two obvious causes:

1. In the first month they seem to be playing 'catchup' with the accounts payable. The solution is therefore a working capital one. Get receivables in quicker, pay payables slower (by agreement), reduce inventory and, lastly, renegotiate temporary increase in bank facility.
2. In month 3 they are using short-term finance (overdraft) to fund long-term assets. They have broken the basic rule of long-term finance for long-term assets. This should be funded by a bank loan or leasing.

## Answer 14

### PAYBACK

Line 1. After five years, this has paid back £750,000, so the next year it needs £100,000 out of £150,000 to complete the payback. Therefore, the payback time would be 5 years plus 100 ÷ 150 × 12 months = 5.67 years.

Line 2. After six years, this has paid back £720,000, so the next year it needs £30,000 out of £120,000 to complete the payback. Therefore, the payback time would be 6 years plus 30 ÷ 120 × 12 months = 6.25 years, so this project would not be considered.

## Answer 15

### ACCOUNTING RATE OF RETURN

Line 1. Average net cash flows after depreciation would be (7 × £150,000 − £850,000) ÷ 7 = £28,570.

Express this as a percentage of average capital employed which is (£850,000 + 0) ÷ 2 = £425,000; this gives £28,570 ÷ £425,000 × 100 = 6.72%.

Line 2. Average net cash flows after depreciation would be (7 × £120,000 − £750,000) ÷ 7 = £12,857.

Express this as a percentage of average capital employed which is (£750,000 + 0) ÷ 2 = £375,000; this gives £12,857 ÷ £375,000 × 100 = 3.43%.

## Answer 16

## NET PRESENT VALUE – OIL WELLS

**Fill in coloured boxes**

**Cheap & Slick**      **Discount Rate**      **15%**

| Year | Cash Flow Factor | DCF | |
|------|------------------|-----|---|
| 0 | −3,800 | 1 | −3,800.00 |
| 1 | 1,500 | 0.8696 | 1,304.35 |
| 2 | 2,000 | 0.7561 | 1,512.29 |
| 3 | 2,000 | 0.6575 | 1,315.03 |
| 4 | 1,000 | 0.5718 | 571.75 |
| 5 | 1,000 | 0.4972 | 497.18 |

| | |
|------|------|
| NPV | **1,401** |
| IRR | **30.98%** |
| Prof Index | **1.37** |

**J R Associates**

| Year | Cash Flow Factor | DCF | |
|------|------------------|-----|---|
| 0 | −5,300 | 1 | −5,300.00 |
| 1 | 1,000 | 0.8696 | 869.57 |
| 2 | 2,500 | 0.7561 | 1,890.36 |
| 3 | 2,000 | 0.6575 | 1,315.03 |
| 4 | 2,500 | 0.5718 | 1,429.38 |
| 5 | 1,500 | 0.4972 | 745.77 |

| | |
|------|------|
| NPV | 950 |
| IRR | 21.87% |
| Prof Index | 1.18 |

## Answer 17

### DISCOUNTED PAYBACK

First, a calculation of simple payback is required.

If the annual cash flow is £2,000, the payback must be between year 3 (£6,000 savings) and year 4 (£8,000 savings). So it is 3 years plus 1,000 ÷ 2,000 × 12 months = 3 years 6 months or 3.5 years. This is within the four-year hurdle rate set.

If the figures are now discounted, we have:

| Year | 0 | 1 | 2 | 3 | 4 |
|---|---|---|---|---|---|
| Cash Flows | −7,000 | 2,000 | 2,000 | 2,000 | 2,000 |
| Factor | 1.00 | 0.8929 | 0.7972 | 0.7118 | 0.6355 |
| DCF | −7,000 | 1,786 | 1,594 | 1,424 | 1,271 |
| | | | | | |
| Net Present Value | | −£925 | | | |

So, four years of discounted cash flows do not give a payback, but five years would look as follows:

| Year | 0 | 1 | 2 | 3 | 4 | 5 |
|---|---|---|---|---|---|---|
| Cash Flows | −7,000 | 2,000 | 2,000 | 2,000 | 2,000 | 2,000 |
| Factor | 1.00 | 0.8929 | 0.7972 | 0.7118 | 0.6355 | 0.5674 |
| DCF | −7,000 | 1,786 | 1,594 | 1,424 | 1,271 | 1,135 |
| | | | | | | |
| Net Present Value | | £210 | | | | |

The payback would therefore be 4 years plus 925 ÷ 1,135 = 4.81 years, which is outside the required payback. Discounting the figures would make the position worse and might change the decision.

# Answer 18

## TOTAL COST OF OWNERSHIP – SOLAR HEATING PANELS

*Alternative Cash Flows*

1) Current Situation

|  |  | Yr 1 | Yr 2 | Yr 3 | Yr 4 | Yr 5 | Yr 6 |
|---|---|---|---|---|---|---|---|
| Panels Replaced | Cost per panel | 5 | 5 | 5 | 5 | 5 | 5 |
| Costs |  | −£2,000 | −£10,000 | −£10,000 | −£10,000 | −£10,000 | −£10,000 | −£10,000 |
|  |  |  |  |  |  |  |  |
| Total Costs | −£60,000 |  |  |  |  |  |  |

2) Alternative Situation

|  |  | Yr 1 | Yr 2 | Yr 3 | Yr 4 | Yr 5 | Yr 6 |
|---|---|---|---|---|---|---|---|
| Panels Replaced |  | 30 |  |  |  |  |  |
| Costs | −£1,800 | −£54,000 |  |  |  |  |  |
| Benefits |  | 750 | 750 | 750 | 750 | 750 | 750 |
|  |  |  |  |  |  |  |  |
| Total Net Costs | −£49,500 |  |  |  |  |  |  |

The figures do not allow for the time value of money or possible inflation; and, of course, the £54,000 (instead of £10,000) would need to be found in year 1.

# Answer 19

## EXPECTED VALUE

We need to work out the expected value, based on the marketing department's historical probabilities, as follows:

| Estimate | Parts | Probability | Weighted Value |
|---|---|---|---|
| Best Case | 3,000,000 | 0.1 | 300,000 |
| Worst Case | 2,000,000 | 0.3 | 600,000 |
| Normal Case | 2,750,000 | 0.6 | 165,000 |
| Expected Value |  |  | 1,065,000          parts |

## Answer 20

## DISCOUNTED CASH FLOW – NET PRESENT VALUE (M/C)

This is a spreadsheet view of the calculations of the relative NPVs for machines A and B:

**Machine Savings**

| Variables | | | | | | |
|---|---|---|---|---|---|---|
| Projected Sales | | £2.00 | £3.00 | £4.00 | £3.00 | £2.00 |
| Sales Sensitivity % | 100% | | | | | |
| Savings % | 50% | | | | | |

| Machine A | | | | | | |
|---|---|---|---|---|---|---|
| Discount Rate | 8% | | | | | |
| Sales(£ million) | | £2.00 | £3.00 | £4.00 | £3.00 | £2.00 |
| Year | 0 | 1 | 2 | 3 | 4 | 5 |
| Cash Flows | −300,000 | | | | | |
| | | 50,000 | 75,000 | 100,000 | 75,000 | 50,000 |
| Net Cash Flow | −300,000 | 50,000 | 75,000 | 100,000 | 75,000 | 50,000 |
| Factor | 1.00 | 0.9259 | 0.8573 | 0.7938 | 0.7350 | 0.6806 |
| DCF | −300,000 | 46,296 | 64,300 | 79,383 | 55,127 | 34,029 |

| | |
|---|---|
| Net Present Value | −20,864 |
| Internal Rate of Return | 5.35% |

| Variables | | | | | | |
|---|---|---|---|---|---|---|
| Projected Sales | | £2.00 | £3.00 | £4.00 | £3.00 | £2.00 |
| Sales Sensitivity % | 100% | | | | | |
| Savings % | 75% | | | | | |

| Machine B | | | | | | |
|---|---|---|---|---|---|---|
| Discount Rate | 8% | | | | | |
| Sales(£ million) | | £2.00 | £3.00 | £4.00 | £3.00 | £2.00 |
| Year | 0 | 1 | 2 | 3 | 4 | 5 |
| Cash Flows | −400,000 | | | | | |
| | | 75,000 | 112,500 | 150,000 | 112,500 | 75,000 |
| Net Cash Flow | −400,000 | 75,000 | 112,500 | 150,000 | 112,500 | 75,000 |
| Factor | 1.00 | 0.9259 | 0.8573 | 0.7938 | 0.7350 | 0.6806 |
| DCF | −400,000 | 69,444 | 96,451 | 119,075 | 82,691 | 51,044 |

| | |
|---|---|
| Net Present Value | 18,704 |
| Internal Rate of Return | 9.74% |

The base case shows that machine B is the best choice, giving an NPV of £18,704, whereas machine A is unviable at a negative NPV of –£20,864.

The cost of capital is shown as follows:

**WACC Calculation**

| Source | Proportion | Cost % | WA |
|--------|-----------|--------|-------|
| Equity | 50% | 12% | 6.00% |
| Loans | 50% | 4% | 2.00% |
| | | Total Cost | 8.00% |

However, if the financial structure changed to 10% equity and 90% loans, it would be as follows:

**WACC Calculation**

| Source | Proportion | Cost % | WA |
|--------|-----------|--------|-------|
| Equity | 10% | 12% | 1.20% |
| Loans | 90% | 4% | 3.60% |
| | | Total Cost | 4.80% |

The cost of finance has therefore fallen to 4.8%, albeit with greater risk due to the higher proportion of borrowed money.

This would now create an NPV for machine A of £4,603, and the NPV for machine B would be £56,904. (Reworking the above, using factors based on 4.8% WACC.)

Finally, we need to rework the above, based again on 8% cost of capital but incorporating the expected values based on the suggested best and worst case probabilities for each machine. This would give the following:

**Machine A**

| | Probability | Values | Weighted |
|--------|-----------|--------|----------|
| Best | 0.2 | 101,956 | 20,391 |
| Normal | 0.5 | −20,864 | −10,432 |
| Worst | 0.3 | −32,029 | −9,609 |
| | Expected Value | | 351 |

**Machine B**

| | Probability | Values | Weighted |
|--------|-----------|--------|----------|
| Best | 0.2 | 29,870 | 5,974 |
| Normal | 0.5 | 18,704 | 9,352 |
| Worst | 0.3 | −65,036 | −19,511 |
| | Expected Value | | −4,185 |

This clearly shows that machine B (due to the perceived risks, as mentioned) would cease to be viable, and machine A would now return a satisfactory positive NPV of £351 as opposed to –£4,185.

# Glossary of Terms

**Absorption costing**: the establishment of the total cost of a product/service by adding the materials, labour and overheads based on an overhead 'absorption' rate.

**Accounting rate of return (ARR)**: a method of investment appraisal that relates the average profit made per year to the initial sum invested in a project.

**Accounting Standards**: standards set by accounting standards boards to ensure comparability and fairness in the way accounts are presented.

**Activity based costing**: a techniques of separating costs into cost pools (rather than departments), so that a more accurate cost of a product/service can be established by allocating costs to a product by the product's demand for that resource.

**Activity ratios**: ratios that describe the speed of turnover, such as inventory, receivables and payables.

**Balance sheet**: also called a statement of financial position (SOFP), it is a summary of assets and liabilities of an organisation at one point in time. It is one of the three main year-end accounting statements.

**Break-even**: the point where sales equal total costs.

**Budget**: a plan of action expressed in financial terms, usually for the next 12 months.

**Capital investment appraisal**: this describes a group of techniques used to assess and compare differing capital projects.

**Capital reserves**: a reserve not created through revenue trading such by the revaluation (upwards) of non-current assets.

**Cash flow forecast**: part of the budgetary control procedures, this is a management accounting statement that summarises other budgets (sales, purchases, overheads, labour, capital) into the predicted effects on the bank balance. It is often confused with the cash flow statement which is a historical statement of what has happened to the cash.

**Cost model**: a model of a supplier's costs for a supply situation showing the approximate breakdown of materials, labour, overheads and profit.

**Cost of sales**: the direct costs deducted before arriving at the gross profit.

**Cost plus pricing**: the total cost of a product or service plus a mark-up to cover profit.

**Cost transparency**: the sharing of costs and margins of both supplier and customer to better improve joint profitability.

**Costing for decision making**: the breakdown of costs between fixed and variable costs, for the purpose of making decisions such as break-even analysis.

**Current assets**: short-term assets used in the trading cycle, such as cash, accounts receivable and inventories.

**Current liabilities**: liabilities due within 12 months, such as creditors and overdraft.

**Debenture loans**: loans to an organisation secured by a debenture trust deed. They may come from a bank or a group of debenture holders.

**Depreciation**: the amount by which a non-current asset is written down during a year.

**Earnings before interest, tax, depreciation and amortisation (EBITDA)**: used as a comparative measure where the level of depreciation and amortisation in some industries can have a distorting effect on comparisons.

**Financial status**: ratios that describe the stability of a company, such as gearing and interest cover in the long term, and current ratio and acid test in the short term.

**Fixed assets**: the former name of the non-current assets section in the balance sheet.

**Fixed budget**: a budget that assumes one level of activity and restricts spending on all cost centres to a 'fixed' level.

**Flexible budgeting**: a budget that allows movement in the variable costs of a budget statement.

**Gearing**: the level of debt expressed as a percentage of its total long-term finances.

**Gross profit**: sales less cost of sales.

**Income statement**: formerly known as the profit and loss account, it shows the sales less the running costs, and hence the profit, of an organisation over a period. It is one of the three main year-end accounting statements.

**Incremental budget**: a budget based on the previous year and adjusted for inflation and other known differences.

**Insolvent**: where a company's assets are less than its liabilities (that is, negative net assets).

**Intangible assets**: those non-current assets that are not 'touchable', such as patents, brand values and goodwill.

**Internal rate of return (IRR)**: this gives an annualised compounded percentage return on a project.

**Investor ratios**: ratios used by investors to assess their investment, such as P/E ratio, dividend cover and yield.

**Ledger**: a book of account.

**Liquidity**: the ability of an organisation to meet its short-term debts on time. It often refers to having adequate short-term cash resources.

**Marginal costing**: the cost of making one more item (in other words, the variable costs).

**Marginal pricing**: pricing a product or service above the variable costs to achieve a contribution.

**Mendelow's Matrix**: a two-by-two matrix used to map stakeholders using their power and level of interest.

**Net present value (NPV)**: this gives the absolute return over the life of a project, after allowing for the time value of money.

**Net profit**: sales less costs. Profit may be before or after interest, tax or depreciation.

**Non-current assets**: assets that are not purchased with the intention of selling in the short term, such as buildings and machinery. They remain in the balance sheet at the year end, as they are not fully consumed.

**Non-current liabilities**: liabilities payable over more than 12 months, such as loans.

**Open book costing**: the sharing of all the costs of a supplier with the customer, with a view to reducing costs through joint initiatives.

**Ordinary shares**: the shares (and shareholders) that control a company and have the highest risk and return.

**Payback**: a technique of investment appraisal that establishes the time it takes to recover the capital costs of a project.

**Preference shares**: shares that are somewhere between ordinary shares and loans usually with a fixed rate of dividend and little controlling interest.

**Profit and loss account**: the former name of the income statement.

**Profit before interest and tax (PBIT)**: the same as earnings before interest and tax (EBIT).

**Profitability ratios**: ratios that measure profitability, such as return on sales, gross profit and return on capital.

**Reserves**: the sum of all the company reserves, such as retained profits plus the capital reserves.

**Retained profit**: profit after all deductions, including dividends paid to shareholders.

**Revenue reserves**: all the retained profits in a company since its commencement.

**Sales**: the amount invoiced to customers during the year. Also called revenue, income or turnover.

**Shareholders' equity**: the balance sheet value of a company expressed as the ordinary shares plus the reserves.

**Solvency**: the ability of a company to meet its debts.

**Stakeholder**: anyone with an interest in an organisation's activities. Can be primary (contractual) or secondary.

**Statement of cash flows (or cash flow statement)**: this shows how an organisation's profit has been converted into cash at the year end, after allowing for capital expenditure and finance-raising activities. It is one of the three main year-end accounting statements.

**Statement of financial position (SOFP)**: another term for balance sheet.

**Total cost of ownership**: also known as life-cycle costing and total cost of acquisition, this establishes the whole-life cost of a product, from purchase through to decommissioning at the end of its life.

**Transfer pricing**: the price at which goods or services are transferred from one division to another within an organisation.

**Variance analysis**: the analysis of the differences between the budget and the actual results.

**Working capital**: defined as current assets less current liabilities.

**Zero based budget (ZBB)**: where a budget for a department is drawn up on the assumption that the 'department' is being set up from nothing to do its required tasks. It does not rely on what resources were used in the past.

# Reading List

Atrill & McLaney, *Accounting and Finance for Non-specialists* (7th Edition, 2010).

Atrill, Peter, *Financial Management for Decision Makers* (6th Edition, 2011).

Drury, Colin, *Cost and Management Accounting: An Introduction* (7th Revised Edition, 2011).

Millichamp, A.H., *Finance for Non-financial Managers: An Active-learning Approach* (3rd Edition, 2000).

# Index

For Product Safety Concerns and Information please contact our EU
representative GPSR@taylorandfrancis.com Taylor & Francis Verlag GmbH,
Kaufingerstraße 24, 80331 München, Germany

Printed and bound by CPI Group (UK) Ltd, Croydon, CR0 4YY
01/05/2025
01858414-0012